D0634550

Using the INTERNET and the WORLD WIDE WEB in Your JOB SEARCH

Fred E. Jandt
Author of *Win-Win
Negotiating* and *The
Customer is Usually Wrong!*

Mary B. Nemnich
Employment Specialist
and Popular Lecturer

Send your comments to authors via e-mail: jobnet@aol.com

JIST Works, Inc.

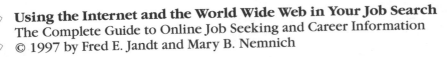

Using the Internet and the World Wide Web in Your Job Search
The Complete Guide to Online Job Seeking and Career Information
© 1997 by Fred E. Jandt and Mary B. Nemnich

Published by JIST Works, Inc.
720 N. Park Avenue
Indianapolis, IN 46202-3431
Phone: 317-264-3720 Fax: 317-264-3709 E-mail: jistworks@aol.com
World Wide Web Address: http://www.jist.com/jist

Other Books by Fred E. Jandt

- *Win-Win Negotiating*
- *The Customer Is Usually Wrong!*

See the back of this book for additional JIST titles and ordering information. Quantity discounts are available.

Cover Design by Honeymoon Image & Design

Printed in the United States of America

99 98 97   9 8 7 6 5 4 3 2

Library of Congress Cataloging-in-Publication Data

Jandt, Fred Edmund.
    Using the Internet and the World Wide Web in your job search /
Fred E. Jandt, Mary B. Nemnich.
        p.   cm.
    Revised edition of: Using the Internet in your job search / Fred
E. Jandt.
    ISBN 1-56370-292-4
    1. Job hunting—Computer network resources.   2. Internet (Computer
network)   3. World Wide Web (Information retrieval system)
I. Nemnich, Mary B., 1951-   .   II. Jandt, Fred Edmund. Using the
Internet in your job search.   III. Title.
    HF5382.7.J36   1997
    650.14'0285'467—dc20   96-46178
                                             CIP

We have been careful to provide accurate information throughout this book, but it is possible that errors and omissions have been introduced. Please consider this in making any career plans or other important decisions. Trust your own judgment above all else and in all things.

ISBN 1-56370-292-4

PREFACE

It was only 18 months ago that we wrote the preface to *Using the Internet in Your Job Search*. In that short time, major changes encouraged us to prepare this new edition:

- In the first edition, we devoted fewer than four pages to the World Wide Web. Today, as the Web has become—for many people—synonymous with the Internet, we've focused the entire new edition on the World Wide Web.

- In the first edition, we mentioned Lynx and Mosaic as World Wide Web browsers. Netscape wasn't in popular use then. In this new edition, we've provided the information you need to use all the resources of the Web.

- In the first edition, we described the locations then available for finding job openings on the Internet. Since that time, job databases and resume databases have grown in number and size. In this new edition, we point you to job and resume databases more and describe several in detail.

- In the first edition, we presented one of the first model electronic resumes. In this edition, we help you prepare your own electronic resume for scanning programs so that you'll be selected over others.

Overall, since that book was published, we've been in contact with job seekers, career placement specialists, employers, and administrators of job and resume data banks. We've included their experiences in this new edition. We think you'll find that this new edition is state-of-the-art and includes advice from the leading-edge users of job search on the Internet.

One word of caution. We've done our best to verify that the information in this book is up-to-date. But because computer technology and the Internet change so fast, by the time you read this, some things will have changed. Some sites we suggest may have new addresses or have been closed and replaced by others. Therefore, we've tried to make this book more a complete guide to the job search process than a listing of sites.

Our objective, then, for this edition remains the same as that for the first: "to help you become more proficient at using the Internet and to give you one more tool for finding that next job." We still take you step-by-step from gaining access to the Internet to finding job listings to applying for those jobs.

CONTENTS

Get On or Get Left Behind

CHAPTER 1

In 1995, we published *Using the Internet in Your Job Search*. Thousands of job seekers, employers, and career counselors have used the book as their guide to jobs and staffing on the Internet.

We have also been able to do many workshops for job seekers, employers, and career counselors since the publication of that book. As you might guess, most of the people in attendance were connected to the Internet and were there to learn how to use the Internet to look for jobs or to post job vacancies.

But there is something else you may not have guessed. We asked the people in attendance to indicate by raised hands how long they had been on the Internet. Here is what we found:

- When we asked how many had accessed the Internet during the past year (1995), almost everyone raised his or her hand.

- When we asked how many had accessed the Internet during the past two years (since 1994), the majority of attendees raised their hands.

- When we asked how many had accessed the Internet during the past three years (since 1993), only two or three hands were still up.

These results are supported by recently published surveys: In 1994, 31 percent of U.S. households had PCs. In 1995, the number rose to 36 percent. About 18 million households have modems, but only about 10 million of those modems are used regularly.

The majority of today's Internet users have had access only since 1994. And even more startling is the reported figure that 50 percent of the people using the Internet in the United States today started using it in 1995!

What Happened?

What we call the Internet today is a product of the Cold War. The Internet was originally designed to link the military, defense contractors, and universities to make it possible to send computer data over telephone lines. More and more computer networks at universities and research centers were established and made a part of the Internet. Most of the information available on the Internet at that time was research-oriented technical information, but it also included notices of job vacancies of interest to the research and computer communities.

Over time, some connections were established by computer networks not located at universities or research centers. But only after the giant commercial computer networks such as America Online and CompuServe provided Internet connections to their users did the Internet become available to anyone who could afford the commercial providers' charges. And as more and more people with all sorts of backgrounds and interests connected, the Internet became increasingly diverse in the information available there. So instead of just research and computer job vacancies, the job vacancies exploded to include all types of jobs—from gardeners to youth ministers and from weekend sports television anchors to nurses—and from full-time jobs to part-time jobs to contract jobs. In a couple of hours one day in 1996, we were able to locate a total of about one-half million job postings. Today you can find job vacancies for any type of job in your city or worldwide!

Why Everyone Wins

Job search and recruitment on the Internet will continue to grow because it offers advantages to both the employer and job seekers. Employers talk about these advantages:

1. **Speed**. Traditional recruiting by publicizing a vacancy in print publications can be very slow. Some publications require that announcements be submitted 30 or more days in advance. Then there is printing and mailing time. Then applicants are given time to apply.

   In contrast, a vacancy announcement posted on the Internet can receive a response minutes after being posted!

2. **Coverage area**. Newspaper classified ads have largely been limited to the newspaper's circulation area. Specialized publications such as industry trade magazines have been limited to their mailing lists.

   In contrast, a vacancy announcement posted on the Internet can be seen by anyone with Internet access worldwide. It's impossible to know exactly, but it is a fairly reliable estimate that some 20 to 40 million people use the Internet regularly.

3. **Cost**. Traditional recruiting is expensive. Publicizing a vacancy using advertisements is costly. A one-time, 2-column by 2-inch display ad in the Monday edition of the *Indianapolis Star*, for example, costs $332.00. A headhunter's fee can be 20 to 30 percent of the new hire's base salary.

In contrast, a vacancy announcement can be posted on the Internet at no cost.

Other advantages exist for employers today; we discuss those advantages in Chapter 14, "Advice for Employers." For now, let's look briefly at the advantages for job seekers. They are the same three advantages: speed, coverage area, and cost.

We've been guests on television shows during which the interviewer challenged us to find a job vacancy for a person. Once in Fresno, California, the host asked Fred to find a vacancy for a person the producers had brought to the studio. The individual said that because of family reasons, he was not able to relocate. This meant that Fred had to find the individual a job in Fresno. The person said also that he wanted a job as a cable engineer. Fred had fewer than five minutes but was able to locate jobs in Fresno and jobs as a cable engineer, but not jobs as a cable engineer in Fresno. Even so, before the five minutes were up, the individual had an accurate idea of what was available in Fresno. Let us repeat that: *Before the five minutes were up, the individual had an accurate idea of what was available in Fresno.* That's speed.

We've found that most job seekers think of using the Internet as a way to locate jobs in other states. That's true—the Internet does make it possible for us to locate jobs in other states—but it also allows us to locate jobs in other countries and in our own home town and ZIP code. The Internet is both international and local!

The costs to the job seeker of searching the Internet can be free. In the next chapter we'll discuss ways to access the Internet, but it's important to note here at the outset that many public libraries provide Internet access to their patrons.

So for both the employer and the job seeker, the Internet has advantages. That's why the Internet job market will continue to grow and grow.

Even More Advantages

At least now in the early years of the Internet job market, there is another advantage to the employer. For now, the applicants coming over the Internet represent a somewhat select group. Think about who has access to the Internet now and what skills are required to use the Internet today. Generally users are well educated, computer literate,

and innovative enough to be early adopters of the Internet as a means of communication.

And that's exactly the type of employees many employers are looking for—well educated, computer literate, and innovative.

Some employers believe that applicants coming to them over the Internet are coming to them prescreened. Recent surveys have supported this assumption. In 1995, it was reported that 81 percent of Internet users and 74 percent of online subscribers are 44 years old or younger. Nearly two-thirds are college graduates (compared to about 28 percent in the general population), and about half are professional or managerial. And Internet users are not all men as is popularly believed. Males do account for about two-thirds of Internet users and about 59 percent of online subscribers. Men do use the Internet more, but by number, the Internet is by no means a male-only domain.

We've often been asked to explain exactly what the Internet is. What we say is to think of the Internet as a very large library. In early 1996, the World Wide Web portion of the Internet contained more than 22 million "pages" with a million more added each month. At that rate, the Internet will soon exceed the information stored at the Library of Congress.

Fortunately for job seekers, the World Wide Web makes it possible to move from one information site to others linked to it. The World Wide Web makes it easy for you to find what you need in this large, unorganized library.

With no librarians, anyone can "visit" and leave material. Some people have left treasures; others have left trash. Each user must learn how to use the World Wide Web to find the material that is useful to him or her. Luckily, the World Wide Web is easy to use.

There is a wealth of up-to-the-minute information available. The job seeker on the Internet can easily find information on occupation employment trends, the unemployment rates in different locations, housing costs in different locations, guides for building a resume, and even order a pizza on the Internet (in California's Santa Cruz area at **http://www.pizzahut.com**) while all this information is being read!

Another way we encourage job seekers to use the information available on the Internet is to study the vacancy announcements and resumes posted on the Internet to reevaluate how job seekers describe their skills in relation to how others describe their skills and to what employers are currently looking for. We've worked with people who have thrown away their resumes after having studied the resumes of their "competition." We've worked with others who have totally changed their employment objectives after having studied what employers are looking for. There's no other way a job seeker could have access to so many job descriptions and so many real resumes.

Using the Internet in a job search presents a way for job seekers to reevaluate how they present themselves to the employers they want to reach for the careers they want to have!

Over the past two years, we've received many e-mail messages from people who have done just that. Here's only one sample:

● ●

```
I found my current job on ba.jobs.offered. I
was looking on the USENET groups for several
months before I found the "pearl." I am not a
software engineer, so it took a long time to
find the job I wanted. I was a video producer
at Ames Research Center, but wanted to move
on. I found an ad for an office administrator
at a start up company. The magic words "start
up" enticed me to send my resume. To make a
long story short, I am the office manager for
a rapidly growing CD-ROM publishing company
and have decided to change my career path to
focus on Human Resources. Quite a change from
a Video Production background. I am the happi-
est I've ever been at work. I work with great
people, and have a great boss. I think the
Internet is a great way to find jobs.
```

● ●

Get On!

There are even more advantages. Consider these facts:

Newspapers across the country have seen the growth of Internet job vacancy announcements. Some have seen these low-cost ads as a threat to their more expensive classifieds. Is it any surprise, then, that six of the country's major newspapers joined together to post their some 35,000 job vacancy announcements on the Internet? Or that in May, 1996, two other newspapers joined in? In fact, by the summer of 1996, the list had grown to include 19 newspapers: You can read the job vacancy announcements from the *Atlanta Journal-Constitution, Boston Globe, Chicago Tribune, The Columbus Dispatch, The Denver Post, The Hartford Courant, Los Angeles Times, The Miami Herald, Milwaukee Journal Sentinel, Minneapolis St. Paul Pioneer Press, Minneapolis St. Paul Star Tribune, The New York Times, The Orlando Sentinel, Philadelphia Inquirer, Rocky Mountain News, The Sacramento Bee, San Jose Mercury News, South Florida Sun-Sentinel,* and *The Washington Post* at `http://www.careerpath.com`. (We describe this more in Chapter 4.)

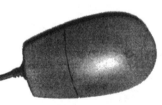

And the April 4, 1996, issue of the *Investor's Business Daily* reported a recent AT&T poll that showed that 80 percent of today's college students plan to use the Internet as a job search tool (page A4). AT&T also announced its own Web site for college students looking for jobs. The AT&T College Network (`http://www.att.com/college/`) offers tips on job-hunting and career strategies and provides links to other Internet job listing sites. (In Chapter 4, we give you even more sites for job listings, and Chapter 13 is directed at college students.)

There have been misunderstandings about the Internet, and there have even been abuses of the Internet. But in the area of the job search, the Internet is a win-win situation for everybody—except, of course, those who haven't gotten online yet!

A Special Word to the Computer-Phobic

So you haven't been able to program your VCR or microwave. You feel intimidated and overwhelmed by technology. The following are some tips for learning to deal with technology.

First, find a teacher you feel comfortable with. Many computer "experts" have no empathy for the computer-phobic. They speak a language you don't understand and have no patience to show you what to do. Find someone who's good with computers and who is a patient teacher. It could be someone at work, a friend at church, or even a neighbor's teenage child. Don't ask them to teach you everything about computers; just ask them to show you something on the computer that they think you could use. Focus on learning one thing that you can use; don't even begin to try to learn everything that could be done.

Then find a class at a local community college or adult education center designed to help beginners learn about computers and software. You can find these classes in course catalogs and by asking at computer stores.

We tell computer-phobic students to explore like a child would. Don't worry about doing something wrong. Explore and see what happens when you try something. The odds are that you're not going to do any harm to the computer. So, try it. Just avoid the "know-it-alls" until you're ready for them!

And you can use the computer itself to learn about computers and the Internet. *NewbieNewz* is an online magazine for beginners. Send an e-mail message to **nn-info@io.com**. If you're not sure how to do this yet, go on to Chapter 2.

In Chapter 2, we present information you need for using the Internet: how to get set up at home, where to find a service provider who connects you to the Internet, and how to use e-mail. If you already have this down, you can go on to Chapter 3 in which we describe the World Wide Web, or to Chapter 4 in which we identify the locations of job vacancy announcements on the World Wide Web.

Getting Connected

What is called the Internet today was started a little over 25 years ago in the Cold War Era by the Defense Department Advanced Research Projects Agency (ARPA) to link researchers with computer centers to share hardware and software resources over telephone lines. Before that time magnetic tapes or punch cards had to be exchanged by mail. Access was limited to the military, defense contractors, and universities doing defense research. In the early 1980s Milnet, an unclassified military network, was spun off ARPAnet, but connections between the two networks continued. That interconnection was known as the DARPA Internet. And what we know as the Internet today is an expansion of the concept of interconnections between these two computer networks.

In the late 1970s and early 1980s more computer networks were developed for the academic and research communities, and these too became a part of the Internet. Established in 1986, the National Science Foundation Network (NSFnet) replaced the original ARPAnet by 1990, and by 1991 NSFnet itself ceased to exist. But what remained was the Internet—the interconnections among computer networks that by then consisted of about 8,000 networks around the world. So in a very real sense, the Internet is not a "thing"; it's the interconnections among separate computer networks worldwide.

When you're on the Internet from your spare bedroom in your home in Texas, you're not aware of the interconnections that allow you to apply for a job in Germany. To the user, the Internet seems to be a direct connection.

You might be wondering who bears the cost. The National Science Foundation has been supporting the backbone of the Internet for upwards of $10 million dollars a year. As the NSF withdraws support and commercial free-market forces take over, the nature of the Internet will certainly change.

Adapting to the Internet

Before we begin, we must discuss the most common mistake job seekers with a little knowledge about personal computers and a little knowledge about the Internet can make. We can see this mistake if we look back to the histories of the introduction of different new technologies. The quality of silent movies in the late 1920s was superb, whereas the talkies were crude and simplistic. But by the 1930s virtually all movies were talkies. Some producers and stars made the transition, but a whole new set of faces with theatrical experience became the new stars because they had the skills that the new technology demanded. Those who didn't adapt to the unique characteristics of the new technology—those who acted the same way and just added speech—weren't successful.

In the 1930s everyone agreed that television would never replace radio. Radio was the "theater of the imagination." But the transition was dramatically fast as major radio stars switched over to the new medium. Some survived, but many didn't adapt to the new visual requirement that the new technology demanded.

What's the lesson from these shifts from silent movies to talkies and from radio to television? It's that each new technology has unique requirements.

How does that lesson apply to job seekers using the Internet? You know how to prepare a resume. If you know how to use a personal computer, you probably have that resume on disk. When you learn the basics of using the Internet, you'll learn that you can send a resume electronically to an employer.

You work carefully on your printed resume to give employers just the right "picture" of you as they review it with your letter of application. You're proud of that resume, and it's probably pretty good—so good in fact that you feel you should use it with your electronic job application. You've just made the same mistake as the silent movie stars who didn't realize that each new technology has unique requirements. An employer looking at a printed resume takes in at a glance the whole page or two. An employer looking at an electronic resume sees only the first screen and will make a judgment based on the first 20 or so lines of your resume!

In this book we want to help you make that transition from silent movie star to the talkies, from radio star to television, from printed resume to electronic resume, from a job seeker relying on out-of-date local print vacancy notices to a job seeker electronically scanning current job vacancies anywhere in the world.

In this chapter we describe the ways anyone can gain access to the Internet. Even if you have access now, perhaps at your current job, you should review this chapter to learn about other ways. Not only does the cost differ, but the extent of your access can vary. And for those of

you planning to rely on your access at work, remember that your
employer may not appreciate your using company time and resources
for your new job search. We end the chapter describing what you're
getting access to and how you'll be identified there.

Using a Computer

What is generally thought of as the first modern computer was the
ENIAC built in 1944. The computer could execute up to 5,000 arith-
metic operations a second and was 100 feet long, 10 feet high, 3 feet
deep, and weighed 30 tons. ENIAC had 17,468 vacuum tubes, 70,000
resisters, and 6,000 switches and used 140,000 watts of electricity. The
advances have come fast. Randall Tobias, former vice chairman of
AT&T, is credited with offering this comparison to help us understand
how far computers have advanced: "If we had similar progress in
automotive technology, you could buy a Lexus for about $2. It would
travel at the speed of sound and go about 600 miles on a thimble of
gas."

Do you have a 486? A new Pentium-based computer? Have you considered buying a PC or Macintosh? It doesn't matter for access to the
Internet. Too expensive? Too complicated? What cost $3,500 in 1991
is now available for $1,500 or less. Even the large discount stores now
sell computers. Factory-equipped personal computers can be running
in less than a half hour. If you need help, the major manufacturers have
toll-free help lines.

If you're ready to purchase, consider getting the same kind of computer your kids use at school or you use at work. Here are some other
things to consider:

- **Invest in a good monitor**. Skimping on a good monitor can
  affect your eyes and cause headaches. Most complete systems
  come with color monitors. Avoid monitors that have dot pitches
  larger than .28—here a smaller number is better. Look for what
  is easy for you to read.

- **Invest in speed**. Speed means how quickly your computer
  processes information. Speed can be indicated by a number
  ending in "86" and by "megahertz" (MHz). For IBM-compatible
  computers today, the Pentium is standard. The newer Pentium
  Pro computers are required to run the latest applications. For
  Macs, the PowerPC is recommended. You can also compare the
  megahertz ratings. The higher the MHz, the faster the computer
  processes information.

- **Invest in storage**. The amount of information a computer can
  hold is measured by "megabytes" (M, MB, or megs) of hard-
  drive memory. The higher the megabytes, the more information
  the computer can store. Today most systems come with 8 MB of
  RAM (the area of the computer where applications and data are
  held while you work with them), which should be considered

the minimum you'll need. A hard drive is the place where the computer stores software and data. Most experts recommend 1 GB ("gig," short for "gigabyte").

Remember, too, that as more and more people buy computers for their homes, more and more people replace their old computers with newer, more powerful ones. This means that many used systems are available. Check the newspaper classifieds and computer swap meets. The advantage of buying a used computer is that the price will be much less, and you should be able to negotiate as part of the price that the seller install your home computer and help you get started on it. The disadvantage is that there is no guarantee, so be sure that the seller agrees to install it and get you going on it.

You don't need to invest in a computer right away to have access to the Internet. Almost all colleges and universities offer computer labs to students. You usually don't have to be a computer science student to use these labs, so check with your local college or university. Learn the conditions for using its computer labs and under what conditions you may have access to the Internet.

If you're not in college now, you can enroll for one class. That will be considerably cheaper than investing in a new computer right away. Some colleges may open their computer labs to alumni. If you're a graduate of a college in your community, check with the alumni office. Someone there may be able to help.

As public libraries become increasingly computerized, some provide computer access to patrons. Some government buildings also provide access to citizens. Do some checking.

Using a Modem

A *modem* is a device that connects your home computer to a computer network through a telephone line. Modems can be internal (inside your computer) or external (a separate unit outside your computer). Technically, a modem converts digital signals produced by computers into analog sound waves that can be transmitted over telephone lines. Modems are rated by speed and such features as error correction and data compression. Error correction features help filter out telephone line noise to ensure error-free transmission.

Speed refers to the time it takes to transmit the information. Many people have modems rated at 2400 bps (bits per second) or baud, which is considered slow by today's standards. Transferring a file from one computer to another that takes 11 minutes at 2400 baud takes less than two minutes at 14,400 baud. Most computers sold since mid-1995 come equipped with a 28,800 baud modem.

Today's modems also allow you to send and receive faxes. If you buy a modem, it will probably come with a trial subscription to one of the commercial online services such as America Online. Keep in mind, though, that your modem's speed is limited to the speed of the modem at the other end of the line.

Installing a Telephone Line

If you're planning to access the Internet from your home, you'll need a telephone line. After you install your modem in or beside your computer, you will plug the modem into a phone jack. Deciding whether you need a separate telephone line should be based on such factors as how many people use the telephone in your home and how many incoming calls you receive. If you have call-waiting on the same line as your modem, for example, an incoming second call will break your modem's connection unless you remember to turn off call-waiting.

Installing Communications Software

Some modems come equipped with the communications software necessary to connect your home computer to another computer. If yours doesn't, you'll need to buy a communications package that works with your modem. The easiest way is to check that the software specifically mentions your modem's brand and model number in its list of compatible modems. If it doesn't, get advice from a knowledgeable dealer so that everything will work for you.

Your communications software must provide terminal emulation, which basically permits your home computer to act as a terminal on the computer system you're connected to. The most commonly used terminal emulation over the years is known as VT-100, the standard for computer-to-computer communications.

Now that you've thought about access, the next step is how you actually get connected to the Internet. There are several ways to get connected: commercial online services, freenets, and bulletin board systems.

Using Commercial Online Services

Commercial information services charge a monthly fee. They themselves provide you with a wealth of information, including news and financial data, bulletin boards to post messages, and mail to other subscribers. Some commercial online services have their own career and job vacancy sections. The commercial online services can also provide gateways to send mail to people on other networks and give you access to the Internet. An *Internet Service Provider* (ISP) is a service that provides you access to the Internet.

CompuServe (about 4.7 million subscribers in 1996), based in Columbus, Ohio, and first launched in 1979, is the oldest of the Big Four commercial online services. It was owned by H&R Block before going public in 1996. CompuServe has a reputation as the most business-oriented and as offering the most breadth and depth of information of the online services. You can access your CompuServe account through the Internet from another computer system. (This is particularly useful when you need to check your e-mail from work.) For World Wide Web access, CompuServe provides CompuServe Mosaic as its browser. CompuServe also provides an Internet-only service called Sprynet. Also in 1996 CompuServe introduced its low-cost, family-oriented WOW! service for $17.95 a month. WOW! requires the Windows 95 operating system, a 486 or faster computer, and at least 8 megabytes of RAM. Call 800-848-8199 for more information or visit `http://www.compuserve.com`.

America Online, based in Vienna, Virginia, is now the largest online service with about 6 million subscribers in 1996. America Online has a reputation for creative content and a "club" feeling. It includes NetNoir, an area devoted to the interests of African-Americans. America Online offers complete Internet applications. For the World Wide Web, Microsoft's Internet Explorer will become America Online's bundled browser, and AOL also offers users the popular Netscape browser. AOL is available at $9.95 a month for five hours and $2.95 an hour over five. Call 800-827-6364 for more information or visit `http://www.aol.com`.

Prodigy (about two million subscribers in 1996) was a joint project of Sears and IBM and is targeted more to home users and entertainment. Prodigy was the first to offer a Web browser and the first to offer its subscribers their own personal Web pages. Call 800-776-3449 for more information or visit `http://www.prodigy.com`.

In 1994 Microsoft, the world's largest personal computer software company, introduced The Microsoft Network (MSN) as part of Microsoft's new personal computer operating system, Windows 95. MSN relies less on its own content but emphasizes its e-mail service and seamless access to the World Wide Web. Users of Windows 95 can subscribe to the service with a couple of clicks of their mouse. Call 206-882-8080 for more information or visit `http://www.msn.com`.

MCI has some two million Internet subscribers chiefly through services it runs for universities and businesses. MCI is offering unlimited access to the Internet for $19.95 a month to customers and noncustomers alike. Call 800-550-0927 or visit `http://www.internetmci.com/`.

In 1996, AT&T announced that it would offer its 80 million regular residential telephone customers five hours of free access to the Internet each month (or unlimited access for $19.95 a month) on its new WorldNet access service. Those who aren't AT&T long-distance customers pay $24.95 a month. WorldNet will allow users to establish their own World Wide Web page with free software AT&T will make available. For more information call 800-WORLDNET or visit `http://www.att.com/worldnet/wis/`.

GEnie Services is one of the oldest of the online services, but has yet to make an impression with consumers. For more information call 800-638-8369 or visit `http://www.genie.com/`.

Netcom is the largest of the independent online services and is growing fast with hookups in 150 cities. Netcom charges a flat monthly fee for 40 hours of use and free use late at night and on weekends. Contact NETCOM On-Line Communications at 800-353-6600 or visit `http://www.netcom.com/`.

In addition there are hundreds of local and regional providers. There are two large nonprofit service providers as well. Institute for Global Communications, probably the best-known and most efficiently coordinated effort for peace and the protection of the environment, provides complete access to the Internet. IGC is the home of PeaceNet, EcoNet, ConflictNet, LaborNet, and WomensNet. The basic rate is $12.50 monthly plus telephone charges for twelve hours of use; the volume rate is $25.00 monthly. Special rates are available for groups, students, and low-income people and organizations. For more information, call 415-561-6100; fax 415-561-6101; or write to IGC at P.O. Box 29904, San Francisco, CA 94129, or visit its home page at `http://www.igc.org`.

The International Internet Association (IIA) is the largest nonprofit provider of free Internet access and services in the world, giving easy access to the Internet. IIA provides 800 access from any point in the United States. For more information, e-mail IIA at `iia.org`.

Using Freenets

Freenets are not-for-profit public access information systems. The guiding principle of freenets is that computer communications and the Internet should be available to everyone. There are scores of public access freenets nationwide. The first and best-known freenet, Cleveland Freenet, was developed at Case Western Reserve University in 1986 to permit thousands of local Cleveland citizens to chat with each other and to visit the courthouse, library, and arts and community centers. The Cleveland Freenet also provides access to the Internet. Some freenets offer Internet access; others are local only and feature discussion groups about local issues. Freenets are the fourth largest consumer online service in the world, with a total of about a half million users worldwide. Freenets play an important role in providing low-cost Internet access.

Another example of a freenet is the Sailor project of the Maryland public library system that calls for terminals to be available in public libraries. Maryland citizens will also be able to call from home using local telephone numbers. Complete access to the Internet will cost a Maryland citizen about $35 a year. Another example is Alaska's State Library and the University of Alaska in Fairbanks' joint project State-wide Library Electronic Doorway (SLED). In time, every public library in Alaska will have computers tied into the Internet for public use.

Most freenets are funded and operated by individuals and volunteers. And most are members of the National Public Telecomputing Network (NPTN), an organization working to make computer network services as freely available as libraries. For more information, call 216-498-4050; fax 216-498-4051; or write to Box 1987, Cleveland, OH 44106.

Using Bulletin Board Systems

An estimated 50,000 to 100,000 public dial-up bulletin board systems (BBSs) are operating in North America today. BBSs come and go depending on user interest and the sysop, or systems operator, the person who runs the Board. The city of Austin has more than 400 BBSs. There is a BBS for every conceivable lifestyle and interest ranging from the law to religion and from home brewers to users of different brands of computer software. Some of the bulletin board systems offer Internet access. Some bulletin board systems are free, some suggest donations, and others charge a fee. Prices range from $30 to $75 a year.

Most bulletin board systems are small operations that provide a low-cost alternative to the national online services. They don't provide anywhere near the services of the online services, but they provide an alternative. Bulletin board systems are linked together through networks such as FidoNet, which was developed by Tom Jennings and basically given away out of his personal philosophy of "radical communications."

One of the most helpful BBSs on the Internet is the WELL (Whole Earth 'Lectronic Link) started by *Whole Earth Review* and located in Sausalito, California. It's an excellent place to learn about the Internet. To join, call 415-332-8410 by modem, log in as new user, and then follow the prompts.

Boardwatch Magazine originally specialized in BBSs. The magazine was founded by Jack Rickard as a hobby in 1987 and has been online since January, 1989. Today, it is a "guide to the Internet, World Wide Web, and BBS." Articles in Boardwatch are diverse and cutting-edge. In a typical issue you'll find monthly reviews of BBSs; articles on self-publishing on the Internet; information about computer viruses; the latest technology in graphics and sound; and book reviews and special articles on education, government, and business.

David Hakala is the self-titled "Editor at Fault" at *Boardwatch*. Mary spoke with him about BBSs and their place in today's World Wide Web.

MN: What has the expansion of the World Wide Web meant to BBSs?

DH: BBS sysops finally have a product that can earn them a decent living—Internet access. Instead of getting $60 a year per subscriber, they can earn $10 to $100 a month selling the same BBS access along with SLIP/PPP access to the Internet.

Their market is dramatically expanded. Dial-up BBSs are limited to local calling area markets. Only 25 percent of BBS users call long distance to reach their favorite boards. By contrast, a BBS that can be reached by telnet has the world as its oyster.

Businesses want Web design and hosting services and are willing to pay much more than they would for boring ANSI/ASCII online presences. Smart BBS sysops are connecting to the Internet. Of the 1447 Internet Service Providers (ISPs) listed in the Boardwatch Quarterly Directory of ISPs, over 40 percent ran a BBS less than a year ago.

BBS sysops have well-established roots in their local communities of online users, which gives them a significant advantage over national ISPs and telcos [telecommunications companies]. Sysops are making money by training and supporting local Internet users in person, something national ISPs are unprepared to do.

MN: How has *Boardwatch* repositioned itself since the expansion of the World Wide Web?

DH: We have led the drive to convert BBS operators to Internet Service Providers. Since 1989, we have reported on new ways to connect a BBS to the Net. We now address the needs of practicing and aspiring Internet Service Providers with or without a BBS component.

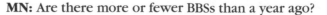

MN: Are there more or fewer BBSs than a year ago?

DH: There are fewer BBS-only sysops than there were a year ago. Membership in FidoNet, the international amateur network of BBS sysops, is declining at the rate of about 100 systems per week. BBS software vendors report sales of "pure" BBS packages are dramatically off. One vendor's DOS BBS software sales dropped from over $600,000 to $30,000 in a single quarter. But all vendors report record sales of software that combine the best features of BBSs and the Web. BBSs are evolving, not dying out. They remain the source of online communities as opposed to sterile, lonely data libraries.

MN: Why do people use a BBS?

DH: First, to communicate with other people. BBSs are living communities, each with its unique culture. Sysops do not sell online access; they sell companionship. Second, because they can't afford Windows-based Internet access, and third, because there is no local Internet service provider.

MN: Do people generally set up a BBS for profit or as a hobby?

DH: Most BBSs established in the last five years have profit-making origins. There has been a dramatic decline in the percentage of online hobbyist systems made available to the public free of charge.

Some people decry this "commercialization" of the BBS community. I hail it as the fuel which makes quality systems possible and the feedback mechanism which eliminates poor efforts. "If it's worth doing, someone will pay you to do it; otherwise, you should find something more useful to do."

MN: What impact have the commercial providers such as AOL and CompuServe had on local BBSs?

DH: The Big Boards have ignited widespread awareness of online communications, creating a mass market in which large and small operators thrive. Instead of taking customers from local BBSs, the Big Boards have made it much easier for local sysops to acquire customers. Many novices start on a large carrier, then quickly switch to a cheaper, less restrictive local BBS/Internet provider. The Big Boards report a 50-percent attrition among trial members. The most frequently asked question on any of the major services is "Where can I find a BBS in my area that offers Internet access?"

MN: What advantages does using a BBS offer?

DH: For one thing, full-speed connections. A dial-up line is used by one user at a time, at the full speed of which the modem is capable. The Internet is a packet-switched network in which multiple users share one link. It is not uncommon on the Net for a file to download at less than 1000 characters per second over a modem link that's capable of achieving 3000 characters per second.

For another, BBSs provide efficient, text-only inter-faces. ANSI/ASCII may be dull compared to GIFs, JPGs, and MOV and WAV files, but BBS screens are displayed almost instantly instead of minutes.

MN: What do you see as the future of BBSs?

DH: ANSI/ASCII BBSs will survive as "training wheels" for aspiring "infopreneurs." It makes sense to develop a working business model on a local level using dial-up BBS technology to learn what users want, how to effectively deliver it, and how to manage a virtual community. The next step, essential to economic viability, is to connect local users to the world via the Internet. The third and most profitable step is to create Web-based virtual communities to address the wants of the enormous neo-literate "mouse potato" market.

MN: How does a user find a local BBS?

DH: Mostly by "word of modem." Users swap e-mail about good BBSs. Local and national lists of BBSs, such as the USBBS list, are widely circulated. Many print publications such as *Boardwatch*, *Computer Shopper*, and local periodicals print monthly lists of BBSs. Some sysops advertise in computer-oriented magazines, others in topic-oriented publications.

You can access *Boardwatch Magazine*'s home page at `http://www.boardwatch.com`, where you can read the full text of their latest issues online simply by registering. You can also subscribe to the magazine online for delivery. You can also reach *Boardwatch* by voice at 303-973-6038, by fax at 303-973-3731, or modem at 303-973-4222.

Looking to join a local BBS? There are ways to find the telephone number you need. In later chapters, you'll find out how to use these tools, but highlight this now so you can find it later:

> On CompuServe, go to the IBM BBS Forum
>
> On America Online, use the keyword BBS
>
> On the Internet, go to any of the BBS newsgroups

Now that you've decided how to get connected, you need to know more about what you're getting connected to.

Your Internet Address

Just as you have a mailing address, you will have an address on the Internet. Actually, the addresses are easy to understand. Let's look at one of Fred's addresses:

> `fjandt@wiley.csusb.edu`

First of all, know how to "read" the address aloud. Fred's address is read aloud as "f-j-a-n-d-t at wiley dot c-s-u-s-b dot e-d-u." A period is read aloud as "dot." Commonly known words—such as wiley—are said as a word; others—such as Fred's name, fjandt—are spelled out letter by letter.

Just as your mailing address tells us what state and city you live in and where in that city you actually get your mail, your Internet address provides location information. Refer back to Fred's address. We'll look at the elements from right to left, which goes from most general to most specific:

- ■ The last part of Fred's address is **edu.** That tells you he's at an educational institution. In other addresses, you may see **com** for commercial, **gov** for government, **mil** for military, **org** for organizations, or **net** for networks.

- ■ Next is **csusb** . This refers to California State University, San Bernardino, the educational institution where Fred teaches.

- ■ Next is **wiley** . There are several computer systems at Fred's university. Wiley is simply the name of one system used on that campus—the system Fred is using.

- ■ Finally, there is the userid, or user name, **fjandt** . That's simply an abbreviation of Fred's full name. Many people like Fred choose to use the first letter of their first name and then as much of their last name as their system permits. For example, Mary uses **mnemnich** for her userid.

Some addresses will have an additional two letters at the end, such as **jp** . That's because most countries require a two-letter country code in addresses. All Internet addresses in Japan end in **jp**—the two-letter code for Japan.

Let's look at another example:

        `jobnet@aol.com`

Reading from the right, you see `aol.com` for the commercial online service America Online, and the userid is `jobnet` . This is the address we use to answer your questions about our book.

In addition to words you can read, every computer on the Internet has a unique number called its IP (Internet Protocol) address. The IP address identifies a specific computer on a specific network. IP numbers look like this:

        `128.174.33.160`

If you know the IP number, you can enter that as the address.

What happens if you enter the address incorrectly? Well, just as with the U.S. Postal Service, your misaddressed mail will be returned to you by a "postmaster." By the way, in one further comparison with the Postal Service, electronic mail is known as e-mail, but print material delivered by the Postal Service is often called *snail-mail*. That comparison shows one definite advantage of the Internet.

Some computer systems are case-sensitive. This means that letters shown in capitals must be entered as capitals and those shown in lowercase must be entered in lowercase. Be careful to copy down addresses exactly as you find them. Computers are very powerful, but very literal—in some systems `FJANDT` would not be recognized as `fjandt`, and `mnemnich` would not be recognized as `MNEMNICH`.

Choosing a Password

One final word: You must have a password. Without the security a password provides, anyone who knew your address could send messages in your name. Also, anyone could order merchandise from JC Penny's in your name. Security is provided by carefully choosing a secret password.

Passwords should be random and not linked to you in any way. For example, if your friends know you love cats and if you use your cat's name Yahtzee as your password, a friend could enter all your pets' names and quickly find your password. In fact, the most secure passwords are not actually words, but random letters and numbers or parts of two or three words put together.

A password should never be shared with another person. You might be able to trust your friend not to use it, but what if your friend accidentally allows a third person to see your password? You don't know whether that third person might use your account for all sorts of things you wouldn't know about or approve!

The Message Header

All e-mail messages are sent with what is known as the header. The header includes a TO: line, a FROM: line, a subject line, and other information. The following is a sample header:

```
Message 646
From carranza@ucssun1.sdsu.edu Sat Nov 12 6:24:42 1994
Date: Sat, 12 Nov 1994 16:24:22 -0800
From: Reyes Carranza <carranza@ucssun1.sdsu.edu>
To: fjandt@igc.apc.org
Subject: Re: permission


Sure, why not. Is there anything special you want me to do?
Reyes
```

Later, in Chapter 10, we stress the importance of carefully wording your subject line. In reviewing messages received, you'll usually see the name of the sender and the subject line. People who receive many e-mail messages a day scan this list for the names they recognize and for subjects of immediate interest to them. Condensing your message into a descriptive and attention-getting subject line is very important.

Finding Others' Addresses

Sending messages to other people means that you need to know their addresses. How can you find out other people's e-mail addresses? Unfortunately there isn't a single, simple directory. The reasons are many: people's e-mail addresses change, some desire security, some organizations prefer to use e-mail for internal use only, some organizations don't have the staff available to compile and update lists, etc. But here are some things you can do:

- Look at business cards and letters. It is becoming very common today to list e-mail addresses on business cards and letters.

- Call and ask. Simply call the receptionist and ask whether an e-mail address is available for the person you're trying to reach.

- Search the Internet. Try the following methods:

1. WhoWhere? is a free e-mail search engine supported by advertising. You can use WhoWhere? to find people and organizations on the Internet. To locate a person's e-mail address, you type in as much of the name as you know and then click the "Start People Search" button. You can also search by company name. If you find that you're not listed, you can add your listing. Visit WhoWhere? at **http://www.whowhere.com/** .

2. Anyone who has posted an article on an Internet newsgroup since July 1991 is probably in the 4.1 million address Usenet Address Database. Visit this site at **http://usenet-addresses.mit.edu/** .

3. Four11 Directory Services is the Internet's largest white page directory with over 6.5 million e-mail addresses and Web pages. Visit this site at `http://www.four11.com/` .

4. InterNIC registers domain names and owners. Directories on InterNIC's site on the World Wide Web (`http://www.internic.net`) contain names, addresses, phone numbers, and e-mail addresses of companies or individuals who have their own domain names.

5. Another method is WHOIS. Enter at a telnet prompt (see Chapter 6) the following:

   `whois.internic.net`

   At a `whois` prompt, enter the last name of the person or the company you are trying to reach. Note that some of the search results you'll see are in the form of e-mail addresses you'll easily recognize or a string of numbers you'll recognize as the IP address.

6. If you know the name of the computer the person you're searching for is on (for example from WHOIS), you can try a finger command to search for a person's userid to complete their address. But, not all computers have finger, and not all those who do have it list all the people on that computer. To try it, enter the following:

   `finger` `<some part of the person's name or userid>@<computer address`

   You'll find limited success.

7. Another method is PSI's White Pages Services. You can telnet (see Chapter 6) to:

   `wp.psi.com`

   and log in as `fred` .

However, don't expect complete success with these methods. The most reliable way to get another person's e-mail address is to ask the individual for it!

The World Wide Web

Realities that lead to this new edition of this book on using the Internet in your job search are the development, growth, and popular adoption of the World Wide Web. The Web's history is short. Its popularity makes it the predominant way people are using the Internet. You need to know only a few things to use this powerful means of retrieving information.

Earlier we described the Internet as a very large library with no librarians. Today's World Wide Web search engines sort through millions of pages to bring to your computer the information you requested. In this chapter, we prepare you to use the World Wide Web on your own.

Web History

The World Wide Web was born of the need to simplify the process of finding and using the vast amount of data on the Internet. The concept of an interconnected, hypertext-driven system originated at the European Particle Physics Laboratory in Geneva, Switzerland. Known simply as CERN, an acronym for the French "Centre European Researche Nucleare," the lab was a brain trust of scientists, students, and researchers from all over the world. The physicists at CERN were looking for a way to share information efficiently and quickly. In 1989, physicist Tim Berners-Lee advanced a proposal for a system that would make the dissemination of data faster and smoother without having to sort through a mountain of unnecessary documents on the Internet.

Until this period, the information on the Internet existed in databases that were cumbersome to search. For example, gopher (which we describe in Chapter 6) was easy in the sense that it was menu-driven with the data neatly organized in lists. However, a search through gopher still necessitated a tedious and time-consuming process of paging through countless screens to get to the desired information. Ftp ("file transfer protocol"—a means of transferring files from one remote machine to another, which we also describe in Chapter 6) consisted not only of lists, but lists of often unintelligible file names. Berners-Lee sought a way to bring order to the chaos for CERN scientists.

What Berners-Lee proposed was a simple means of finding information by following a series of links from one piece of data to another. Prior to this time, the metaphor most often used to describe the Internet had been a "tree," where users made their way to information by going from branch to branch up a "trunk" of menus. The gopher system used this hierarchical means of organizing information. Searches accomplished in this manner were time-consuming as one often had to climb the same tree again and again each time new information was sought. Berners-Lee envisioned his more efficient process as a "web" of "information nodes" that CERN scientists could use to move quickly from one piece of information to another. He called this concept of interconnected links "hypertext."

In his proposal, Berners-Lee laid out the entire picture of a web that could be interconnected among several different machines. As early as 1989, Berners-Lee conceived of a broad-based use for his system—a "world wide web." He also raised the notion of "hypermedia," the idea that, not just text, but pictures, sound, graphics and animation could be transmitted across the web.

The Browsers

It wasn't until 1990, however, that the first World Wide Web browser—that is, the software that allows users to explore or "browse" the information on the WWW—was developed. By 1991, the Web browser was in wide use at CERN.

It was time to take the Web to a more generalized level. Word had been spreading on discussion groups on the Internet (known as *newsgroups*) about this remarkable new tool. CERN began to make its browser available to anyone by ftp. Software development rapidly followed and, by early 1993, 50 Web servers were in existence. By late 1993, that number grew to more than 500 servers.

The early part of 1993 saw the emergence of a new browser, developed by Marc Andreesen and Eric Bina, undergraduate students at the University of Illinois at the National Center for Supercomputing Applications (NCSA) in Champaign, Illinois. It was called Mosaic, and it soon became almost synonymous with the web itself. When Mosaic was licensed commercially, web browsing (or what is popularly called "surfing") became available to a wider group, and traffic on the World Wide Web took off. Mosaic is the basis of the commercial browsers of Spry/CompuServe and Microsoft.

The next year, Andreesen and former Stanford University professor Jim Clark formed Netscape and by the end of that year released the Netscape Navigator. In the fall of 1994, the Mosaic browser accounted for 60 percent of all traffic on the World Wide Web. By the spring of 1995, Mosaic accounted for 5 percent of the traffic, and Netscape accounted for 75 percent of all Web visitors. Netscape had become the Microsoft of the Internet.

With the explosion of information available on the Internet, the need for a standard location system became apparent. You'll see this referred to as an URL–Uniform Resource Locator. The locations for Web sites are URLs. The URL for CareerPath, for example, is

```
http://www.careerpath.com
```

The elements of a URL are these:

`http:`	Hypertext terminal protocal–the type of application used to access the information
`//www.careerpath.com`	Here, the World Wide Web and the host name

Getting on the World Wide Web

To "browse the web," you need a service provider and a software package. If you're a subscriber to a commercial online service, you can have assess to the World Wide Web with the software the service provides. The major full-service Internet software packages available today are these:

- **Netscape Navigator Personal Edition 3.0**. Regarded as the best by experts and novices alike, Netscape has a "hand-holding" program for new users, leading them through the process of selecting and signing up with a service provider. The program also has a full range of advanced features. Contact 800-638-7483.

  Netscape Navigator (or just Netscape for short) has many features. With Netscape, you don't need to type in the entire Web address. To reach Microsoft's home page, for example, you could enter its complete Web address:

  ```
  http://www.microsoft.com
  ```

Netscape will get you there with:

```
microsoft.com
```

or even just:

```
microsoft
```

One of Netscape's most useful features is its Bookmarks feature. Pull down Bookmarks and choose Go to Bookmarks. Pull down File, click What's New?, and Netscape will check in with your bookmarked sites to see whether they've changed since your last visit.

- **Internet in a Box**. As the original browser of choice (Mosaic), Internet in a Box looks dated already, but it is user-friendly and easy to install and includes an off-line tutorial and complete instruction manual. Contact Spry/CompuServe at 800-557-9614.

- **CommSuite 95**. Integrates voice, fax, e-mail, and its Web browser, Cyberjack. CommSuite 95 uses Windows 95's Microsoft Exchange to manage e-mail. Contact Symantec at 800-441-7234.

- **Netcruiser Plus 2.1**. A simple, easy-to-use interface with a full set of Internet products (not integrated), provided by Netcom, a major national service provider. Contact Netcom at 800-638-2661.

- **Internet Explorer 2.0**. This is Microsoft's product and has seamless integration with the Windows 95 desktop. Free on Microsoft's Web sites (`http://www.microsoft.com`).

- **Internet Suite**. A fast system with a search umbrella Webcompass that includes over a dozen different search engines. Contact Quarterdeck at 800-354-3222.

- **Emissary 1.2**. This has been described as an ideal software program for anyone who uses many different parts of the Internet; however, it might be difficult for the novice. Contact Attachmate at 800-872-8649.

With each one of these, you load the software on your computer. You'll be shown on your screen some of the Internet service providers and asked for charge information. You can enter your credit card number and be on the Web.

Search Engines

Just a few years ago the World Wide Web was populated by physicists and computer programmers. Today it's a mass of information for anyone. How do you find what you want in this maze?

The popular phrase *search engine* refers to electronic directories that search for documents, pages, or sites on the World Wide Web based on keywords. And the miracle of the Web is that you simply have to point and click to go to any of the sites the search engine gives you. Many are in use; here are some samples:

Alta Vista at `http://www.altavista.digital.com` was developed by Digital (see fig. 3.1). Alta Vista has been online since December, 1995. It receives more than two million hits per day (see fig. 3.2). With 21 million pages, it is the largest of the Web search databases.

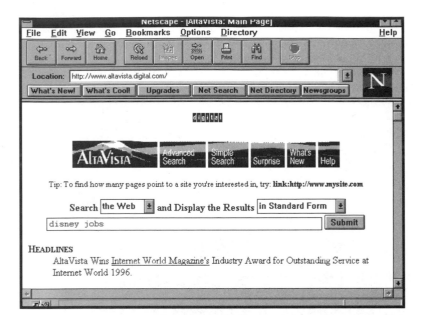

● ● ● ● ● ● ● ● ●

Fig. 3.1. Alta Vista
home page with
keywords "Disney
jobs" entered.

● ● ● ● ● ● ● ● ●

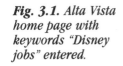

Excite at `http://www.excite.com` has a full text database of
1.5 million pages. Excite also searches newsgroups.

InfoSeek Guide at `http://guide.infoseek.com` allows very
detailed search requests. InfoSeek has a limited database of full text of
about one million pages. It offers complete displays of search results
including the URL, the title of the Web page, the size of the file, and a
summary.

Lycos at `http://www.lycos.com` is one of the oldest search engines (see fig. 3.3). Its name comes from *lycosidae*, Latin for "wolf spider," a family of wandering ground spiders. You can enter a search string at the main box, or you may narrow your search specifications by controlling several different fields in the search options area. Lycos searches yield comprehensive results (see fig. 3.4).

Fig. 3.3. *Lycos home page with keywords "medical secretary" entered.*

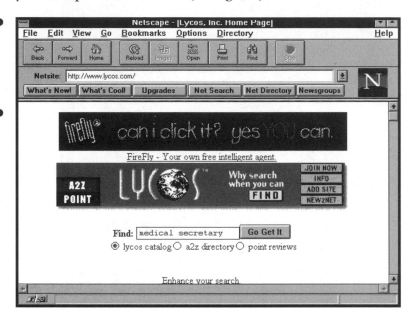

Fig. 3.4. *Lycos results screen showing first hit.*

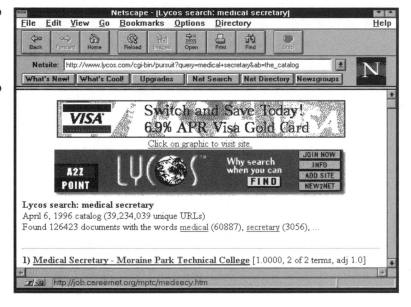

Open Text at `http://www.opentext.com` offers a "power search" option where you may enter up to five search terms and five Boolean operators (words that aid in information retrieval, such as *or*, *and*, and *not*). You can also search on one term or refine your search by specifying relevance of particular terms.

Yahoo (an acronym for "Yet Another Hierarchical Officious Oracle") at `http://www.yahoo.com` is a very popular search engine (see fig. 3.5). Graduate students David Filo and Jerry Yang started Yahoo as a personal list of their favorite Internet sites. Yahoo has become one of the most important organizing forces on the Internet (see fig. 3.6).

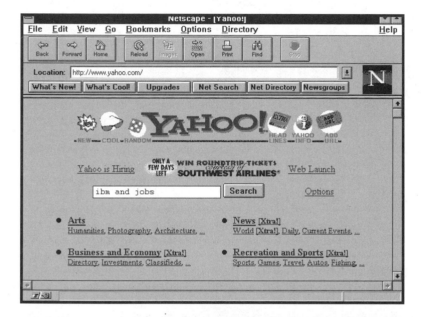

Fig. 3.5. Yahoo home page with the keywords "IBM" and "jobs" entered.

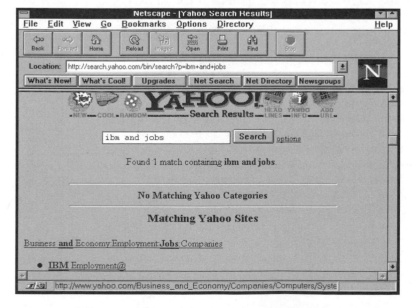

Fig. 3.6. Yahoo search results screen showing first hit.

In addition, there are now available a few search engines that combine several different search engines at their site. Your one request at a single site activates a search using several of the search engines. One of these, called Savvy Search, consolidates seven search engines at its site. Savvy Search is located at `http://www.cs.colostate.edu/~dreiling/smartform.html`.

Another of these multi-threaded multiple search sites is the MetaCrawler. This one uses eight different engines at its site. It's a bit slow. You can find MetaCrawler at `http://www.metacrawler.com`.

We've only shown you a few of the several hundred search engines available on the World Wide Web. For a list of more than 350 of them, look at the URL `http://www.mihnelson.com/MSfram.html`.

The Multimedia Web

Why has the World Wide Web become the major way to visit the Internet? Think of a page of text that has a footnote. Imagine that just by pointing at the footnote, whatever is referenced in the footnote magically appears on the next page. Imagine that that page also has a footnote. You could point at it and magically see what it referenced on the next page. This is the magic of the World Wide Web. It's called "point and click." Click on any highlighted text and your Web browser magically takes you to that site.

The second reason is that the Web provides you with multimedia. We've mentioned sound as an advantage of the World Wide Web. Sound on the Internet used to involve a three-step process: Download an audio file, decompress it, then play it. On the Web, RealAudio enables everything to happen instantly while you're online.

RealAudio software was developed by former Microsoft vice president Rob Glaser in 1994 to receive and decode sound via modem. The RealAudio software can be downloaded free from this site:

`http://www.realaudio.com`

The RealAudio site provides National Public Radio shows, ABC headline news, and links to some 500 other sites.

It's also possible to use the Internet for your telephone calls—real-time conversation. NetPhone is one application that makes it possible for you to place audio calls over the Internet. You and the person you wish to talk with must have the same brand of software. With that in place, you can talk live to anyone anywhere in the world for no cost other than your service provider's regular access charge. You can visit the NetPhone home page at this URL: `http://www.emagic.com`.

Video over the Internet is available now, too. CU-SeeMe is a videoconferencing program that allows users to see one another. The quality of the video is similar to surveillance video cameras. CU-See-Me was developed at Cornell University. (For more on CU-SeeMe, see Chapter 12.) You can learn more about it at the site: `http://cu-seeme.cornell.edu/`.

The Internet started to change the job search; and the ease of use of the World Wide Web is making the change complete. You can use the search engines we've described in this chapter to find job listings and career information on the Internet. In the next chapter, we'll identify and describe some of the major sites for job listings.

The World Wide Web Classifieds

Now that you've got an idea of how to use the World Wide Web, in this chapter we turn our attention to the sites on the World Wide Web that contain actual job vacancy announcements.

The Corporate Home Pages

Many companies and public organizations have established—or are in the process of setting up—their own home pages on the World Wide Web. And many of these organizations now include their vacancy announcements on their home pages.

The typical vacancy announcement on an organization's home page has more detail than a classified ad would have. You'll notice that many companies are putting their Web addresses in their display ads (see fig. 4.1). The home page typically has more information about the organization—its mission statement, product descriptions, recent press releases, etc.

● ● ● ● ● ● ● ● ●

Fig. 4.1. An increasing number of employers reference their home page in their newspaper ads.

● ● ● ● ● ● ● ● ●

THE FUTURE IS HUGHES.
THE CHANCE IS YOURS.

Hughes Space and Communications Company, a world leader in satellite communications and wireless technology, seeks the talents of a Compensation Specialist.

The successful candidate will maintain existing pay and classification systems, consult with senior management, provide expertise on compensation policies and practices, and perform various human resource functions. Other responsibilities include: departmental planning, policy development and deployment, implementing salary incentives, designing compensation packages, conducting surveys, and coordinating special projects.

A Bachelor's degree in Human Resources or related field and seven years of current experience in domestic and off-site/international compensation, performance management programs, and compensation surveys is desired, as is the ability to coordinate organization change and transition plans. A working knowledge of CCP designation and compensation/statistical methodology is essential. Must have ability to prioritize projects in a multi-task environment. Familiarity with MS Word, Excel, and related software is preferred.

Hughes offers a competitive benefits package which includes a variety of options in health and life insurance.

For immediate consideration, please fax or e-mail your resume to: (310) 364-4026. E-mail: staffup 1@ccgate.com. Or mail it to: **Hughes Space and Communications Company, Dept. MAY 12-LAT-PW/CS, Bldg. S10, MS 368, P.O. Box 92919, Los Angeles, CA 90009**. See us on the World Wide Web at http://www.hughespace.com. Proof of U.S. Citizenship may be required. We are an Equal Opportunity Employer.

HUGHES

SPACE & COMMUNICATIONS
A HUGHES ELECTRONICS COMPANY

Figure 4.2 shows the Hughes Space and Communications home page. When you click the icon that says "Want to work here?" the employment area of the Web site appears. When you click the Opportunities icon, you are presented with a list of opportunities available at that company (see fig. 4.3). Clicking any item on the list brings up a job announcement, as figure 4.4 shows. At the end of the announcement, you'll find instructions on how to apply.

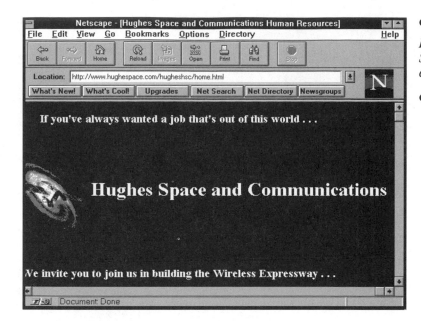

Fig. 4.2. The Hughes Space and Communications home page.

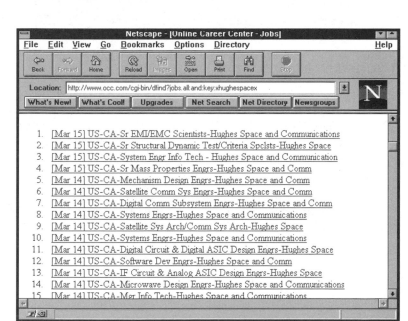

Fig. 4.3. A list of opportunities at Hughes Space and Communications.

Fig. 4.4. Clicking an item in the list brings up a job announcement.

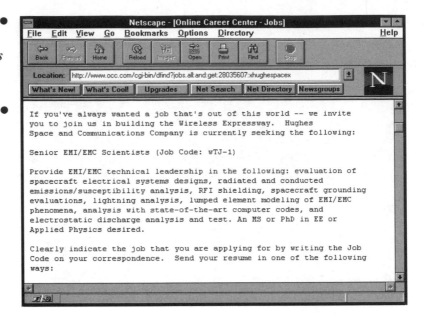

```
         Netscape - [Online Career Center - Jobs]
 File   Edit   View   Go   Bookmarks   Options   Directory                    Help

  Back  Forward  Home    Reload  Images  Open   Print  Find    Stop

 Location:  http://www.occ.com/cgi-bin/dfind?jobs.all:and:get:28035607:xhughespacex

 What's New!   What's Cool!   Upgrades   Net Search   Net Directory   Newsgroups

 If you've always wanted a job that's out of this world -- we invite
 you to join us in building the Wireless Expressway.  Hughes
 Space and Communications Company is currently seeking the following:

 Senior EMI/EMC Scientists (Job Code: wTJ-1)

 Provide EMI/EMC technical leadership in the following: evaluation of
 spacecraft electrical systems designs, radiated and conducted
 emissions/susceptibility analysis, RFI shielding, spacecraft grounding
 evaluations, lightning analysis, lumped element modeling of EMI/EMC
 phenomena, analysis with state-of-the-art computer codes, and
 electrostatic discharge analysis and test. An MS or PhD in EE or
 Applied Physics desired.

 Clearly indicate the job that you are applying for by writing the Job
 Code on your correspondence.  Send your resume in one of the following
 ways:
```

If you have a particular employer in mind, use one of the Web search engines to search for that company's home page. If you don't have a particular employer in mind, but you want to review corporate home pages, start with the following:

- The Commercial Sites Index, started in 1994 and located at `http://www.directory.net`, lists about 28,000 small and large companies with Web pages. You can go to these sites directly from the CSI home page. The Index doesn't indicate, however, which companies have job vacancies.

- Yahoo lists home pages with employment postings in a separate category. Go to `http://www.yahoo.com` and select "Business and Economy." Then select "companies" from the subcategory listing.

You might want to visit some sample company Web pages. Disney, for example, is located at `http://www.disney.com`. Figure 4.5 shows the Disney home page. Click "contents" to get started.

Fig. 4.5. *The Disney home page.*

Under "Disney Business Information" in the table of contents, there is a heading titled "Team Disney." Click it, and it brings you to Disneyland Job Opportunities (see fig. 4.6).

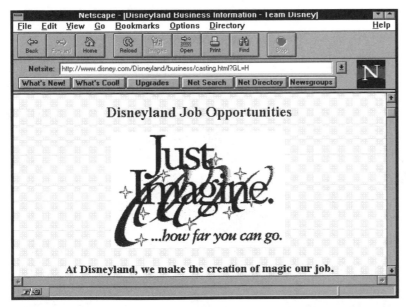

Fig. 4.6. *Displaying Disneyland Job Opportunities.*

Scroll down, and you will access the job postings. Here you will find job descriptions, minimum requirements, and application deadlines (see fig. 4.7). The end of the document provides an address for mailing resumes and a hotline number.

Fig. 4.7. The job postings on the Disney Web site.

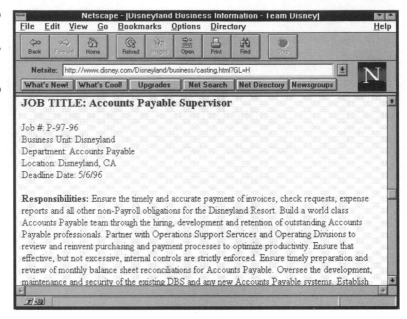

Netscape - [Disneyland Business Information - Team Disney]

File Edit View Go Bookmarks Options Directory   Help

Back Forward Home Reload Images Open Print Find Stop

Netsite: http://www.disney.com/Disneyland/business/casting.html?GL=H

What's New! What's Cool! Upgrades Net Search Net Directory Newsgroups

JOB TITLE: Accounts Payable Supervisor

Job #: P-97-96
Business Unit: Disneyland
Department: Accounts Payable
Location: Disneyland, CA
Deadline Date: 5/6/96

Responsibilities: Ensure the timely and accurate payment of invoices, check requests, expense reports and all other non-Payroll obligations for the Disneyland Resort. Build a world class Accounts Payable team through the hiring, development and retention of outstanding Accounts Payable professionals. Partner with Operations Support Services and Operating Divisions to review and reinvent purchasing and payment processes to optimize productivity. Ensure that effective, but not excessive, internal controls are strictly enforced. Ensure timely preparation and review of monthly balance sheet reconciliations for Accounts Payable. Oversee the development, maintenance and security of the existing DBS and any new Accounts Payable systems. Establish

Some of the corporate home pages invite you to apply online. The Good Guys is a retailer of audio, video, and personal electronics in California, Nevada, Oregon, and Washington. Their home page is actually a part of two employment databases. Visit their home page at

`http://www.thegoodguys.com`

At the time we accessed The Good Guys home page, the company was running a promotional game. This is what it looked like (see fig. 4.8).

Fig. 4.8. The Good Guys home page.

Netscape - [the good guys!]

File Edit View Go Bookmarks Options Directory   Help

Back Forward Home Reload Images Open Print Find Stop

Location: http://www.thegoodguys.com/

What's New! What's Cool! Upgrades Net Search Net Directory Newsgroups

ALIEN ABDUCTION! (THE REAL STORY)   Find Rob & Enter Here

Help find where our sales counselor Rob has been transported by Aliens, and you will be automatically entered into a drawing for a Home Theater System that's out of this world. (Hint: He's somewhere in our website)
How to Play...

We scrolled down just a bit and found all the icons for accessing the various areas of their Web site (see fig. 4.9). Click the Employment Opportunities icon, and you receive the Employment Opportunities screen (see fig. 4.10).

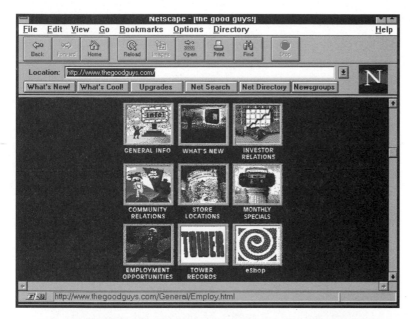

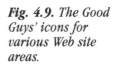

Fig. 4.9. The Good Guys' icons for various Web site areas.

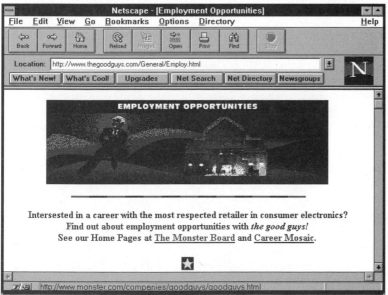

Fig. 4.10. The Employment Opportunities screen of the Good Guys home page.

The Good Guys use Monster Board and Career Mosaic for recruitment. You are given links to both sites. We clicked Monster Board and were sent to The Good Guys' home page at that site. We then scrolled down to reach job opportunities and clicked Corporate Jobs. On the next screen, there is a View and Apply button. Click it, and you access the job opportunities list by Monster Board. All the jobs are numbered, and you can check off those for which you want to apply (see fig. 4.11).

Fig. 4.11. Jobs displayed on the Monster Board.

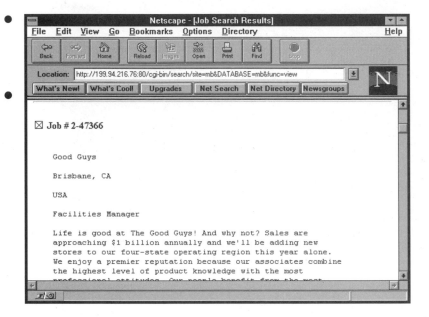

After making a selection, you can simply click GO to apply right there online for the jobs you've checked. When the Submit Resume screen appears, click Apply. You are then led through a series of fill-in-the-blanks prompts. At the end, you simply click "submit resume online."

Employment Databases

In Chapter 1, you read about CareerPath, the employment database of the help wanted classifieds from 19 major newspapers—*Atlanta Journal-Constitution, Boston Globe, Chicago Tribune, The Columbus Dispatch, The Denver Post, The Hartford Courant, Los Angeles Times, The Miami Herald, Milwaukee Journal Sentinel, Minneapolis St. Paul Pioneer Press, Minneapolis St. Paul Star Tribune, The New York Times, The Orlando Sentinel, Philadelphia Inquirer, Rocky Mountain News, The Sacramento Bee, San Jose Mercury News, South Florida Sun-Sentinel,* and *The Washington Post.* Job seekers register with their real names and e-mail addresses. There is no charge. This database can be searched by job classification or by newspaper and is updated daily. CareerPath is located at

`http://www.careerpath.com`

Other employment databases include these:

America's Job Bank, a service of the U.S. Department of Labor and the states' public employment service agencies, links 1,800 state employment service offices. The Job Bank contains one of the largest listings of active jobs available—one quarter of a million job listings from all over the country—and it includes professional, technical, blue-collar, management, clerical, and sales positions. In February, 1996, visits to America's Job Bank Web site approached four million hits. The Job Bank is located at

> `http://www.ajb.dni.us`

BPL Internet Index - JOBS is a well-organized mega-list located at

> `http://www.ci.berkeley.ca.us/bpl/bkmk/jobs.html`

Career Magazine is a unique databank. It combines job postings from newsgroups into a database that can be searched by location, skills, and titles. Career Magazine can be located at

> `http://www.careermag.com`

Career Mosaic is sponsored by Bernard Hodes Advertising. Career Mosaic can be searched by job description, company name, and location. This site is located at

> `http://www.careermosaic.com`

Employment Opportunities and Job Resources on the Internet is a mega-list with guides to Internet job searching compiled by librarian Margaret Riley. You can locate this site at

> `http://www.jobtrak.com/jobguide/`

Employment Opportunities and Resume Postings is a mega-list with links to other mega-lists. Not all URLs include the letters www, so enter this one carefully. This Web site is located at

> `http://galaxy.einet.net/GJ/employment.html`

ERISS provides a listing of job search software sources and Web sites focusing on job listings, resumes, career resources, and government agencies. You can visit it at

> `http://www.eriss.com`

E-Span's Interactive Employment Network includes job listings. You can access this site at

> `http://www.espan.com`

Help Wanted is a private company specializing in "university arena, management and marketing." The company's Web site is located at

>   http://www.helpwanted.com

Job Hunt at Stanford University contains sections with jobs in academia, science, engineering, and medicine from the classified ads in major metro newspapers. This Web site also includes job listings from newsgroups and resume banks. You can visit it at

>   http://rescomp.stanford.edu/jobs.html

JOBTRAK is used by over 10,000 college students and recent graduates and over 170,000 employers and is available to students and alumni of over 400 colleges and universities nationwide. The job vacancies here are specifically targeted to college students and recent graduates. JOBTRAK can be searched by keywords and provides skill assessment tools, resume writing tips, interviewing techniques, and salary negotiation advice. This Web site is located at

>   http://www.jobtrak.com

Mainstream Career Center, a service of Mainstream Access, provides career, human resource, and entrepreneurial information on the Microsoft Network. The service is available on the Internet as well. The site contains electronic job matching, online support groups, electronic networking, self-assessment tests, interview preparation, job market information, recruiter contacts, company information, and advice from experts. This site is located at

>   http://www.worklife.com

Monster Board is a job database of jobs worldwide. The database is searchable by keyword. You can also use Monster Board to keyword search through various job-related newsgroups. Monster Board is located at

>   http://www.monster.com

A Look at Monster Board

Monster Board is a large, user-friendly online recruiting service that was established in October of 1994 as the 455th registered site on the World Wide Web. Mary spoke with Thom Guertin, Associate Creative Director of Monster Board.

MN: How did the Monster Board come about?

TG: The Monster Board was the brainchild of Jeff Taylor, who is now the Executive Vice President of Interactive Services for TMP Worldwide, Inc. Jeff and the rest of us were looking for another way to expand the recruiting reach of corporations and shorten their hiring cycle. The Web's inherent capabilities and ease-of-use appealed to us. The Monster Board was a way for job seekers and recruiters to meet halfway along the info highway and speed up the process of a traditional career search.

MN: How are you positioned in the online recruitment market?

TG: The Monster Board is the premier career site on the World Wide Web. We offer job seekers free access to over 50,000 career opportunities, along with the ability to apply online instantly. The Monster Board is a cost-efficient, real-time recruiting tool utilized by leading corporations worldwide to attract highly qualified candidates online.

MN: Is there a charge to job seekers?

TG: The Monster Board is absolutely free to job seekers. Candidates can search for and apply online to over 50,000 jobs in minutes. They can also submit their resumes to our international database, research potential employers, and read up on the latest career trends at no cost.

MN: What is the cost to employers for using the Monster Board?

TG: The Monster Board offers a number of corporate value packages to increase a company's online presence. Individual job listings are priced at $125 each for the first four jobs, $100 thereafter. Each job runs for eight weeks at a time. Corporate brochures (Employer Profiles) and Online Open Houses are also extremely effective recruiting tools used by companies to attract candidates to their open positions. Users can conduct research on specific employers when making their decisions to apply online.

> **MN:** How did the Monster Board get to be so big, so fast?
>
> **TG:** I think a big part of how we got here is that we never stop pushing the medium. The Monster Board is always looking for innovative ways to utilize Internet technology in the best interests of the candidates and companies. We've held virtual interviews and career fairs, as well as featured online surveys.
>
> **MN:** We're curious about your graphics. They give a certain message. Why a monster?
>
> **TG:** The Monster Board started out as a big idea and turned into a "monster idea" in no time flat. The Monster Board tries to make the job search/hiring process less stressful and more fun for all involved. Our friendly user interface, bold graphics, and unique name serve as differentiators online. The monsters are your guides, watching out for your career and making a connection between candidates and companies. Our mantra in-house is "functional, fast, and fun."

Figure 4.12 shows Monster Board's home page. In this example, we selected "Career Surfari" and then "Monster Search" to find job openings. The Monster Board allows you to search for job listings by location and discipline (see fig. 4.13).

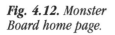

Fig. 4.12. Monster Board home page.

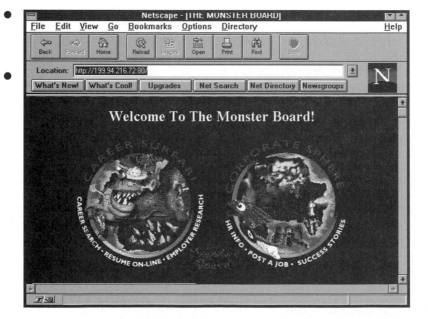

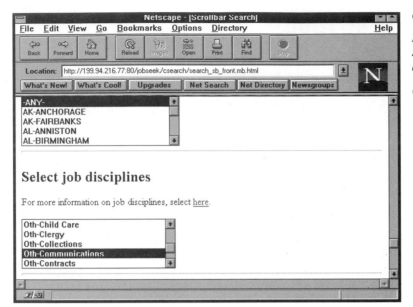

Fig. 4.13. You can select location and discipline.

Our search using ANY for location and Other—Communications for discipline located 36 jobs. You can narrow the search parameters even further by selecting individual companies and specific job titles. You then are presented with a list of jobs and may apply by clicking the positions you're interested in and using a fill-in-the-blanks resume as we showed you for the Good Guys' Web site.

The National Association of Graduate and Professional Students representing 150 universities established a job bank and career development Web page for graduate and professional students. The site contains job listings and links to commercial placement services and university career centers. If you're a graduate or professional student, first request a password by sending an e-mail request to nagps@netcom.com. Then you'll be able to visit their site at

        http://nagps.varesearch.com/NAGPS/nagps-hp.html

Online Career Center is a nonprofit employer association funded by employers. The Online Career Center allows the job seeker to search for jobs by city, state, or industry. This site is located at

        http://www.occ.com

Recruiting Links is a database of links to employment opportunities anywhere on the World Wide Web. Access this site at

        http://www.recruiting-links.com

Some employment databases specialize in one profession.

Education

National Educators Employment Review lists job openings in schools and educational institutions. The Web site is an abbreviated version of the *National Educators Employment Review* newspaper. This site includes information on state certification requirements, salary reviews, and a forum for job search and interviewing tips in education. You'll find this site at

        http://www.teacherjobs.com

Academe This Week is a service of *The Chronicle of Higher Education* and can be found at

        http://chronicle.merit.edu/.ads/.links.html

Financial/Accounting/Insurance

The NationJob Network reaches over 125,000 job seekers a month. The Network's Financial/Accounting/Insurance Jobs Page is located at

        http://www.nationjob.com/financial

Law

National Federation of Paralegal Associations provides information to the legal community including jobs. Access the Web site at

        http://www.paralegals.org/

The TSW (The Seamless Website) Legal Job Center is located at

        http://seamless.com/jobs/

The number of job databases continues to grow and evolve. The U.S. Department of Labor's America's Labor Market Information System (ALMIS) is sponsoring several projects, including one to develop a nationwide talent bank to help employers and prospective employees make their first contact through the Internet.

Even More Databases

The number of job and resume databases continues to grow. In the following list, we've provided even more you might want to review. Remember how quickly things can change on the Internet. There will be more; some will change their addresses; and others may disappear.

Find this database:	At this location:
4Work	http://www.4work.com
Adams JobBank Online	http://www.adamsonline.com
Airline Employee Placement Service	http://www.aeps.com/aeps/aepshm.html
American Federal Jobs Digest Listings	http://www.jobsfed.com/
America's Help Wanted	http://www.jobquest.com/
Arizona Careers Online	http://amsquare.com/america/arizona.html
BAMTA (Bay Area Multimedia Technology Alliance) Job Bank	http://www.bamta.org/BAMTAJB/
bioScience Career Fairs	http://recruit.sciencemag.org/science/feature/classified/career-fair.shtml
Business Job Finder	http://www.cob.ohio-state.edu/dept/fin/osujobs.htm
C.E. Publications Job Search	http://www.ceweekly.wa.com/
Capital Region Employment Network	http://www.crisny.org/~cren/
Career Connections	http://www.crisny.org/~cren/
Career Network	http://www.careernetwork.com/
Career Web	http://www.cweb.com/
CareerLynx-USA	http://gold.lsn.com/home.htm
Career Mosaic Asia	http://www.careerasia.com
CareerNet	http://www.careers.org
CareerSite: The Smart Way to Find A Job	http://www.careersite.com/

The Catapult on JobWeb	`http://www.jobweb.org/catapult/catapult.htm`
Cell's Positions Available	`http://www.cell.com/cell/posi/`
Classified Ads from JOM (Minerals, Metals, & Materials Society)	`http://www.tms.org/pubs/journals/JOM/classifieds.html`
College Grad Job Hunter	`http://www.collegegrad.com/`
Colorado Online Job Connection	`http://www.peakweb.com/jobs.html`
Commonwealth Jobsearch	`http://www.corpinfohub.com/cjs.htm`
Computer Software/Systems Jobs Page computers	`http://www.nationjobs.com/computers`
Contract–Jobs.Com	`http://www.ContractJobs.com`
Corsair Job Lead Reports	`http://www.interstat.net/corsair.html`
Department of the Interior Automated Vacancy Announcement Distribution System (AVADS)	`http://www.usgs.gov/doi/avads/index.html`
Direct Marketing World Job Center	`http://www.dmworld.com`
The Directory	`http://www.aone.net.au/the diretory/`
Electronic Job Guide	`http://none.coolware.com/search/../jobs.html`
Emploi	`http://www.login.net/%7Ewaxocom/ann.jobs.html`
Employment Edge	`http://www.employmentedge.com/employmentedge/`
Employment Online	`http://www4.nando.net/classads/employment/`
Employment Opportunities in Australia	`http://www.employment.com.au/`
Entry Level Job Seeker Assistant	`http://members.aol.com/Dylander/jobhome.html`

Executive International Employment Available Positions	`http://bizserve.com/greenlake/ERI/`
Executive Taskforce	`http://exectask.co.nz/`
Federal Jobs Central	`http://www.fedjobs.com`
GETAJOB	`http://www.getajob.com/`
GetNet International-Employment	`http://www.getnet.com/employment/`
Heart Career Connections	`http://www.career.com/`
Hospitality Industry Job Exchange	`http://www.hospitalitynet.nl`
Hotflash Jobs	`http://iquest.com/~ntes/jobslist.html`
Information Systems Job Search	`http://walden.mo.net/~devino/ads.htm`
IntelliMatch	`http://www.intellimatch.com`
Interactive Employment Network	`http://www.espan.com`
International Headhunters Guides	`http://www.universal.nl/jobhunt/`
InterNet Job Locator	`http://www.joblocator.com/jobs/`
JobBoard	`http://wfscnet.tamu.edu/jobs.html`
Job Center	`http://www.jobcenter.com/`
The Job Connection	`http://www.jobconnection.com/`
JOBLine...OnLine LA	`http://www.joblineonline.com/`
Job Listing at tamu.edu	`http://ageninfo.tamu.edu/jobs.html`
Job.net	`http://www.vnu.co.uk/vnu/cc/`
JobNet: Human Resources Online	`http://www.jobnet.org/`
The Job Server	`http://www.jobserve.com/`

Job Web	`http://www.jobweb.com`
Jobs and Career Opportunities with the Federal Government	`http://www.jobweb.org/ fedjobsr.htm`
JobsNorthwest	`http://www.jobsnorthwest. com/`
Jobs Online	`http://www.ceweekly.wa.com`
Marketing Classifieds	`http://www.marketingjobs. com/`
MedSearch America	`http://www.medsearch.com`
MMWire Classifieds	`http://www.mmwire.com/ classifieds.html`
National Diversity Journalism Job Bank	`http://www.newsjobs.com`
National Education Employment Review	`http://www.netgrafx.com/ neer/default.htm`
National Employment Job Bank	`http://www.nibbs.com/ ~najoban/`
NationJob Network	`http://www.nationjob.com/`
Navy Jobs	`http://www.navyjobs.com`
NYWorks	`http://www.nyworks.com/`
Online Sports Career Center	`http://www.onlinesports. com/pages/careercenter.html`
Pencom Career Center	`http://www.pencomsi.com/ careerhome.html`
People Bank	`http://www.peoplebank.com`
Recruiter Online Network	`http://www.ipa.com`
Reed Employment	`http://www.reed.co.uk/ employment/jobs/index.htm`
Training and Development Job Mart	`http://www.tcm.com/trdev/ jobs/`

Walking Through
Commercial Services

In Chapter 2, we talked about getting connected to the Internet.
Because many people will gain access through commercial services,
we'll take a step-by-step look at CompuServe and America Online in
this chapter. We are using these two services as examples, but bear in
mind that there are several other Internet services providers from
which to choose. Prodigy, for example, has a careers bulletin board
where subscribers can discuss job-hunting tips and also a classified
advertising department with a help-wanted section.

Once you get access through whatever means, how you use the
Internet is the same. This chapter is just for the new user accessing the
Internet through a commercial provider.

Accessing the World Wide Web
Through CompuServe

If you select CompuServe as your provider, you will be given two disks
for your initial setup and log on. CompuServe provides these disks
free, usually through a computer publication. We found ours in
Internet World magazine. You are given free hours, usually 10. Just
insert the disks, one at a time, and follow the simple directions for
setup on your screen. One screen simply says, Sign Me Up. You will be
asked for the agreement number and the serial number that are provided on the package. There are spaces for you to fill in your name,
address, phone number, and other information plus your credit card
number.

Next, a screen appears that explains how to select the communications
program your modem uses. You'll be asked for your modem's baud rate
(see Chapter 2). Select Proceed if you don't know it.

After setup, CompuServe dials an 800 number that automatically installs your local access number. You are then given your userid and password. These are selected for you. You do not choose them yourself. The userid is a long number that looks something like this:

```
543210.789
```

Your CompuServe e-mail address will contain this number and be constructed like this:

```
543210.789@compuserve.com
```

Typically, the password is two words, separated by a hyphen, such as **frame-pen**. (Previously, the words were separated by a slash: i.e., frame/pin.) Be sure to write these down and keep them in a safe place. You will need them if you ever need to re-subscribe.

Next, you will be given a prompt to enter your userid and password. Notice that when you enter the password, the letters do not appear on the screen. That prevents a person looking over your shoulder from learning your password. After you've entered your userid and password, you will be logged out. From the next time you log on to CompuServe and every time after that, you will never need to enter these again. (Previously, users had to enter their userid and password each time they logged on. Not so in the new version.)

Now, let's find our way to the World Wide Web and a job opening.

An icon called CompuServe Information Manager is automatically installed on your Windows Program Manager. You click this icon to log on. The first screen you see is Connect to CompuServe as figure 5.1 shows.

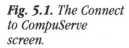

Fig. 5.1. The Connect to CompuServe screen.

Click Connect. This brings up a What's New window, superimposed
on the Explore CompuServe window (see fig. 5.2). If there is nothing
in particular you'd care to look at, simply click Cancel, and the Explore
CompuServe screen is revealed (see fig. 5.3).

*Fig. 5.2. The What's
New window.*

*Fig. 5.3. The Explore
CompuServe screen.*

At the top of the Explore CompuServe screen is a toolbar containing
different icons. One of these is a globe, CompuServe's symbol for the
Internet and World Wide Web. Click this icon, and you are taken
directly to the CompuServe Mosaic Web browser (see fig. 5.4).

Fig. **5.4.** *CompuServe Mosaic Web Browser screen.*

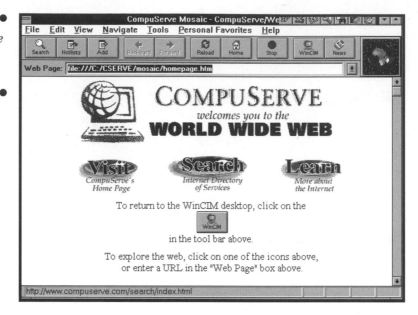

Click Search, and you receive a screen called Search Gizmos where you may enter keywords to search the Web. You are given a choice of several different search engines, including Excite, Yahoo (which is one of the best known), and CompuServe's own search engine. We chose Excite, the first one listed, and entered the keyword **employment** (see fig. 5.5).

Fig. **5.5.** *Excite search screen with keyword "employment" entered.*

At the top of the resulting screen, we found a message window containing the logo for IntelliMatch Online Recruiting with the message, <u>Your perfect job is a CLICK away!</u> We clicked it (see fig. 5.6).

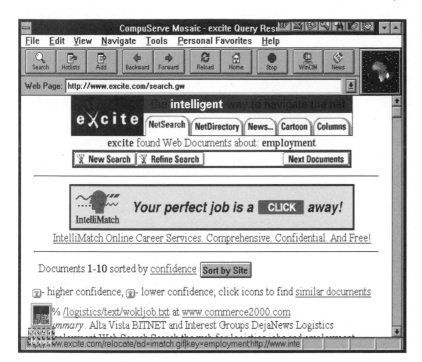

Fig. 5.6. *Message window for IntelliMatch Online Career Services.*

● ● ● ● ● ● ● ● ●

We retrieved IntelliMatch's home page and clicked Hot Jobs! (see fig. 5.7). At the Current Job Listings screen, we selected Human Resources (see fig. 5.8). We received a list of Human Resource positions and selected the one shown in figure 5.9.

● ● ● ● ● ● ● ● ●

Fig. 5.7. *IntelliMatch home page showing Hot Jobs button on lower left.*

● ● ● ● ● ● ● ● ●

Fig. 5.8. *Current Job Listings screen with Human Resources as a list item.*

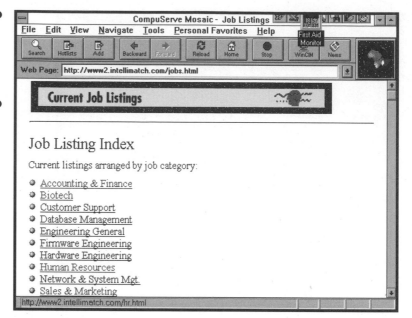

Fig. 5.9. *A Human Resources job opportunity.*

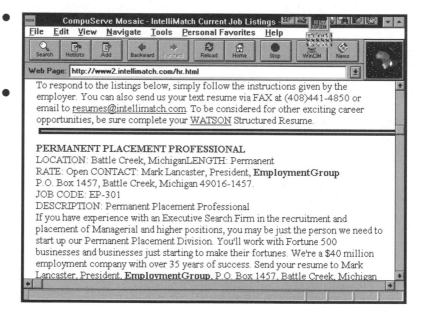

To access jobs through CompuServe, you can simply use the "go" feature. At the toolbar, select the streetlight icon. This opens a window with a prompt for a keyword. Enter jobs (see fig. 5.10). You'll open a window with the words "Access Classifieds" highlighted. Click "Select" (see fig. 5.11).

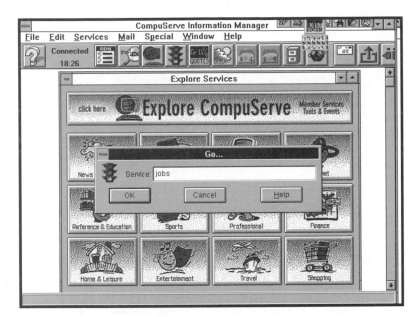

Fig. 5.10. *Go . . . window with keyword "jobs" entered.*

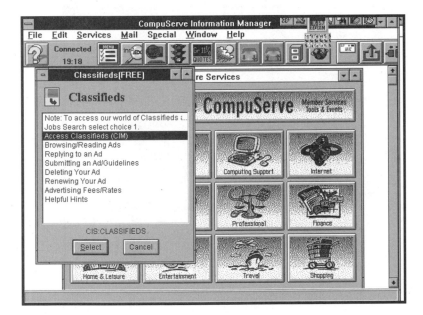

Fig. 5.11. *CompuServe Classifieds window.*

Here, you are offered several options for searching the classifieds. Select Job Search(E-Span) and click Browse (see fig. 5.12). This puts you in contact with E-Span's database of jobs. This database is searchable by occupation and geographic area. We chose Banking, Account, Finance (see fig. 5.13) and U.S. North Central (see fig. 5.14) and found a Purchasing Operations Manager in Minnesota (see fig. 5.15).

Fig. 5.12. Browse Job Search to access E-Span database.

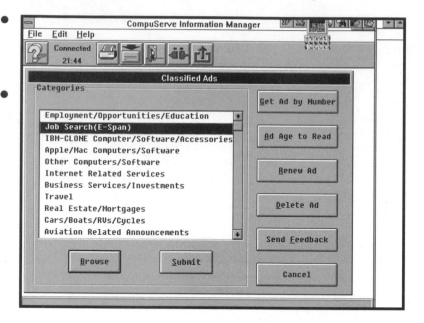

Fig. 5.13. Select your general occupational category.

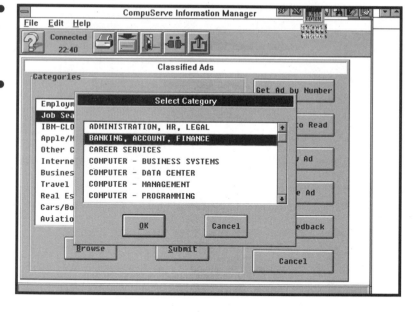

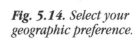

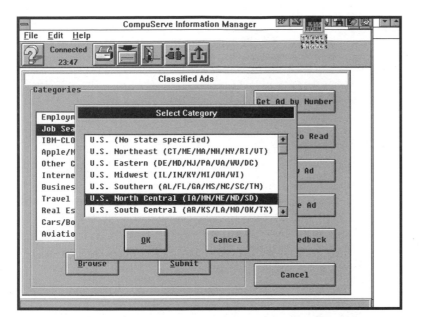

Fig. 5.14. *Select your geographic preference.*

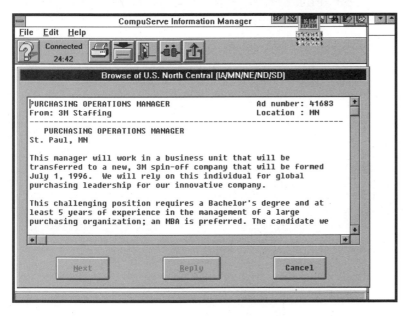

Fig. 5.15. *A job opportunity meeting selected criteria.*

On this position, the instructions were to apply directly by mailing a resume. An e-mail address was also provided.

Note: At the time this is being written, CompuServe has just announced plans to shift its content to the World Wide Web. Up until this time, CompuServe has utilized proprietary software to deliver its service to customers. According to the company, CompuServe subscribers who already have access to the World Wide Web should experience little difference in service and will benefit with easier and faster access to the Web.

Accessing the World Wide Web Through America Online

America Online (AOL) provides a disk for your first sign-on. It comes with a preassigned numerical userid and alpha password like this:

```
48-6284-5667
CUBS-CURIAE
```

Before you log on, you will be asked for your userid and password, and then led through a series of questions, asking for the baud rate of your modem, and personal information, such as your name, address, phone number, and credit card information. You will also be asked to enter a new password of your choosing, along with the name you want to use online. Your userid will then look like this:

```
name@aol.com
```

Generally, AOL provides disks for several hours of free service as a preview. You can often find these disks free in computer magazines. (We found ours in *PC World* magazine.)

For your first logon, the disk packet contains the following instructions:

1. Insert the enclosed disk in your floppy disk drive.

2. From your Windows Program Manager, click File and select Run. At the prompt, type **A:/SETUP** (or **B:/SETUP**) and press Enter.

3. When the installation is complete, click the **America Online** icon, and you're ready to go!

The first screen to come up shows your name and a prompt for your personal password. Type your password. (Again, your password does not show on the screen for security reasons. Notice the asterisks.) From this point on, each time you log on, your screen will look like the one shown in figure 5.16.

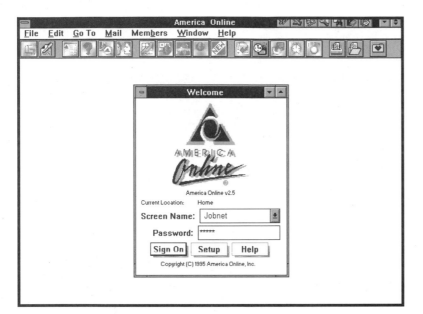

Fig. 5.16. *The AOL Sign-On screen.*

Next comes a Welcome screen (see fig. 5.17). If your system has a sound card, you will also hear a voice say, "Welcome!" The same voice will also inform you if you have mail.

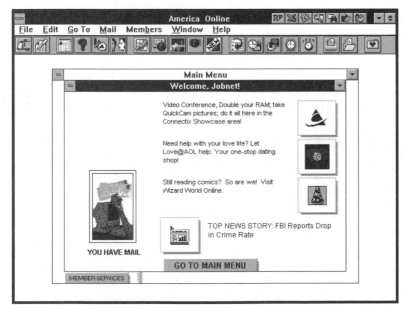

Fig. 5.17. *The AOL Welcome screen.*

Note: With the release of AOL's new 3.0 version in late 1996, the screens shown in this chapter will change. However, the same information can still be accessed.

Notice that there is a toolbar at the top of this screen containing several different icons. One of these is a globe. If you put your cursor there, the message <u>Internet Connection</u> is displayed. Click the message, and it opens the Internet Connection window (see fig. 5.18).

Fig. 5.18. The AOL Internet Connection.

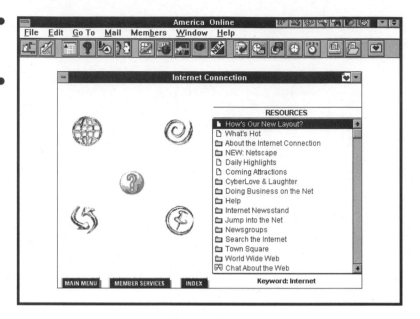

AOL has its own Web browser (Microsoft's Internet Explorer). However, Netscape is also available through AOL. If you plan to use Netscape, you will need to download it following very simple instructions on-screen. Under Resources, there is a menu containing the heading Netscape. Click Netscape, and it will lead you to the download instructions. Make sure you have the latest version of AOL that will run Netscape.

If you want, you can simply use AOL's own Web browser. To get there, click the globe icon on the Internet Connection screen (see fig. 5.19).

Fig. 5.19. The AOL home page.

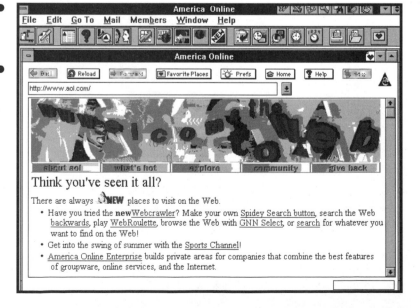

Notice that just above the graphic saying <u>Welcome to the Web</u> is a space. If you know the URL for a particular Web site, you may type it in here. Place your cursor at the start of the line and type the address, such as `http://www.jobcenter.com`, and press Enter.

This will take you directly to the site.

To do a search, click the highlighted word <u>webcrawler.</u> This brings up a screen with an area for typing keywords. At this screen, you are given two prompts besides the keyword. You may search the Web for "titles" (the web resource name) or "summaries" (the title and a brief description) and control for the number of search results. We chose "titles" and "25" results. We typed in the keyword **recruiters** (see fig. 5.20).

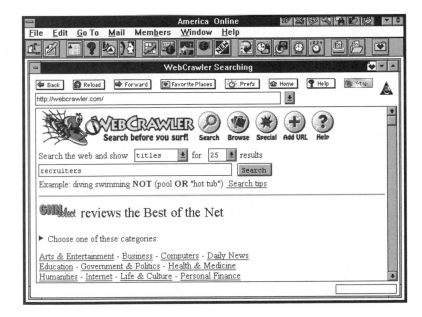

Fig. 5.20. *AOL WebCrawler search page.*

We clicked on search and retrieved the screen shown in figure 5.21. The search yielded 962 hits. From the list of the first 25, we selected JobHunt On-Line Job Meta-List. That selection returned the screen shown in figure 5.22.

Fig. 5.21. Search results for keyword "recruiters."

Fig. 5.22. The JobHunt Meta-List.

We scrolled through JobHunt's list of job resource categories, as figure 5.23 shows, and selected General (see fig. 5.24). We received an extensive alphabetical listing of job resources, including everything from the major ones, such as E-Span, Online Career Center, and Job Trak to more specific ones, such as Summer Job Web (for—what else?—summer jobs) and Platsautomaten (jobs in Sweden.) Best Jobs in the USA was a database of employment ads from *USA Today* newspaper. FedWorld contained jobs within the federal government.

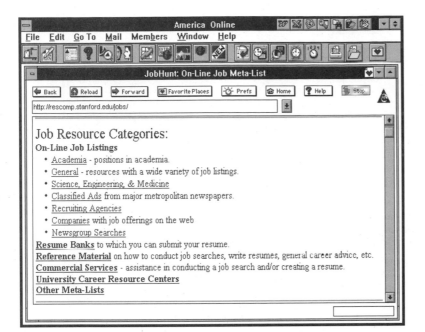

Fig. 5.23. *List of Job Resource Categories.*

Fig. 5.24. *General Job Listings–resources with a variety of listings.*

We selected Adams JobBank Online from near the top of the list (see fig. 5.25). From the list of choices on Adams' home page, we elected to go to its search engine. For keywords, we entered **Arizona** and **medical secretary** (see fig. 5.26). As figure 5.27 shows, our search yielded one match: a medical secretary in Arizona.

Fig. 5.25. Adams JobBank Online home page.

Fig. 5.26. Adams JobBank Online Search screen with keywords.

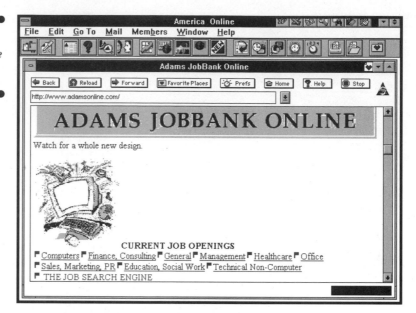

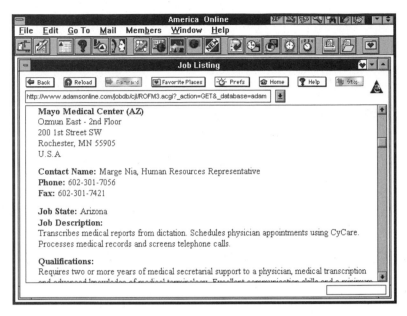

Fig. 5.27. Medical
secretary job listing.

We've shown you how to navigate through several screens to get to a
jobs area. There are different ways to do this, using AOL's Go To
feature. Simply select Go To from the menu bar at the top of the
screen. Click Go To to open the window. Select "keyword" from the
list of options. Enter an employment-related keyword to go directly to
a job area. If you type **jobs**, you get a listing of options where jobs may
be searched, including E-span database, Help Wanted - USA, and the
classified ads area. Typing **career** at the Keyword prompt gives you
two options: The Career Center and Career Web Sites (see fig. 5.28).

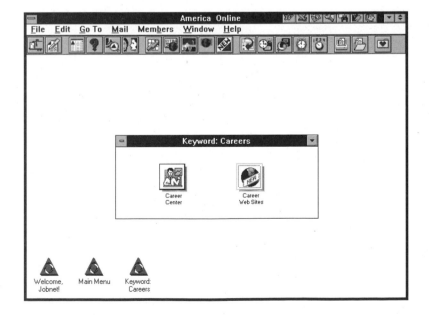

Fig. 5.28. AOL
Keyword window.

In the Career Center, you can access jobs, plus career guidance and other help (see fig. 5.29). Selecting Career Web Sites, shown in figure 5.30, gives you a list of career and job resources available on the World Wide Web. We selected Virtual Job Fair, clicked Open and were sent immediately to its Web site, shown in figure 5.31.

Fig. 5.29. The AOL *Career Center.*

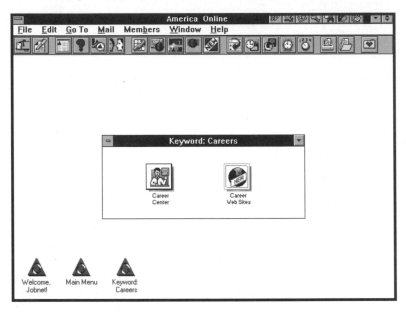

Fig. 5.30. Career *Center Web site* *options.*

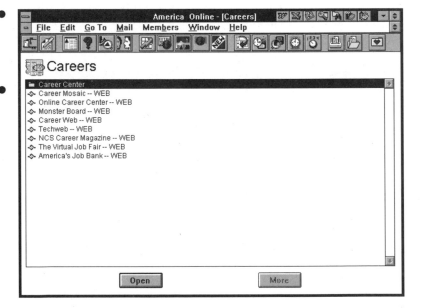

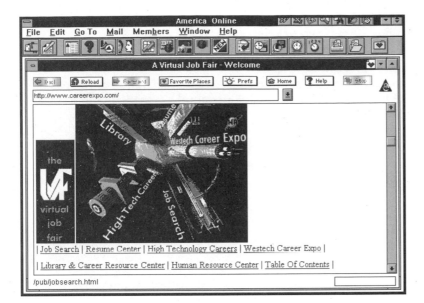

Fig. 5.31. Virtual Job Fair Web site options.

From Go to ... Keywords, if you type **classifieds** at the Keyword prompt, you enter the AOL Classifieds section. Here, you can select an option called Employment (see fig. 5.32).

Fig. 5.32. AOL Classifieds menu screen.

Career Resources on AOL and CompuServe

The commercial online services make a great deal of material easily available for members to access. For example, America Online's Career Center provides the following:

- Articles on issues important to career development

- Employer Contacts Database Information on thousands of employers and potential employment opportunities

- Career Guidance Services exercises and database with thousands of career options to determine a career direction

- Occupational Profiles Database Information on more than 700 occupations

- Career Resource Library and Employment Agency Database

- Hoover's Handbook detailed analyses of 500 U.S. corporations

- Business and Economic News updated throughout each day.

CompuServe's Career Management Forum addresses topics of concern to job seekers, including

- Today's job market

- Career workshops

- Resume and interview help

- Networking

- Salary issues

The forum's Industry and Professional publications section contains online versions of

- Dun and Bradstreet

- Hoover's Company Database

- The Thomas Registry

These are all valuable resources for serious job seekers.

Using E-Mail in CompuServe and AOL

One feature of online services you will frequently use is e-mail. Many employers request that you e-mail resumes; and, as you will learn in Chapter 12, much interviewing, both formal and informal, takes place over e-mail.

Let's take a look at the e-mail features of CompuServe and AOL.

CompuServe E-Mail

In the menu bar at the top of the first CompuServe screen, Explore Services, you will find the heading Mail. Click Mail and you receive the list of options shown in figure 5.33.

Fig. 5.33. The Mail pull-down menu.

When you click Create/Send Mail, you first retrieve a window called Recipient List, which enables you to save in an address book the name and e-mail address of the person to whom you are sending a message (see fig. 5.34). Simply type in the name and e-mail address and indicate which address type (CompuServe, Internet, etc.) you are using to send mail.

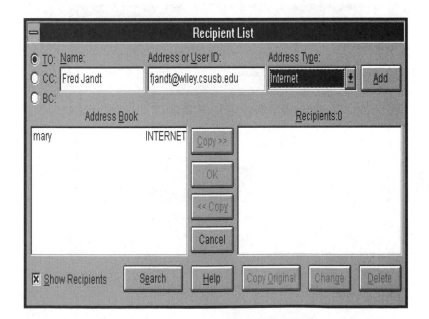

Fig. 5.34. The Recipient List window.

After you have added the address, click OK, and you will be taken to the Create Mail screen, with the address already entered. Then, all you need to do is enter a subject line–something that briefly titles your message–press Tab to move to the part of the screen where you enter the body of the message, and type your message (see fig. 5.35). Click Send Now and it's on its way.

Fig. 5.35. Complete e-mail message.

To check new mail, just click the envelope icon in the toolbar. That will take you directly to the Get New Mail window (see fig. 5.36).

Fig. 5.36. The Get New Mail window.

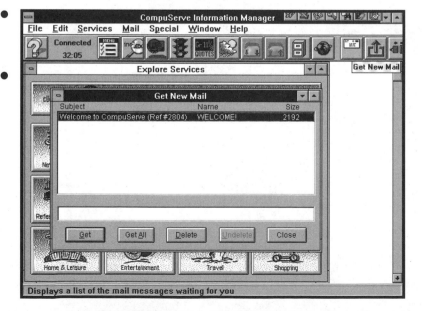

CompuServe now also has voice e-mail available. This feature has special meaning for job seekers especially. We'll take a closer look at it in Chapter 12.

America Online E-Mail

AOL has an easy-to-use e-mail system. When you first log on to AOL, you will see (and hear, if you have a sound card installed) a message telling you whether you have mail. Just click the mailbox icon, and you will retrieve your new mail (see fig. 5.37).

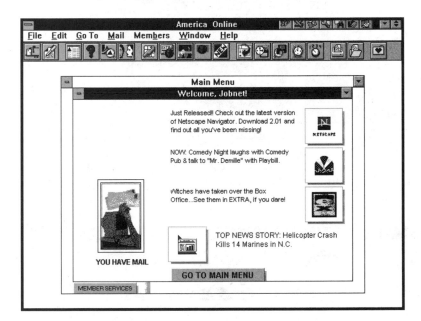

Fig. 5.37. AOL Welcome screen showing mailbox icon.

To compose an e-mail message, click Mail in the menu bar at the top of the Main Menu screen. Click Compose Mail in the pull-down Mail menu (see fig. 5.38).

Fig. 5.38. Compose Mail selected.

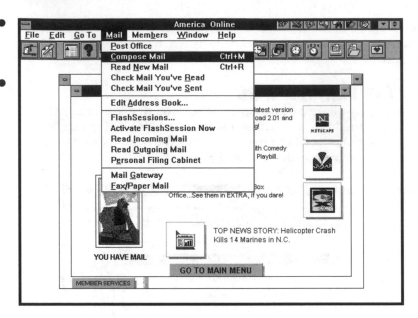

You will see the Compose Mail window with the cursor blinking at the address line (see fig. 5.39). Now, just type the address, subject line, and message. When you have finished, click Send (see fig. 5.40).

Fig. 5.39. Compose Mail window.

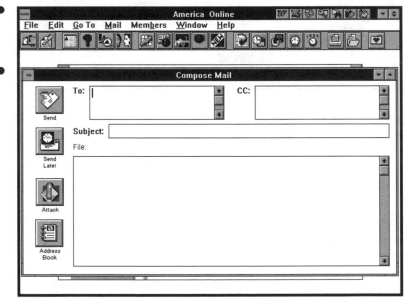

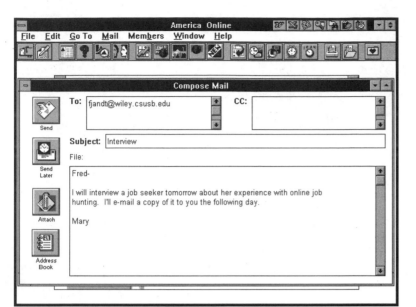

Fig. 5.40. *Completed e-mail message.*

As with the other features of commercial Internet service providers, the e-mail function is fast and very user-friendly. Rediscover the joy of correspondence. You'll find yourself using it often.

Using Resources Available Through Online Providers

Every job seeker needs information about employment trends as well as vacancies and employers. By using CompuServe, America Online, and other commercial Internet service providers you can learn what occupations are growing or shrinking, unemployment rates for any part of the country, and housing costs in any part of the country. This kind of information is essential if you want to succeed in today's labor market.

Mary worked with career military officers at a base that was closing. After having been out of the civilian job market for many years, the officers were amazed at the amount of research that is necessary to find the right job. They had to learn about civilian pay structures and benefits packages, as well as company philosophies. For many of these people, a new career also meant relocation. The kind of resources available through Internet service providers such as CompuServe and America Online can put you in touch with all this information and more.

Remember commercial service providers differ in the amount and range of Internet services they deliver to you. Before you subscribe to any service, evaluate your needs and what the services can provide—and at what cost.

In the following three chapters, we present you with the world of options available to you on the Internet.

Venturing "Outside" the World Wide Web

Before the World Wide Web, your primary means of making your way around the Internet were telnet, a tool for retrieving text from remote computers; gopher, a menu-based search tool; and ftp, a tool for retrieving text from another computer. These methods still exist, but Netscape has made them easier to use.

Newsgroup Job Listings

Don't let the word "newsgroup" mislead you. What is referred to as "news" does not refer to current events but instead to what we might more appropriately call "bulletin boards."

Think of a bulletin board on a college campus or even in a neighborhood grocery store or laundry. Let's say your dog is missing. You can post a message on a bulletin board for people to read as they pass by. If someone has seen your dog, that person might copy down your telephone number and call you to report where he or she saw your dog. Another person with a dog of the same breed might leave you a message to tell you about some available puppies. And because bulletin boards are visible to anyone who passes by, another person might write graffiti on your posting. Think of a newsgroup as the electronic equivalent of a bulletin board in your local grocery.

In newsgroups, you'll find more than 18,000 discussion groups on topics from the Bible to bestiality. Newsgroups (sometimes referred to as *network news*) are transmitted on USENET (User's Network). Just because you have Internet access doesn't mean you have access to USENET newsgroups. Any even if your Internet service provider provides access to USENET, that doesn't necessarily mean that you have access to all the thousands of newsgroups. Commercial Internet service providers may provide you access only to their own newsgroups.

Newsgroups are identified by topic. Some of the newsgroups are serious discussions on serious topics; others are just for fun; still others are frank, explicit discussions of adult topics. Under a topic on the first screen for a newsgroup, you'll see postings (also known as *articles*) that can be as recent as five minutes old or several months old, depending on how many postings the group receives. So be sure to check out when each article was posted. In addition to the date, each posting is identified by its subject line. You decide which article you want to read by its subject line.

If you have no experience with newsgroups, one place to begin is the newsgroup

> `news.announce.newusers`

which provides articles on how to best use newsgroups.

Some of the newsgroups with job listings are predominantly computer-related job openings. If you go to one of those newsgroups and if you're not looking for one of those positions, you'll just have to look through a lot of job listings for people with computer skills before you find a job opening more appropriate for you.

With the advent of the World Wide Web, some of the job databases can search through some of the job-related newsgroups by keyword. Read through their screens carefully; you may have to select Search Newsgroups or go to a separate part of the search screen designated "Usenet Search."

For example, CareerMosaic offers keyword searches of some 57,000 job postings on:

`ab.jobs`	Alberta, Canada
`alt.building jobs`	trade jobs (not really in use)
`atl.jobs`	Atlanta
`aus.ads.jobs`	Australia
`aus.jobs`	Australia
`austin.jobs`	Austin, Texas
`az.jobs`	Arizona
`ba.jobs.contract`	San Francisco Bay area
`ba.jobs.direct`	San Francisco Bay area
`ba.jobs.offered`	San Francisco Bay area
`balt.jobs`	Baltimore/Washington, D.C.
`bc.jobs`	British Columbia, Canada

`bermuda.jobs.offered`	Bermuda
`bionet.jobs`	biotechnology
`bionet.jobs.offered`	biotechnology
`biz.jobs.offered`	primarily business
`can.jobs`	Canada
`chi.jobs`	Chicago
`cmh.jobs`	Columbus, Ohio
`co.jobs`	Colorado
`comp.jobs`	computer-related
`comp.jobs.offered`	computer-related
`dc.jobs`	Washington, D.C.
`de.markt.jobs`	Germany
`dfw.jobs`	Dallas/Fort Worth
`dod.jobs`	U.S. Department of Defense
`euro.jobs`	Europe
`fl.jobs`	Florida
`fr.jobs.offres`	France
`hepnet.jobs`	high energy and nuclear physics
`houston.jobs.offered`	Houston, Texas
`hsv.jobs`	health services and related positions
`il.jobs.offered`	Illinois
`in.jobs`	Indiana
`israel.jobs.offered`	Israel
`ithaca.jobs`	Ithaca, New York
`kw.jobs`	Kitchener-Waterloo, Ontario, Canada
`la.jobs`	Los Angeles
`li.jobs`	Long Island, New York
`lou.lft.jobs`	Louisiana
`mi.jobs`	Michigan
`milw.jobs`	Milwaukee
`misc.jobs`	computer-related
`misc.jobs.contract`	computer-related and others
`misc.jobs.offered`	computer-related and others

`misc.jobs.offered.entry`	computer-related and others
`nb.jobs`	Nebraska
`ne.jobs`	New England
`ne.jobs.contract`	New England
`nj.jobs`	New Jersey
`nm.jobs`	New Mexico
`nv.jobs`	Nevada
`nyc.jobs`	New York City
`nyc.jobs.contract`	New York City
`nyc.jobs.offered`	New York
`oh.jobs`	Ohio
`ont.jobs`	Ontario, Canada
`ott.jobs`	Ottowa, Canada
`pa.jobs.offered`	Pennsylvania
`pdaxs.jobs.computers`	Portland, Oregon
`pdaxs.jobs.construction`	Portland, Oregon
`pdaxs.jobs.engineering`	Portland, Oregon
`pdaxs.jobs.management`	Portland, Oregon
`pdaxs.jobs.sales`	Portland, Oregon
`pdaxs.jobs.secretary`	Portland, Oregon
`pdaxs.jobs.temporary`	Portland, Oregon
`pgh.jobs.offered`	Pittsburgh
`phl.jobs.offered`	Philadelphia
`qc.jobs`	Quebec
`sdnet.jobs`	San Diego
`seattle.jobs.offered`	Seattle
`stl.jobs`	St. Louis
`stl.jobs.offered`	St. Louis
`tor.jobs`	Toronto
`triangle.jobs`	Research Triangle, NC
`tx.jobs`	Texas
`uk.jobs`	United Kingdom
`uk.jobs.contract`	United Kingdom

`uk.jobs.offered`	United Kingdom
`us.jobs.contract`	U.S.A.
`us.jobs.offered`	U.S.A.
`vegas.jobs`	Las Vegas
`za.ads.jobs`	South Africa

You'll notice that there are general, national newsgroups as well as some more specialized ones. Most of the newsgroups that list jobs are specialized for a particular city, state, country, occupation, or employer.

Just as the Internet is dynamic and ever-changing, so are the newsgroups. Some become inactive; many new ones will be added. We've identified from the many thousands of newsgroups those that are job-related. Keep in mind that your service provider may not provide access to all newsgroups.

U.S. Cities

`atl.jobs`	Jobs in Atlanta, Georgia
`austin.jobs`	Jobs in Austin, Texas
`ba.jobs.contract`	Contract jobs in the San Francisco Bay area
`ba.jobs.misc`	Jobs in the San Francisco Bay Area
`ba.jobs.offered`	Large listing of jobs in the San Francisco Bay area
`balt.jobs`	Jobs in the Baltimore and Washington, D.C., area
`chi.jobs`	Jobs in Chicago
`cmb.jobs`	Jobs in Columbus, Ohio
`dc.jobs`	Jobs in the Washington, D.C., area
`dfw.jobs`	Jobs in the Dallas-Ft. Worth area
`houston.jobs.offered`	Jobs in Houston, Texas
`la.jobs`	Jobs in Los Angeles
`li.jobs`	Jobs in Long Island, New York
`memphis.employment`	Jobs in Memphis, Tennessee
`ne.jobs`	Jobs in Boston and the Northeast
`nyc.jobs.contract`	Contract jobs in New York City
`nyc.jobs.offered`	Jobs in New York City

`pdaxs`	Jobs in Portland, Oregon (*Note*: insert job title such as clerical, management, etc.)
`pgh.jobs.offered`	Jobs in Pittsburgh
`phl.jobs.offered`	Jobs in Philadelphia
`sdnet.jobs`	Jobs in San Diego
`stl.jobs`	Jobs in St. Louis
`triangle.jobs`	Jobs in the Triangle Park area (North Carolina)

States

`fl.jobs`	Jobs in Florida
`il.jobs.misc`	Jobs in Illinois
`il.jobs.offered`	Jobs in Illinois
`mi.jobs`	Jobs in Michigan
`nm.jobs`	Jobs in New Mexico
`tx.jobs`	Jobs in Texas

Nationwide

`misc.jobs.contract`	Large listing of contract jobs
`misc.jobs.offered`	Very large listing of primarily computer-related jobs, but others listed as well
`us.jobs.contract`	Contract positions in the U.S.
`us.jobs.offered`	Jobs in the U.S.

Outside the U.S.

`ab.jobs`	Jobs in Alberta, Canada
`aus.ads.jobs`	Jobs in Australia
`aus.jobs`	Jobs in Australia
`can.jobs`	Jobs in Canada (also see local newsgroups: ab.jobs, kingston.jobs, kw.jobs, ont.jobs, ott.jobs, qc.jobs, and tor.jobs)

`de.markt.jobs`	Jobs in Germany
`dk.jobs`	Jobs in Denmark
`fr.jobs.offres`	Jobs in France
`gn.jobs`	Green Net's small listings of jobs in Europe
`kingston.jobs`	Jobs in Kingston, Canada
`kw.jobs`	Jobs in Kitchener-Waterloo, Ontario, Canada
`ont.jobs`	Jobs in Ontario, Canada
`uk.jobs`	Small listing of jobs in the U.K.
`uk.jobs.offered`	Listing of jobs in the U.K.
`web.jobs`	Small listing of jobs in Canada
`relcom.commerce.jobs`	Jobs in the former Soviet Union
`swnet.jobs`	Jobs in Sweden
`tor.jobs`	Jobs in Toronto, Ontario
`za.ads.jobs`	Jobs in South Africa

Occupation

`bionet.jobs`	Very large listing of jobs in the biological sciences
`biz.jobs.offered`	Very large listing of all types of jobs
`comp.jobs.offered`	Listing of computer-related jobs
`cr.jobs`	Small listing of jobs in conflict resolution and dispute mediation
`edu.popular`	Some job listings for people interested in education for democratic social change
`gen.jobs.usa`	Listing of jobs in environmental and social change
`misc.jobs`	Small listing of computer-related jobs
`misc.jobs.misc`	Mostly computer-related job listings
`misc.jobs.offered`	Very large listing of primarily computer-related jobs, but others listed as well

Employer

`dod.jobs`	U.S. Department of Defense jobs
`su.jobs`	Jobs at Stanford University
`ucb.jobs`	Jobs at the University of California, Berkeley
`ucd.cs.jobs`	Jobs at the University of California, Davis
`uiuc.misc.jobs`	Jobs at the University of Illinois, Urbana-Champaign
`umn.general.jobs`	Jobs at the University of Minnesota
`ut.jobs`	Jobs at the University of Texas

Here are some job postings we've taken off various newsgroups:

```
Subject: US-MO HelpDesk Persons Needed

From: McDonnell Douglas Technical Services Company
(MDTSC)

Date: 13 May 1996 00:53:22 GMT

Message-ID: <4n6162$61j@consolidated.ccinet.net>

    McDonnell Douglas Technical Services Company
    is a large provider of information technol-
    ogies in the St. Louis and Los Angeles areas.
```

We currently have several different openings for experienced help desk persons.

Experience with one or more of the following areas is desired: MS-Office, Windows, Novell, Lan/WAN, and/or NT.

The ideal candidate must have proven technical experience along with the ability to manage various projects. This person must have excellent communication skills, be customer responsive, possess a positive attitude, and have a desire to grow technically.

We offer competitive salary along with excellent benefits.

This opening is in the St. Louis Missouri area.

For confidential consideration please send your resume to:

E-Mail: rjones @ezl.com

Please include day time/night time phone along with the best time to call.

Add HelpDesk to the subject line.

Subject: Japan-Tokyo, System Administrator Manager

From: auxtech@futuris.net (AUX Technology)

Date: 12 May 1996 15:16:51 -0400

Message-ID: <4n5df3$2f4@kiwi.futuris.net>

JOB: JR22

POSITION TITLE:

System Administrator

SALARY RANGE:

Open - Based on experience and relocation package

JOB DESCRIPTION:

A major financial firm is looking for a talent to lead
its UNIX, PC, LAN teams in all aspects of rolling-out,
maintaining and supporting their information technology
systems. The successful candidate must have a
consultative approach to solving business problems with
excellent communication skills. This position requires
prior experience implementing IT solutions in a financial
environment. Past experience in an Investment Banking
firm would be a plus as would experience in front and
back office systems and managing a multinational staff.

Must have a strong knowledge of UNIX, Real-Time Trading
Systems and SunWork Stations. This person will fully be
conversant in all Sun hardware and software. Development
experience is a plus. This opportunity is at the senior
management level.

It would be valuable if the candidate comprehended the
Japanese language or would be willing to learn.

This is a great opportunity for a person who is looking
for a leading-edge opportunity and wants to pursue a
career in Asia. This firm has an excellent reputation
worldwide.

To be considered, please E-mail resume ASCII format or
fax with salary history and REFER TO POSITION#JR22.

AUX Technology, Inc. is an executive search firm. Our
expertise is within IT Networking/Telecommunications/
Client Server and Internet environments.

We have both permanent and consulting positions
available.

We take pride in finding the best opportunities for our
applicants and in making their career move a good
experience. All of our contacts are kept confidential; no
resume is sent out without your proper authorization so
that we can ensure that your privacy is respected.

If you do not find an opening that meets your needs but
feel that you have a strong background within the
technical field, we will also help you seek out

opportunities in other companies. We deal with a multitude of companies that can not possibly be all posted.

AUX Technology, Inc.
Website: http://www.futuris.net/aux/
Email: auxtech@futuris.net
209 Seventh Street, Suite 101
Jersey City, NJ   07302-2017
Telephone: 201-222-0260
Fax: 201-222-2156

———————————————————————

Subject: Harbor Pilots - Saudi Arabia

From: rhp <rhp@rhp.com>

Date: Sun, 12 May 96 20:01:57 PDT

Message-ID: <NEWTNews.831956599.8129.rhp@rhp.rhp.com>

HARBOR PILOTS

We are seeking candidates to fill up to six immediate openings for Harbor Pilots experienced in handling large tankers in confined water and narrow channels. This opportunity has just been opened to include former Navy Harbor Pilots.

Qualified applicants should contact Ross Williams at one of the following addresses/numbers as soon as possible:

Mail: 13704 Turkey Foot Road, North Potomac, MD   20878-3983
Tel.: (301) 948-9549 (Business)/(301) 258-0921 (Residence)
FAX: (301) 948-9549
E-Mail (INTERNET): rwilliams@rhp.com or rhp@rhp.com
E-Mail (SPRINTMAIL): RN.WILLIAMS/MEP.1
(INTERNET): /PN=ROSS.N.WILLIAMS/O=MEP.1/ADMD=TELEMAIL/
C=US/@sprint.com
TELEX: AC:23, TLX:7402427, ANS:WILL UC

———————————————————————

Subject: Printing Plant Manager

From: Ron Schwisow <crs@mail.moran.com>

Date: Sun, 12 May 1996 18:28:02 -0700

Message-ID: <31969022.5AE1@mail.moran.com>

West Texas manufacturer of credit cards, and other promotional products seeking plant manager. Assoc. degree min. plus 5 years experience minimum in MANAGEMENT of a printing plant required. Experience in offset, electronc pre-press, silk-screen and other graphics background desirable.

email or fax resume to: Ron Schwisow crs@teraco.com or FAX 915-689-0129

Subject: GOURMET FOOD DISTRIBUTOR

From: australo@aol.com (AUSTRALO)

Date: 10 May 1996 06:16:05 -0400

Message-ID: <4mv515$av4@newsbf02.news.aol.com>

We are looking for a gourmet food distributor to sell
Havoc Maker Products, a line of hot sauce and soup mixes
to gourmet and/or health food stores. Catalog available,
currently advertised in Chile Pepper Magazine. Display ad
in upcoming Gourmet News.

Email address for catalog and wholesale list.

Thanks.

Ernie Neri

Havoc Maker Products of ME & CT

Subject: TalentBank CD-ROM

From: wmhartzer@aol.com (WM HARTZER)

Date: 9 May 1996 02:15:50 -0400

Message-ID: <4ms2im$83e@newsbf02.news.aol.com>

CD-ROM TalentBank(tm)

Highfield Marketing Group, Inc. continues to accept
resumes for their national CD-ROM TalentBank distributed
to over 1000 top U.S. employers and recruiters. Never a
fee to applicants. E-mail text or postscript resume only
to CDTALENT@AOL.COM or mail 3.5 inch diskette. Or send
your resume to the following address:

CD-ROM TalentBank
Highfield Marketing Group, Inc.
9839 W. Valley Ranch Parkway
Suite #1027
Irving, Texas 75063
USA

You may FAX your resume to: 214-506-0111 24 HRS. 7 DAYS
or call (voice) 800-664-3251 for more information. Get
your resume to us in any way and it will be included in
the next edition!

We now have employers searching our CD-ROM TalentBank for
applicants in the following industries:

healthcare

business

software development

sales and management

general management

office

administrative

executive management

high-tech

Future editions of the CD-ROM TalentBank will include one industry per CD-ROM.

Please note that if you have recently sent your resume to a resume-related newsgroup, an ASCII resume (actually it's in 10 pt. courier) may or may not appear in the next edition.

■■■■■■■■■■■■■■■■■■■■■■■

Subject: Midtown Copy Shop Help WTD

From: spirit38@aol.com (Spirit38)

Date: 10 May 1996 07:41:04 -0400

Message-ID: <4mva0g$c8h@newsbf02.news.aol.com>

Full-time Midtown Copy/Printing Shop Help. Experience w/ Xerox 1090, CLC's, knowledge of offset printing desired. (This is not a pressperson's position). Salary commensurate w/experience.

Fax Res. to 212-397-9600

■■■■■■■■■■■■■■■■■■■■■■■

Subject: Video Video Video

From: cfs3@ix.netcom.com

Date: Sun, 12 May 1996 21:17:29 GMT

Message-ID: <4n5km7$m1n@dfw-ixnews6.ix.netcom.com>

VIDEO   VIDEO   VIDEO   VIDEO

Join the top games company in the Bay, if not the country! "You think we're joking."

Well, we are not. We are, however, searching for a Project Lead to join one of our core games groups. Prefer someone who has had Coin Op. Experience (lots and lots). If not, we would like to see some top-notch Video Game Developers....

Are you good enough? Do you want a challenge? Do you want to be the one making major decisions? Do you want to make a whole lot of money? If you answered yes, you just might have what it takes to join our team.

We are a bunch of hot shots, out to make great games, lots of money, lots of fame, and have a great time doing it!!!!!!!!!!!!!!!!!

DO I HAVE YOUR INTEREST? IF SO, FORWARD A COPY OF YOUR RESUME A.S.A.P.

FAX: 415-903-3418

cfs3@ix.netcom.com

Subject: I Want A New Boss: Funny Stories of Bad Bosses + Best Job$ Links

From: mystory@myboss.com (Moe Money)

Date: Wed, 01 May 1996 18:45:39 -0500

Message-ID: <mystory-0105961845400001@ivyland119.voicenet.com>

We've compiled the best job opportunities, jobs sites and job links on the 'Net. We search the 'Net day and night finding, evaluating and reporting the best job sites. You'll find them at — http://www.myboss.com/newboss.html

New job opportunities and job sites appear daily*

But there's more — much more!!

On a daily basis we receive worldwide submissions of Funny Jokes and True Stories about Bad Bosses. It seems Bad Bosses are everywhere. So far, surfers from 75 countries have visited the site to submit their own stories and to vote on submissions by others.

We post new stories, jokes and one liners every Monday.*

Please VISIT, VOTE and Submit your own story — http://www.myboss.com

Have a laugh. Get a job. Get Even.

Subject: ENVIRONMENTAL LAB MGR SAUDI ARABIA

From: Leslie Corporation <tlc@nettap.com>

Date: Tue, 30 Apr 1996 13:54:21 -0500

Message-ID: <318661DD.292B@nettap.com>

We have a current opening for an Environmental Lab Manager in Saudi Arabia working for the Royal Commission of Saudi Arabia. Requires 5+ years experience managing an environmental lab and a BS or higher.

Visit our web site at http://www.nettap.com/~tlc for more details on the job.

We are the leading recruitment firm to the Middle East since 1977.

There are never any fees for our services.

━━━━━━━━━━━━━━━━━━━━━━━━

Subject: General Managers (Plant Team Leaders) Correction
See my WEB site for more

From: RAYOSB@worldnet.att.net (Ray Osborne)

Date: Sun, 12 May 1996 01:08:12 GMT

Message-ID: <4n33c3$c3v@mtinsc01-mgt.ops.worldnet.att.net>

An EXCELLENT OPPORTUNITY for a GENERAL MANAGER

A large division of a Fortune 100 Company is seeking
General Managers for several of their corrugated
container plants. The company is one of the world's
largest manufacturers of paper, producing more than 1.3
million tons annually for printing and business use. This
division produces paper corrugating medium used in
shipping containers. The division operates eight
corrugated container plants. The medium is used directly
by the division's eight container plants, traded for
liner board (the outer ply of corrugated containers) or
sold on the open market to other box converters. This
division is on track to be the preeminent high-quality,
low-cost producer of both heavy and ultra-light weight
medium. The company is an established leader in coated
paper-board, containerboard, and multiple unit packaging.
This company's three key drivers are customer
satisfaction, productivity improvement and high
performance management.

TITLE: GENERAL MANAGER

POSITION RESPONSIBILITIES: The General Manager (Plant
Team Leader) will provide team leadership and strategic
focus to the plant. Specifically, will lead the
coordination of sales, customer service, and operations
to target the right number and mix of customers so that
plant profitability and efficiency are maximized. Also,
will provide long-term strategic direction and focus to
ensure proper decisions are made (e.g., training,
employment, capital investments, and organizational
structure) to meet the emerging needs of the local
market.

* This position gives the candidate the opportunity to
basically 'run their own business.'

* Opportunity to join an exciting and expanding business
organization.

* Join a team-oriented business.

* Career opportunities to grow within company.

SKILLS NEEDED: Candidate must have at least 8-10 years
experience in paper or package manufacturing, sales and/
or administration, with at least a portion of that time
in a general management role.

```
* Excellent written and verbal communication skills

* Strong work ethic, integrity, and honesty

* Strong leadership skills with ability to work and
motivate a team

* Safety awareness

* Technical and professional knowledge

* Persuasiveness

* Keen Judgment


COMPENSATION:    Possible six-figure salary plus
management incentive plan.

TRAVEL:    Minimal

EDUCATION: Bachelor of Science or Arts degree in
business, marketing or liberal arts

GEOGRAPHY: Positions available in Milwaukee, WI.;
Chicago, IL.; Washington Courthouse, OH.; Ft. Smith, AK.;
Spartanburg, SC.; Covington, GA.; Atlanta, GA.; and
Lewisburg, TN.

ALL INTERESTED CANDIDATES PLEASE CONTACT THE FOLLOWING:

Lisa Wilson
Project Manager
Innovative Search Group LLC
1080 Holcomb Bridge Rd. Bldg. 100, Suite 210
Roswell, GA 30076-4348
800-589-3574 ext. 109   Fax: 770-552-4777   InterNet:
search@america.net

"mailto:search@america.net"

Visit my WEB site for more Top Jobs http://
www.netctrl.com/~rko/
```

Look at the examples carefully. The return address of the person who posted the announcement will be shown differently depending on your reader. It may be in the upper-left corner in two lines, such as:

fjandt

(at igc.apc.org)

You know that to send a message to that person, the e-mail address would be:

fjandt@igc.apc.org

Read the complete job announcement for instructions for applying. Some will specify an e-mail address to send applications; others request that resumes be faxed or mailed.

Some newsgroup readers may have a reply function. You'll be able to choose to send that reply to the whole group or just to the original poster. If you reply to the whole group, your message will be public and be available for anyone to read as a reply. If you reply to the original poster, your message goes only to the poster.

In some of the newsgroups, you'll notice that people have posted their own job-wanted announcement. Even if you don't have access to the newsgroups on these pages, you can still post a job-wanted message to a newsgroup by e-mail. For example, suppose that you want to know job vacancies in stores that sell exotic birds and you know that a popular newsgroup for bird enthusiasts is

```
rec.pets.birds
```

You address an e-mail message to

```
rec.pets.birds@decwri.dec.com
```

Include in your request your name and e-mail address and request that any responses not be posted on the newsgroup but be sent to you directly by e-mail. Be sure to use a subject line that correctly describes your request, such as

```
Experienced exotic bird store attendant
available now
```

In some of the newsgroups, you'll notice that people have posted their resume. You can do the same thing, but we'd encourage you to also post your resume in the job databanks we've identified for you in Chapter 10. These are more likely to be seen and searched by employers. If you're set on one particular location, however, a local newsgroup is appropriate too. Chapters 9 and 10 give you the information you'll need to post an effective electronic resume.

LISTSERV Job Listings

LISTSERV takes its name from "list server." List servers are automatic programs that accept commands requesting different actions, such as subscribing to a list or listing members of a group.

Think of LISTSERVs as newsletters that you ask to receive. The newsletters come to your e-mail address until you unsubscribe. LISTSERVs are free.

Some LISTSERVs are put out by one individual or organization; some are composed totally of messages written by subscribers to the LISTSERV. LISTSERVs can be moderated, that is, a real live person receives messages from subscribers to be posted on the list. The moderator accepts some, edits some, and rejects others.

LISTSERVs cover a wide variety of topics. Most LISTSERVs do not list job vacancies. How do you find the one that has jobs you're interested in? One way is to ask colleagues in the field if they know of one. Another way is to wade through the long list of LISTSERVs until you find the right one. One way to get a list of LISTSERVs is to send an e-mail message to

> `LISTSERV@BITNIC.bitnet`

The message you send should contain only the words

> `list global`

The list server picks up your e-mail address from the header. You don't include it in the message itself.

Another way is to send an e-mail message to

> `MAIL-SERVER@SRI.COM`

In the message, you enter only

> `Send Netinfo/Interest-groups`

You can also find LISTSERVs using gopher. (Using gopher is described later in this chapter.) Here are two gophers to try that list academic discussion lists:

> `gopher nysernet.org`
>
> `path: New York State Education and Research Network (NYSERNet)/Special Collection: Higher Education/Scholarly Electronic Conferences [Kovacs]`

and

> `gopher gopher.austin.unimelb.edu.au`
>
> `path: Austin Hospital, Melbourne/Research Related Information [Directory of Scholarly E-conferences] (ACADLIST)`

A more extensive list can be searched using this gopher:

> `gopher gopher.cni.org`
>
> `path: Coalition for Networked Information/ Coalition FTP Archives (ftp.cni.org)/Publicly Accessible Documents (/pub)/Guides to Network`

```
Use/Strangelove, Michael:  Directory of
Electronic Journals and Newsletters
```

After you've found the LISTSERV that might have jobs you're interested in, you need to subscribe to the list. Let's say you're interested in jobs in criminal justice. Your criminal justice instructor tells you to check out the UNCJIN-L bulletin board. (The "-L" tells you it is a LISTSERV list.) UNCJIN is the United Nations Criminal Justice Information Network. Your instructor gives you its Internet address.

An e-mail note that reads "Please send me a copy of UNCJIN-L" cannot be accepted by the automatic list server. List servers require that you subscribe in a certain way. First you address an e-mail message to

```
LISTSERV@UACSC2.ALBANY.EDU
```

If your mail program requires a subject line, just enter a period.

In the body of the message, you enter only the following:

```
SUBSCRIBE UNCJIN-L <followed by your
name as you usually write it>
```

Shortly you'll receive an acknowledgment of your subscription in your e-mail. Keep this acknowledgment because it will contain information about the list. It will also tell you how to unsubscribe from the list. For this particular LISTSERV, you unsubscribe by addressing an e-mail message to the same address as before. This time the message in the body should read only

```
SIGNOFF UNCJIN-L
```

The acknowledgment will also explain what other commands the LISTSERV can accept–for example, how to put your subscription on hold when you're on vacation, how to get a list of all the subscribers to the list, and how to find old issues of the LISTSERV known as its "archive."

Another LISTSERV contains job listings in television. Don Fitzpatrick Associates' *Shoptalk*, an industry newsletter, contains job listings. This LISTSERV is distributed on the Internet by the S. I. Newhouse School of Public Communications at Syracuse University. To receive it as a LISTSERV (or unsubscribe), you'd send an e-mail message to:

```
LISTSERV@LISTSERV.SYR.EDU
```

On the first line of the message you'd enter

```
SUBscribe SHOPTALK <then your real
first and last name>
```

To unsubscribe, you'd enter

```
SIGNOFF SHOPTALK
```

Some LISTSERVS also have World Wide Web locations. For example, Shoptalk can be visited at

```
http://www.tvspy.com/
```

BBS Job Listings

Some BBSs have job databases. As you'll remember from the interview with David Hakala of *Boardwatch Magazine* in Chapter 2, BBSs are changing, so we can't guarantee that this information will stay correct.

One BBS that we do recommend you look at is Ward Christman's Online Opportunities in Philadelphia. It's one of the best, and we'll come back to it in a later chapter.

Here's a list of some we've found.

BBS Name Location Telephone Number(s) and Maximum Baud Rate(s)	Description
Career Connections Los Altos, CA 415-917-2129 (2400) 415-917-2125 (14,400)	Worldwide job listings No fee required
Career Link, Inc. Phoenix, AZ Voice: 800-453-3350	Nationwide and worldwide job listings Updated weekly Fee required; call 800 number for information
Career Systems MA 413-592-9208 (9600)	Nationwide job listings No fee required
Careers Online San Jose, CA 408-248-7029 (14,400)	Job listings and resume fax service No fee required
Careers Online MA 508-879-4700 (9600)	*Computer World* newspaper listings of DP jobs nationwide
Contractors Exchange San Francisco, CA 415-334-7393 (2400)	No fee required Construction and contractor jobs Updated daily No fee required
Dallas Opportunity Network 214-444-0050	Unable to verify— authors

BBS Name Location Telephone Number(s) and Maximum Baud Rate(s)	Description
D.I.C.E. National Network Des Moines, IA 515-280-3423 (14,400)	Nationwide job listings Updated several times daily
Newark, NJ 201-242-4166 (9600) Sunnyvale, CA 408-737-9339	No fee required
DP NETwork (Toner Corp.) San Francisco, CA 415-788-8663 (2400) 415-788-7101 (9600)	DP jobs in the San Francisco and Sacramento areas Updated daily No fee required
ECCO BBS San Francisco, CA 415-331-7227 (14,400)	Nationwide job listings
Employment Board San Diego, CA 619-689-1348 (9600)	Employment information for the San Diego area No fee required
Exec-PC BBS WI 414-789-4210 (9600)	Large variety of job listings in all areas No fee required to access Job Search door
Federal Job Opportunity BBS 912-757-3100	Service of U.S. Office of Personnel Management
Jobs BBS 404-992-8937	Unable to verify— authors
JOBS-BBS Portland, OR 503-281-6808 (9600)	Listings of all sorts of jobs nationwide Updated several times daily No fee required
International Systems Source Denver, CO 507-645-2394 (14,400)	Mostly jobs for information engineers in the Denver area No fee required
Mouse House Anaheim, CA 714-535-3761	Devoted entirely to Disney, includes job openings
National Technical Search Amherst, MA 413-549-8136 (14,400)	Nationwide job listings with forums and career guides
Online Opportunities Philadelphia, PA 215-873-7170 (14,400)	All kinds of jobs nationwide Updated weekly Registration fee

BBS Name Location Telephone Number(s) and Maximum Baud Rate(s)	Description
OPM FEDJOBS - Philly Philadelphia, PA 215-580-2216 (14,400)	Federal job listings (BBS operated by U.S. Office of Personnel Management) Updated daily No fee required
ouT therE BBS San Jose, CA	San Francisco Bay Area Job listings
408-263-2248 (9600)	Updated every two days No fee required
Résumé Exchange 602-947-4283	Phoenix area resumes and job listings
The Resume File 805-581-6210	Nationwide jobs and resume database and federal job opportunities.

Using Telnet

Telnet is what allows you to access another computer through the Internet. Telnet is similar to using a modem to dial another computer, but it is easier and faster, and doesn't result in any telephone toll charges. Telnet was originally developed to allow users to access their own computer from remote locations. Now, though, telnet is used largely to access databases on other computers.

Telnet is very easy to use. You simply type telnet, press the space bar to create a space, type the address of the computer you want to access, and press Enter.

The next screen you'll see is from the remote computer. Follow the directions on this screen. It may request that you log in and that you enter a password.

Here are some job-related sites you can reach using telnet:

U.S. government data is largely decentralized on the Internet and requires some searching to find what you need. Federal job openings can be accessed by telnet at the following three addresses:

```
telnet marvel.loc.gov
```

Use **marvel** as the log in.

To access the Federal Job Opportunity Board, use this address:

```
fjob.mail.opm.gov
```

FedWorld was established in 1993 to provide a single gateway to more than 100 government agencies. FedWorld is overburdened, and often it is difficult to get a connection. You can try to reach FedWorld at this telnet address:

```
fedworld.gov
```

The Career Connection's Online Information System H.E.A.R.T. (Human Resources Electronic Advertising and Recruiting Tool) can be accessed by telnet. New college graduates and entry-level job seekers should try this address:

```
telnet college.career.com
```

Others should use the following telnet address:

```
telnet career.com
```

This menu-driven system is supported by member companies to enable them to reach the most qualified candidates for advertised positions. This service is free to job seekers.

You can search for positions on Career Connections by geographic location or job title. You can also apply for jobs through this system. You'll be asked to register and select a password so that a private e-mail and profile account can be created for you.

Other telnet addresses include

```
window.texas.gov
```

which provides access to several Texas state agencies including the Texas Employment Commission.

Using Gopher

Gopher is an application that allows you to browse and search documents. It was developed at the University of Minnesota and named after the school's mascot—the Golden Gopher. Gopher is simple to understand and easy to use. Imagine a tree. You scale the trunk to the lower branches and choose to climb one of the branches. You then reach another group of branches and choose to continue along one of these. This is exactly what a gopher does.

The first gopher screen gives you a menu of choices. You pick one. The new screen then gives you a new set of choices. You select one, and that new screen gives you some more choices. The selections you make are recorded as a path, or each selection you make from each menu in a series of menus. In a path the selections are separated by a slash (/). For example:

```
Extension Service USDA Information/USDA and
Other Federal Agency Information/Job Openings in
the Federal Government.
```

The first phrase is the selection you make on the first menu; the next is the selection from the second screen, etc.

Perhaps the only problem some people encounter with gopher is getting lost in the tree—that is, they want to jump from branch to branch in the tree. You can make those kind of jumps on the World Wide Web, but you can't do that in a gopher search. You must go back down the tree until you find a new branch that can take you to another part of the tree.

There are gopher sites all over the world. It's recommended that you choose one close to you. Here are a few examples:

Hostname	IP Number	Log in Id	Location
cat.ohiolink.edu	130.108.120.25	gopher	North America
consultant.micro.umn.edu	134.84.132.4	gopher	North America
gopher.msu.edu	135.8.2.61	gopher	North America
gopher.uiuc.edu	128.174.33.160	gopher	North America
gopher.uwp.edu	131.210.1.13	gopher	North America
panda.uiowa.edu	128.255.40.201	panda	North America
seymour.md.gov	128.8.10.46	gopher	North America
info.anu.edu.au	150.203.84.20	info	Australia
tolten.puc.cl	146.155.1.16	gopher	South America
gan.ncc.go.jp	160.190.10.1	gopher	Japan

Let's work through an example together. (*Note*: As gopher screens are updated, sometimes daily, the option numbers change accordingly.) Enter this:

    gopher.uiuc.edu

You'll see the Root gopher server screen (see fig. 6.1). It's the gopher at the University of Illinois at Urbana-Champaign. The cursor has been moved using the arrow keys to option 11—Other Gopher and Information Servers.

Fig. 6.1. Internet
Gopher Information
Client v2.0.14. The
Root gopher server:
gopher.uiuc.edu
screen.

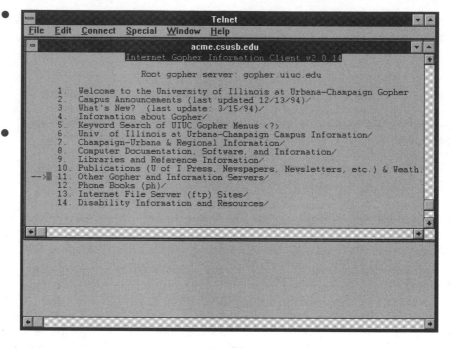

After you choose this option, you'll see the Other Gopher and
Information Servers screens (see fig. 6.2).

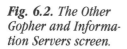

Fig. 6.2. The Other
Gopher and Informa-
tion Servers screen.

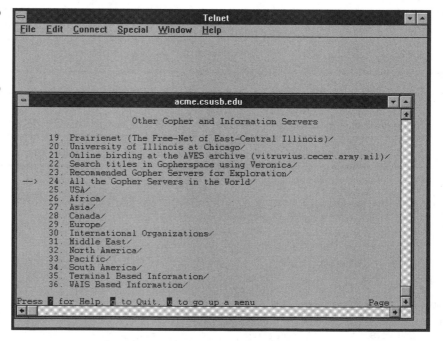

If you move the cursor to option 24—All the Gopher Servers in the
World—and choose this option, you soon see the All the Gopher
Servers in the World screen (see fig. 6.3).

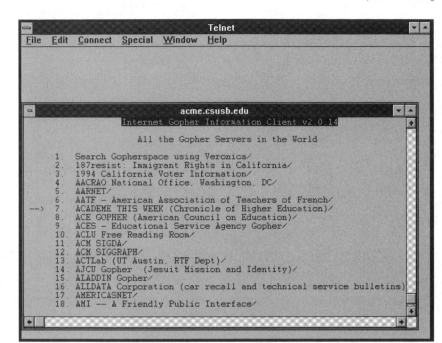

Fig. 6.3. The All the Gopher Servers in the World screen.

The cursor now has been moved to option 7—ACADEME THIS WEEK from the publication the *Chronicle of Higher Education.* If you choose option 16, you see the ACADEME THIS WEEK (Chronicle of Higher Education) screen (see fig. 6.4).

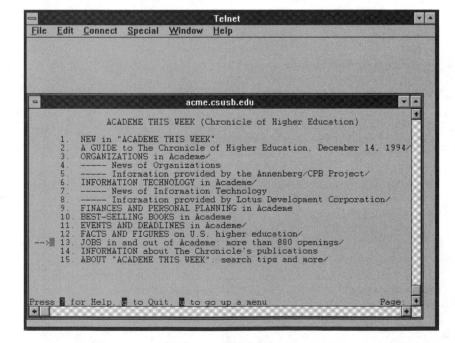

Fig. 6.4. The ACA-DEME THIS WEEK (Chronicle of higher Education) screen.

In figure 6.4 the cursor is at option 15—JOBS in and out of Academe: more than 880 openings. Should you choose option 15, you see the Jobs in and out of Academe: more than 880 openings screen (see fig. 6.5).

Fig. 6.5. The Jobs in and out of Academe: more than 880 openings screen.

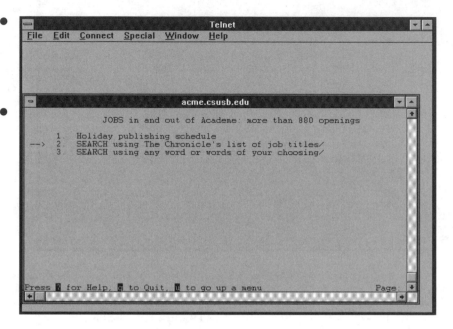

The cursor in figure 6.5 is at option 2—SEARCH using The Chronicle's list of job titles. If you choose this option, you see the SEARCH using The Chronicle's list of job titles screen (see fig. 6.6).

Fig. 6.6. The SEARCH using The Chronicle's list of job titles screen.

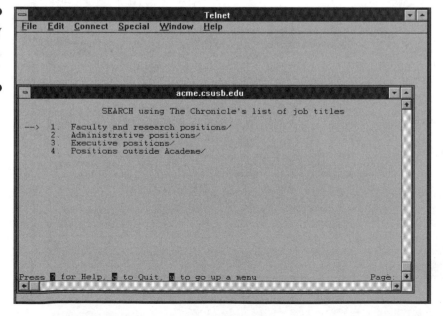

In figure 6.6 the cursor is beside option 1–Faculty and research positions. If you choose this option, you see the Faculty and research positions screen (see fig. 6.7).

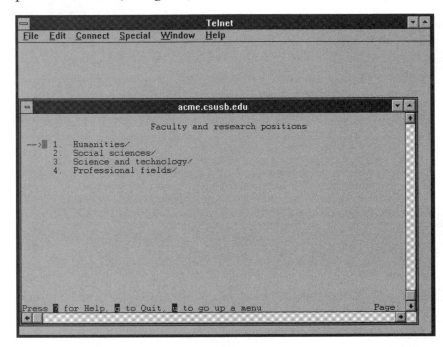

Fig. 6.7. *The Faculty and research positions screen.*

The cursor in figure 6.7 is at option 1–Humanities. Choose this option, and you see the Humanities screen (see fig. 6.8).

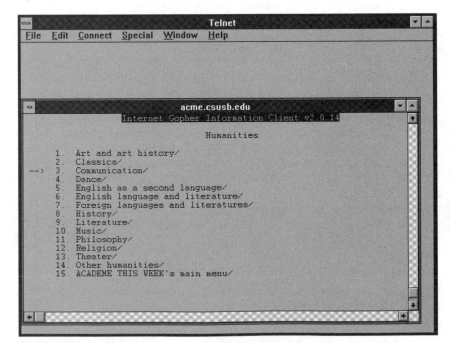

Fig. 6.8. *The Humanities screen.*

If you move the cursor in the Humanities screen to option 3—Communication and choose this option, you soon see the Communication screen (see fig. 6.9).

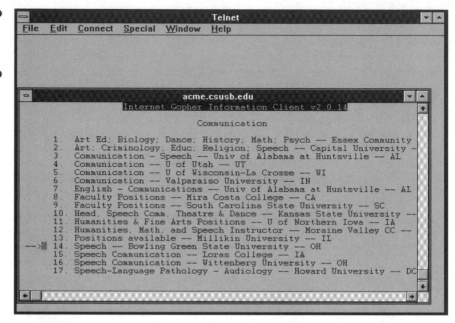

Fig. 6.9. The Communication screen.

In figure 6.9 the cursor has been moved to option 14—Speech — Bowling Green State University — OH. If you choose this option, you finally get to the job announcement. You see the first of two screens that describe this particular Speech position (see fig. 6.10).

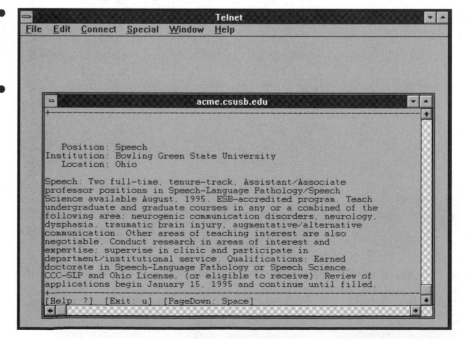

Fig. 6.10. The first screen describing the Speech position.

You can go through the list of All the Gophers in the World to find interesting information of all kinds, but here are some gophers with employment listings:

`gopher chronicle.merit.edu`	Academe This Week (The *Chronicle of Higher Education*)
`gopher cwis.usc.edu`	Gopher Jewels from the University of Southern California
`gopher.dartcms1. dartmouth.edu`	Federal job openings from the Office of Personnel Management
`gopher e-math.ams.com`	American Mathematical Society
`gopher esusda.gov or zeus.esuda.gov`	Federal job openings
`gopher garnet.msen.com`	OnLine Career Center (Msen, Inc.)
`gopher msen.com`	Msen, Inc. main server
`gopher gizmo.freenet. columbus.oh.us`	Columbus, Ohio Freenet Ohio state jobs
`gopher gopher.indiana.edu`	Indiana University (For international information use path: The University: Information Services/University Life/International Center/ International Career EmploymentNetwork)
`gopher gopher.mountain.net`	A wide variety of information for West Virginia
`gopher nightingale.con. utk.edu`	Nursing positions
`gopher gopher.usdoj.gov`	Jobs for attorneys from the U.S. Department of Justice
`gopher gopher.utdallas.edu`	University of Texas-Dallas
`gopher gopher.uth.tmc.edu 3300`	American Physiological Association
`gopher justice 2.usdoj.gov`	U.S. Department of Justice and Inspection General's Offices

`gopher marvel.loc.gov`	Library of Congress employment opportunities
`gopher millkern.com`	Federal, state, and universities with job listings from Millkern Communi cations
`gopher riceinfo.rice.edu`	Rice University and pointers to many more employment listings
`gopher stis.nsf.gov`	National Science Foundation
`gopher gopher.utexas.edu`	University of Texas-Austin Central Gopher; job listings from universi ties and government agencies
`gopher wcni.cis.umn.edu:11111`	Academic Position Network

The following are some career information gopher sites.

The Department of Energy gopher includes a list of federal bulletin boards:

```
gopher gopher.ns.doe.gov

path:  Federal Government Information/General
Information Resoures/Frederal Bulletin Boards
(list)
```

Access the U.S. Department of Labor's *Occupational Outlook Hand-book* (which includes the Dictionary of Occupational Titles codes) and U.S. Industrial Outlook at this gopher:

```
gopher umslvma.umsl.edu

path:  University of Missouri-St. Louis/The
Library/Government Information
```

The Economic Bulletin Board contains more than 700 daily updated files on current economic and trade information, economic indicators, U.S. treasury auction results, and employment statistics at this gopher:

```
gopher gopher.lib.mich.edu

path:  Directory:  Social Sciences Resources/
Economics/Economic Bulletin Board
```

For information about Congress, such as directories and committee assignments, go to

```
gopher gopher.lib.umich.edu
```

```
path:   Directory:   Social Sciences Resources/
U.S. Government Resources:   Legislative Branch
```

or

```
gopher info.umd.edu
```

```
path:   Directory:   Educational Resources/United
States/Government/Congress
```

White House information is available at

```
gopher esusda.gov
```

```
path:   Directory:   White House and Congress/
White House papers
```

And for a listing of all state employment offices, go to

```
gopher gopher.dartmouth.edu
```

```
path:   Dartmouth College/Career Services/Job
Openings in the Federal Government/Misc. Infor-
mation/All State Employment Offices by state
```

or

```
gopher esusda.gov
```

```
path:   Extension Service USDA Information/USDA
and Other Federal Agency Information/Job
Openings in the Federal Government/Misc.
Information/All State Employment Offices by
state
```

You can use Netscape now to reach the same gopher sites. All you do is type in the name of the gopher site with all its colons and slashes. If the word *gopher* isn't part of the gopher's address, insert it in the beginning.

Finding Information

Search engines on the World Wide Web are easy to use. Earlier ways of finding material on the Internet–such as Veronica, WAIS, Archie, and ftp–require the user to do more of the work.

Veronica. On some gopher main menus, you'll see the option Veronica, which was developed at the University of Nevada, Reno, and is an acronym for Very Easy Rodent Oriented Network Information Comput-erized Archives. If it is available, you can request it to search the menus of all known gophers in the world for a keyword. The result is pre-sented as a gopher menu.

WAIS. WAIS (pronounced "ways") or Wide Area Information Service allows you to search databases using keywords. Unlike Veronica, WAIS looks through the contents of documents, not just titles.

If your online server does not have WAIS, you can telnet to public WAIS at this address:

```
quake.think.com
```

and log in with the following:

```
wais
```

You'll be asked to supply keywords separated by a space, such as in the following example:

```
Indiana job
```

Don't use the word *and* in place of the space because WAIS will look for that word too! WAIS will search and then show you sources it has found. The first source listed will be the one that meets your criteria most closely. WAIS takes a little practice, but you can master it. When you find exactly what you want, you can have it mailed to you by entering **m**. WAIS will then prompt you for your e-mail address.

Archie. Archie (the name was derived from the word *archive*) was developed at the McGill University (Montreal) School of Computer Science. Archie servers maintain lists of stored files at every known public archive site. An archie search will give you the location of files; it will not give you the document itself. We'll explain how to do that in the next section on file transfer.

There are public archie sites all over the world. Pick one that's close to you.

Location	Archie Server Name
U.S. Southeast	archie.sura.net
U.S. West	archie.unl.edu
U.S. Northeast	archie.rutgers.edu
New York	archie.ans.net
Australia	archie.au
UK/Ireland	archie.doc.ic.ac.uk
Europe	archie.funet.fi

Let's try the McGill server. Telnet to this address:

> `archie.sura.net`

and log in as **archie**. Remember, you can always enter help to get a list
of the commands. If you enter the following:

> `prog jobs`

You'll see screens flash before you with information that looks like
that in figure 6.11.

```
Host mc.lcs.mit.edu      (18.111.0.179)
Last updated 03:55    5 Nov 1994

Location:              /its/ai/tar
  FILE  -r--r--r--     1993 bytes  19:00  6 Dec 1989  jobs.xmail.Z

Location:              /its/ai/devon
  FILE  -r--r--r--     2557 bytes  19:00  30 Mar 1989 jobs.x-mail.Z
jobs.xmailk.z

Location:              /its/ai/ray
  FILE  -r--r--r--    41463 bytes  18:00  3 Oct 1988   jobs.babyl.Z

Location:              /its/ai/sys2
  FILE  -r--r--r--     4556 bytes  19:00  31 Mar 1985 ts.jobs

Location:           /its/ai/sysen1
  FILE  -r--r--r--     6164 bytes  19:00  31 Mar 1985 jobs.87
```

● ● ● ● ● ● ● ● ●

*Fig. 6.11. Result of
an archie search.*

● ● ● ● ● ● ● ● ●

Remember to use your Scroll Lock key to freeze and unfreeze your
screen.

In the preceding example the file name is on the far right. Next to it
are the date and time the file was created, and next to that is the size of
the file in bytes. You can easily fill up your disk space by transferring
too many files. Delete files you don't need, or learn how to compress
them.

On the far left at top, "Host" is the site, and "Location" is the name of
the directory. You'll need this information to get a copy by file transfer
protocol (ftp) discussed below.

If you don't have telnet, you can send an e-mail message to this address:

> `archie@nearest archie serve`

Enter only the word **help** in the message. You'll get information back
on the commands you can use. You'll use the next section to actually
get a copy of the file itself.

Using File Transfers

File transfer (from *ftp*, or *file transfer protocol*) simply means the act of moving a file from one computer to another. Files can be text, software, photographs, or even digital music. Actually, file transfer is one of the most common uses of the Internet. Many organizations connected to the Internet provide publicly accessible files and allow you to copy those files to your computer by ftp.

The very first thing you need to learn in order to use ftp is the difference between two types of files: ASCII (American Standard Code for Information Interchange) and binary. An *ASCII* file is a simple text file only. It contains no formatting codes, such as tabs, underlining, etc. A *binary* file, however, does contain all the internal codes for formatting.

When you transfer an ASCII file between computers that store information differently, ASCII automatically adjusts the file during the transfer so that the file on the receiving end will be in text. A binary file is transferred as is with no changes. Some network packages come with programs that can convert from one format to another after the file has been received.

To use ftp, you first need the host name. In the preceding example, you'd enter this:

```
ftp mc.lcs.mit.edu
```

Next, you need a log in name and password. For publicly accessible files, you log in as **anonymous** or **ftp** and use your e-mail address as a password; or, if that is not accepted, try this:

```
guest
```

At the first ftp prompt, tell the host computer to use either ASCII (by entering **ascii**) or binary (by entering **binary**). The response to ASCII will be an A; the response to binary will be an I.

At the next ftp prompt, enter this:

```
cd </the/path/name>
```

To list the files in the directory, enter **ls**. To download a file, enter **get <filename>**. For example, when you log in to the host, **mc.lcs.mit.edu,** you'd enter **cd** and the following location:

```
cd /its/ai/tar
```

Sometimes you'll have to do it in steps, such as the following steps:

```
cd its

cd ai

cd tar
```

Ftp is case-sensitive, so remember to enter lowercase words in lowercase letters and uppercase words in capitals. The host computer will
let you know if you have been successful.

Now, you're ready to ask for the file. Sometimes you can see what files
are at your directory location by entering this:

    dir

If you already know the name of the file you want, simply enter its
name, such as in this example:

    get ts.jobs

Again, the host computer will let you know if you have been successful
by a message such as "transfer complete." This means that the file is
now on your computer for you to access and read.

If your system requires you to rename files, simply do that at the get
command, as in the following example:

    get ts.jobs newname.txt

The file would then be named on your computer as **newname.txt** and
not as **ts.jobs.**

You'll notice that some files end in the letter Z or in ZIP. That means
the file has been compressed. To be able to read that file, you'll first
have to uncompress it with a utility file like PKUNZIP.EXE.

Ftp takes a little practice, but it's well worth it. There's a gold mine of
information out there for you to bring home free!

If your access to the Internet doesn't include ftp, you can still use it.
Some Internet hosts provide ftp by e-mail service. One at Princeton
University is this:

    bitftp@pucc.princeton.edu

But first send a help message to verify that the host can send messages
to you.

Netscape makes ftp easier. To use ftp on Netscape, simply type in the
ftp address with all its colons and slashes. If "ftp" is not part of the
address, simply enter it before the ftp address.

Although we titled this chapter "Venturing 'Outside' the World Wide
Web," you've seen here that the World Wide Web is making it easy to
explore all of the Internet.

Career Resources

In Chapter 1, we described the Internet as a very large library. This library has valuable information for the job seeker and for the employer. Let's review ways to use the information in the resume databases and job databases you now know how to access.

Others' resumes are valuable information. So valuable, in fact, that before the Internet some job seekers would place fictitious newspaper advertisements for a position they themselves were looking for. Their ads contained no employer information and asked applicants to mail their resumes to a post office box. Of course, these applications were never acknowledged. People placed the ads merely to get copies of their competitions' resumes and then carefully studied them. This unethical and expensive tactic made it possible for those who placed the ads to rewrite their own resumes to stand out from the others.

You can learn a great deal about how to present yourself in a resume by studying how others present themselves. On the Internet others' resumes can be reviewed honestly and freely.

In the same way, job databases are valuable information. The search engines make it easy to search the job databases by job title. That lets you see those—and only those—job announcements. If you follow this job search strategy on the Internet, you'll probably find a position like your last one. That's okay sometimes, but at other times you may want to expand your job search. Carefully studying vacancy announcements may encourage you to change your employment objective to stress the skills that employers are looking for today.

There's much more out there. We just need to know what's there and how to use it.

Information

In his book *The Road Ahead* (Viking, 1995), Microsoft cofounder Bill Gates defined information as the "reduction of uncertainty." Many years earlier, the linguist and novelist Walker Percy observed in *The Message in the Bottle* (Farrar, Straus and Giroux, 1975) that information is not all of equal value. Percy asks us to imagine a man who finds himself a castaway on an island. Walking the beach each morning, he comes upon bottles washed up by the ocean waves. Each bottle contains a message. Percy examines the differences between knowledge and information and defines information as that communication which has a bearing on the person's predicament. A message that says "A ship passes east of this island once a month" is valuable information to the castaway. But a message that says "Chicago is on Lake Michigan" is of no use to him. Information to one person may be just noise to another.

Percy was foreseeing the Internet, where it is possible to miss seeing information in a sea of knowledge. There is so much material available that it's easy to get lost or be distracted by the trivial and overlook what you really need. Sometime in the future, user-oriented Web agents will continually perform automatic searches of the entire World Wide Web for only the information the user specifies.

Some sites are able to do something like that for you now. For example, the *Los Angeles Times* Web site at `http://www.latimes.com` offers Hunter, the golden news retriever who fetches the most recent stories in the areas you've specified. For example, I've told Hunter to watch for stories on the Internet. In late May, 1996, I signed onto the *Los Angeles Times* Web site and clicked Hunter and my interest area of Internet stores. The first story Hunter brought me was "Number of Job Listings on the Net Rising." The first sentence read "up to 95% of all major newspapers' classified job listings now available on the Internet." By the way, I had read the *Los Angeles Times* that morning and hadn't seen that story!

Researching the Employer

Frequently referred to as "doing homework," this often overlooked step is crucial to a successful job search. Employer research can be accomplished through either formal or informal means, on the Web or at your local public library.

Here's our list of standard sources:

Dun and Bradstreet Million Dollar Directory (annual) Information on public companies with sales volume over $25 million, 250 or more employees, or a net worth of at least $500,000. Dun and Bradstreet has a WWW database of millions of U.S. companies. Visit it at `http://www.dbisna.com/`.

Hoover's *Handbook of American Business*. Profiles of over 500 major U.S. companies.

Moody's Manuals (annual, updated weekly). U.S. and foreign companies traded on the national and regional exchanges and over-the-counter.

Standard & Poor's Corporation Records (annual, updated daily). Includes information on many smaller companies not included in Moody's.

Thomas Register (annual) Manufacturing company profiles. (Thomas has a WWW site.)

Ward's *Business Directory of U.S. Private and Public Companies*.

And don't forget to check corporate annual reports and 10-K Reports (reports that companies file with the Securities & Exchange Commission).

Here are some more specialized publications we recommend:

The Almanac of International Jobs and Careers. Information about international employers.

American Jobs Abroad. U.S. corporations, nonprofits, and government agencies that employ U.S. citizens abroad.

The Best Companies for Minorities. Companies that promote diversity in employment, training, and career advancement.

The Best Companies for Women. Benefits and policies on 52 companies.

Directory of Executive Recruiters. Lists job search firms in the U.S., Canada, and Mexico.

Directory of Overseas Summer Jobs. Summer job openings worldwide.

The Job Hunter's Guide to 100 Great American Cities.

Peterson's Job Opportunities in Business.

Peterson's Job Opportunities in Engineering and Technology. Hiring needs and descriptions of the fastest growing and most successful companies in engineering and technology.

The 100 Best Companies to Work for in America.

Business publications, such as *Fortune, Inc., Money,* and *The Wall Street Journal* are all excellent sources for information on corporations. A truly serious job seeker will make it a point to subscribe to at least one business publication and should continue to do so on a job. These publications often provide data beyond a simple statement of the annual earnings and general financial picture of a company. Here, you can also learn about such things as a company's benefits package and employee perks, and even get an occasional glimpse at the nebulous, hard-to-define concept—corporate culture. *Inc.* magazine publishes its annual "*Inc.* 100," a ranking of the fastest-growing, small, public companies. These surveys include valuable personal interviews with the CEOs of the featured companies.

■ *Working Mother* magazine publishes articles profiling companies that are most "family friendly." It spotlights those that have child care arrangements, family health plans, and advancement potential, evaluating them and comparing them to other organizations. This sort of information contained in these and other articles can help you assess the context of an interview by showing you in advance how the company operates and "thinks."

For the smaller or locally owned businesses, other means of research are available to you. You might simply call or write and ask for a brochure or newsletter on the company. Most small companies regard such written data as good PR for their organizations. Many make their annual reports available to the public for the same reason. Another way to learn about a company informally is to become a consumer of the goods or services it provides. Being able to speak knowledgeably about its products goes a long way toward cementing you as the favored candidate.

Finally, an excellent way to research a potential employer is to talk directly to the people who work there. You can accomplish this simply by chatting with employees of the organization. The purpose here is to find out about the workings of the company, its corporate philosophy, the general working environment, and the salary and benefits structure.

Government Sites

The federal government is a major source of information on the Internet. Explore these general sites:

■ **Library of Congress**. In addition to access to the Library of Congress itself, this site provides easy links to information maintained at practically every government agency. To reach the Library of Congress, telnet to `marvel.loc.gov` or on the WWW at `http://marvel.loc.gov`.

■ **Central Intelligence Agency**. *The CIA World Fact Book* offers information about other countries. This site is located at `http://www.odci.gov/cia/publications/95fact/index.html`.

■ **The White House**. In addition to a photograph of Socks, the First Cat, you'll find the President's press releases, Cabinet information, and more. Visit this site at `http://www.whitehouse.gov`.

The following more specific federal government sites may have information of value to the job seeker.

One very important information site for the job seeker is O*NET—The Labor Department's Employment and Training Administration's Occupational Information Network, available beginning in 1997.

O*NET--The Occupational Information Network

DOL's New, Automated Replacement for the *Dictionary of Occupational Titles*

Click **here** to link to the **O*NET Web Server** (under construction).

THE O*NET VISION

☐ **O*NET will replace** the outmoded *Dictionary of Occupational Titles* (DOT).

☐ **O*NET** will be a **comprehensive database** that identifies and describes important information about **occupations, worker skills and training requirements**.

☐ **O*NET** will be a **timely, easy-to-use database** that will support national efforts to revitalize the American workforce.

☐ **O*NET** will help millions of **employers, workers, educators and students** make informed decisions about education, training, careers and work.

☐ **O*NET** is **the link** to the nation's primary source of occupational information.

O*NET'S ROLE

The value of **O*NET** is illustrated by its potential to serve as the *data infrastructure* supporting a variety of key workforce development initiatives. **O*NET** can be used by:

☐ One-Stop Centers and Employment Service Offices to develop a job match system by providing timely, high-quality data on worker skills and job requirements;

☐ The National Skill Standards Board (NSSB) and other industry-based groups to create skill-based occupational clusters for setting voluntary skill standards based on empirically derived data from job incumbents;

☐ Employers to develop/create customized job descriptions that reflect such contemporary concepts as virtual workplaces;

☐ Employers and workers to identify the specific skills and knowledge required to perform individual work activities and tasks;

☐ Employers, dislocated workers and/or others interested in changing jobs or careers to identify transferable skills across occupations and industries;

☐ Educators and business mentors to identify and prioritize skills for use by school-to-work transition programs;

☐ Educators and training providers to identify skills needed to develop curricula and train people for the workplace;

☐ Counselors to assist millions of students and workers with career decision making at multiple times in their lives;

☐ Researchers and policy makers to more quickly understand rapid changes in skill requirements in the workplace;

☐ Public and private vendors to develop value-added applications and software; and

☐ A variety of other efforts that likely will build on the DOT's extensive use in disability determination, foreign labor certification and vocational rehabilitation.

O*NET AS COMMON LANGUAGE BENCHMARK

Using scientifically-verified data to define all skills and occupational terminology, **O*NET** can serve as a national benchmark providing a *common language* for all users of occupational information. This will help standardize occupational terminology for consistent use across sectors and enhance efforts to bridge the gap between people and jobs. **O*NET's** *common language* will improve communication among students, educators, employers and workers and help integrate learning, training and work in ways not currently possible.

O*NET'S CONTENT FOR COMPREHENSIVE DATA

The new **O*NET** includes a variety of cross-job descriptors that will enable users to **organize job-specific information into broad,** *empirically-based* **occupational clusters** and allow a better understanding of issues of skills transferability and general performance.

O*NET descriptors will be hierarchically arranged at different levels of specificity so that users can **examine skills at broader cross-job levels** for job matching and retraining purposes **as well as at the occupation specific levels** needed for human resource applications.

O*NET will serve as a **truly viable occupational information system**, in a rapidly changing workplace. Content descriptors will not be rigidly referenced to existing job titles but will be collected and aggregated across positions to identify emerging jobs and occupational families.

O*NET content descriptors:

☐ Worker Requirements, including basic skills, cross-functional skills, general knowledge, education;

☐ Worker Characteristics, including abilities, interests, work styles;

☐ Experience Requirements, including training, experience, licensing;

☐ Occupational Requirements, including generalized work activities, organizational context, work conditions;

☐ Occupation Characteristics, including labor market information, occupational outlook, wages; and

☐ Occupation Specific Information, including occupational knowledges, occupational skills, tasks, duties, machines, tools, and equipment.

O*NET'S USES

O*NET used alone can:

☐ Identify job skill requirements

☐ Create skill-based occupational clusters

☐ Identify National Job Analysis Survey work behaviors

☐ Search databases by alternative classification codes (e.g., DOT, GOE, SOC, OES, MOS, OPM, CIP, SIC, etc.)

☐ Sort occupations by skill requirements

O*NET as part of an application software product can:

☐ Make job-person matches

☐ Create job counseling systems

☐ Develop customized education and training curricula

☐ Develop talent bank and resume systems

O*NET PROJECT SCHEDULE

1994: **O*NET** *common language* terms defined.

1995: *Prototype* **O*NET** *testing begins*, using computer-based collection and dissemination methods, as well as information on jobs in high-performance organizations.

1996: **O*NET** *available to limited users*, with rapid expansion of services planned.

1997-1999: **O*NET** *full system completion*.

For further information, contact:

O*NET Project
DOL/Office of Policy and Research
Division of Skills Assessment and Analysis
200 Constitution Ave., N.W., Mail Stop N5637
Washington, D.C. 20210

Or send e-mail to: *O*NET@doleta.gov*

Last updated: August 22, 1995

This site is the automated replacement for the *Dictionary of Occupational Titles*. Its database identifies and describes information about occupations, worker skills, and training requirements. O*NET can be used to ensure that the job seeker uses the common language for occupational information. Using recognized job titles is critical today because, as we have seen, employers are searching resume databases by occupational keywords.

Another very important information site for the job seeker is the *Occupational Outlook Handbook* compiled by the Department of Labor. This resource is located at

> `http://www.espan.com/docs/oohand.html`

This site details the educational requirements, earning potential, and job conditions for some 250 occupations that make up more than 85 percent of the jobs nationwide.

The Department of Labor's home page is located at

> `http://www.dol.gov`

This site provides information from the Employment and Training Administration, the Bureau of Labor Statistics, OSHA, and other Department of Labor programs. The Employment and Training Administration has its own site at

> `http://www.doleta.gov`

At this site, you'll find O*NET (the replacement for the *Dictionary of Occupational Titles*) as well as information on programs such as the Unemployment Insurance Technology Support Center and America's Labor Market Information System (ALMIS). The ALMIS home page is located at

> `http://www.ecuvax.cis.ecu.edu/~lmi/lmi.html`

The ALMIS site contains information for labor market analysts. It also includes a list of state-maintained bulletin boards and links to many state Labor Market Information divisions. These state sites provide unemployment statistics, industry employment, occupational projections, and wages. Some of the state sites break down the data into areas of the state.

The Bureau of Labor Statistics is located at `http://stats.bls.gov`. At this site, you'll find state, area, and nationwide labor market information.

The Training Technology Resource Center (TTRC) is located at `http://www.ttrc.doleta.gov`. At this site, you'll find information on federal and state employment and training activities.

The U.S. Census Bureau is located at `http://www.census.gov`. This site offers a wealth of information, including data about jobs, income, housing, recreation, and more, which can be viewed on a national, state, or county level. There are tables about employment in the fastest-growing and declining occupations, population estimates and projections, migration, journey to work, and educational attainment demographic information. This site also includes the *Statistical Abstract of the U.S.* and *County Business Patterns*.

To learn about the finances of public companies, look up Edgar–the Electronic Data Gathering, Analysis, and Retrieval system–at `http://www.sec.gov/edgarhp.htm`. Edgar contains documents files with the Securities and Exchange Commission since January, 1994, including the 10-Ks, which describe a company's performance during the fiscal year and all developments that shareholders have a right to know. You'll also find information about top executive compensation packages, stock trades made by corporate insiders, and merger and acquisition activity.

Public and Commercial Sites

Career Magazine provides employer profiles, daily job updates, discussion groups, and news articles. You'll find the Web site at

> `http://www.careermag.com`

Career Mosaic not only contains job listings but also such information as employer profiles and a career resource center with resume and interviewing advice. This site is located at

> `http://www.careermosaic.com`

CareerNet is located at `http://www.careers.org`. CareerNet provides links to more than 1,300 career-related Web sites including employers, newsgroups, colleges, and government job sources. This site also contains lists of career-related associations and organizations and career libraries.

Career Resources Page at Rensselaer Polytechnic Institute is a meta-index of Internet career resources including the "Internet Job Surfer" (job databases on the Internet), *Employer's Direct* (job databases and information of more than 100 employers), professional associations, and career services at colleges and universities, and other Internet job lists. Find the Career Resources Page at

> `http://www.rpi.edu/dept/cdc/homepage.html`

The Catapult (National Association of Colleges and Employers) is a clearinghouse of career and job-related sites. It lists Web career guides and library resources, job postings, professional associations, Web search tools, and college career centers. The Catapult is located at

> `http://www.jobweb.org/catapult/catapult.htm`

ERISS provides a listing of Web sites for job listings, resumes, career resources, and government agencies. ERISS is located at

`http://www.eriss.com`

E-Span's Interactive Employment Network provides a range of career services, including salary guides and other information. You can visit this site at

`http://www.espan.com`

Job Hunt at Stanford University is another list of online job search resources and services. This Web site is located at

`http://rescomp.stanford.edu/jobs.html`

The Smart Business Supersite has a great deal of career advice and links to even more Web resources. This site is located at

`http://www.smartbiz.com`

The section News/Columns includes columns on job search skills. The section Jobs/Careers has more articles, reports, checklists, and a lengthy list of related World Wide Web sites. The People Finder section connects to National Consultant Referrals for a list of career management counselors. The People Finder section also has a link to the New Market Forum for an online directory of more than 10,000 professional associations and membership groups. This site also has a directory of electronic mailing lists and newsgroups that specialize in various career topics.

Relocation Information

In addition to career guides, the Internet is an excellent way to research cities that you'd consider relocating to for a new job.

In your search engine, simply enter the name of the city. A survey by the National Center for Supercomputing Applications found that 80 percent of the material on municipal Internet home pages focuses on tourist information, such as hotels, restaurants, and museums. Your browser will bring up many home pages with material related to that city. Here are some sample home pages from selected cities:

Houston <u>`http://riceinfo.rice.edu`</u>

Los Angeles <u>`http://www.ci.la.ca.us`</u>

San Diego <u>`http://www.sannet.gov`</u>

An easy way is to log on to City Net, which allows you to visit pages for cities all over the country. Use this address:

`http://www.city.net/`

The city home pages may have links to other local information sites. If not, search for the local newspaper's home page. Local newspapers on the Internet include local stories and their classifieds. Search for the newspaper by name.

There is also a site for apartment rentals. Corporate Housing Connection's Apartments For Rent On-Line shows apartment rentals, short-term leases, and corporate housing by location and price with floorplans and photographs. Visit their site at

`http://www.aptsforrent.com`

Real estate listings are all over the Internet. Try Listinglink at `http://www.listinglink.com/` as an example. This site allows you to search by price range, community, number of bedrooms, and more.

Job seekers and employers alike today are in need of timely and accurate information on the labor market and careers. Job search professionals today stress that a most critical need job seekers have is access to factual information and the skills in using that information.

You may feel there is just too much information available and that you couldn't possibly deal with all of it. The characters in James Joyce's famous novel *Ulysses* (1922) are constantly sending letters, telegrams, even writing messages in the sand on the beach. Joyce was foreseeing a picture of life as "sending, carrying, and receiving information." Today we would say that the job search process is the same.

Using Internet Support Groups

During the early '90s, California was decimated by huge losses in the aerospace and defense industries. Mary worked extensively with many workers who were downsized out of successful careers. At the local Air Force base, a special department known as the Employment Resource Center (ERC) was established to address the reemployment concerns of workers affected by the base closure. Located on the base, the center became a networking hub for civilian employees and active military personnel. In the center were job postings that included online services, fax machines, word processors for composing resumes, and a State Employment Development Department (EDD) representative who provided placement assistance. Additionally, the ERC conducted special workshops in job search, interviewing, and resume writing, plus a host of other work-related topics. The ERC also conducted on-site classes on how to start a business, pass the California certification test for teachers, and survive life in the civilian world, among others.

There were many ad hoc meetings in the ERC where participants swapped tips as well as success and horror stories. They also passed on valuable information, warned each other about job-hunting pitfalls, shared leads on jobs and training opportunities, and generally supported one another through a traumatic transition period.

At state EDD offices around California, there are special networking groups called Experience Unlimited or the Professional Experience Network, in which persons work together to try to get back to work. These are unemployed people from the professional sector with contacts in different industries at various levels. These individuals, too, have access to job listings, fax machines, word processors, and special workshops through EDD.

Here again, the constant business being informally conducted involves networking with each other and acting as a support group for all the members. When someone gets a lead on a job that's not relevant, the individual passes it along to the other members. When they hear of a special program or training opportunity, they post it on the announcement board. When one member is feeling depressed or has had a particularly bad job-hunting experience, the other members rally around to help the person through it.

The Need for Support

Searching for work is hard. It is a time of frustration, anxiety, high hopes, and low self-esteem. People often take comfort in just knowing that others are going through the same thing. Frequently, job seekers who have been looking for work unsuccessfully for some time will ask hesitantly whether something is wrong with them. When Mary tells them that, many others have been looking even longer, these individuals immediately feel better. Shared misery is somehow easier to bear. That's why job seekers often form support groups. There are the informal ones, such as the networking contacts you make among your family, friends, and business acquaintances; and the formal ones, such as the ERC and Experience Unlimited. You can seek advice, job leads, and consolation from them.

A Supportive Net

There is such a support group available to you over the Internet. There are people out there who have stories to tell you, both good and bad, about their job search and employment experiences. We decided to do a little canvassing on the net to learn some of those stories for you.

We posted a message to a number of employment newsgroups and asked people to share their horror and success stories about Internet job hunting. The response was overwhelming. People contacted us from all over the country and the world.

Like other aspects of Internet culture, we found our correspondents to be generous with their information; supportive of each other as job seekers; and, for the most part, very willing to help. We were chided a couple of times for posting our survey wherever the business of finding jobs was going on—whether in a resume group, jobs group, or purely a discussion group. We got scolded for not adhering strictly to the usage guidelines of some particular group. But we were never flamed, or criticized with abusive language.

In those few instances when we were corrected, we still sensed that the Internet "neighbors" were once again looking out for one another.

A rich resource of wisdom is out there. People are eager to show you the ropes, and we have compiled several of their responses in this section.

Success Stories

Responses in this category ranged from simple praise for electronic job hunting to suggestions for changes to the system to tales of outright success at finding a job on the Net. We heard stories of how people had been searching for a job for several months and then found one over the Net in a matter of weeks. One fortunate job seeker found his job, was interviewed, and was hired all in the same day! Another wrote that she not only found her own job on the Internet, but continues as a recruiter to use the Net for finding applicants.

In many cases the applicant was in the final stage of waiting for word on a job. In a couple of cases, people e-mailed the good news that they had been hired after the survey was completed. Here are some examples of success stories:

● ●

Date: Mon, 13 May 1996 15:22:16 -0700

To: Mary Nemnich <mnemnich@wiley.csusb.edu>

Subject: Re: Tell us your success/horror stories!

Hi, Mary.

I was ready, not only for a job change, but for a CAREER change. I was a systems administrator, but wanted to stop working with computers and start working with people.

I first started looking in the classifieds in the local newspaper. I would read the ads aloud to my husband: "Could I be a ... Karate Instructor?? Pizza Chef??? How'bout an inline skating instructor"

"You can't skate, and don't even talk about your cooking!!!"

OK, so I went online and discovered job searching on the internet. I saw an ad for a technical recruiter. I had the technical expertise, yet I would work with people! I replied to the ad and within the day I had a telephone number of the firm.

I am now a very successful recruiter and use the Internet DAILY for our searches.

I always tell our applicants that I found my job on the Internet, and send them a list of resume and job listing newsgroups and web sites.

I can truly say (even tho it is corny) that it has changed my life AND CAREER!

Hope this helps,

Jennifer Moss

● ●

● ●

Subj: Horror Stories

Date: 96-05-04 17:17:14 EDT

From: (William C. Grosch II)

To: jobnet@aol.com

How about a success story?

I have more work than I can do. Pretty short sweet and simple.

GOOD RATES AND GREAT WORK!!!

● ●

Subj: Re: Horror Stories!!!!

Date: 96-05-05 15:41:40 EDT

From: (Mark Baartse)

To: jobnet@aol.com (Jobnet)

Hi.

I got a good contract as a freelance HTML author thru Usenet. I starting working with the guy for quite a while, via email, before we ever met in the flesh.

Mark

● ●

Subj: Re: Tell us your success/horror story! (New book!)

Date: 96-05-15 11:25:39 EDT

From: (Jon Peterson)

To: jobnet@aol.com (Jobnet)

This is short and sweet.

I am a freelance html/perl writer. I saw an add in uk.jobs.offered at 10.30 am. I sent a reply by email including a CV and saying that I could do half what they wanted to a very high standard, and didn't know a thing about the other stuff.

At 11.AM I get a phone call from the company asking if I could come over at 6.00 PM. After talking to the woman hiring me for 15 minutes, we agree on £300/week and I get the job.

Hardly earth-shattering but it sure beats buying the daily paper, waiting two weeks to hear that you have an interview in another two weeks, or dealing with shady agencies that are charging out at double your fees.

Jon Peterson: WWW Authoring, Consultancy

● ●

••

Subj: Re: Horror Stories!!!

Date: 96-05-03 11:31:48 EDT

From: Payter

To: jobnet@aol.com

Hi, My name is Payter Versteegen, and I graduated from the University of Maryland, Baltimore County (UMBC) in June 1991, with a degree in Computer Sciences. My first job was with a computer company in Rockville/Gaithersburg, Maryland. The late spring of 1994 was an extremely hectic time for over 1200 (employees in my company) since this was when the first wave of layoffs [attacks?] commenced. While my company was quite heroic in its efforts to place "surplused" workers elsewhere in the Organization, its most noteworthy effort to move them met with failure. Those workers would become simply out of luck.

I made it past the first two waves of layoffs, but destiny would have my job, as well as everyone else's; it was only a matter of time. In the month I had to find work either within or without the company, I turned to the Usenet newsgroups for help and found numerous opportunities. An employee (of a computer company) got hold of my resume and simply sent my account an e-mail. I responded, we met, and he hired me.

No doubt a success story for me. Good luck with your book. :)

L8r, P8r.

••

From: Richard Brown

To: mnemnich@wiley.csusb.edu

Subject: [miscjobs.offered] HORROR STORIES JOBS

Actually, my only story about job hunting on the net is good. I started reading miscjobs.offered, checked in with the career.com (online career center) daily, and subscribed to the optimist mailing list. Within one month, I had 3 job offers, and contacted a company in the exact location I wanted to work in, who is now MAKING a position for me.

••

From: a Bay Area Jobseeker

To: mnemnich@ wiley.csusb.edu

Subject: Re: HORROR STORIES JOBS

I've found my last three jobs over the Internet. I was laid off from one of the three, when the company fell prey to the California recession and the up-and-downness of tech companies in the Bay area. But the current one is all right, and I'm still occasionally looking for that perfect job. The first job was a contract job, which lasted for a year. As I want to work in Internet-related jobs, I suppose this is the only way to go!

••

● ●

From: Andrew Snow

To: Mary Beth Nemnich <mnemnich@ wiley.csusb.edu>

Subject: Re: HORROR STORIES JOBS

Hi,

I'm a contractor, so I don't know if this is appropriate, but I met my most recent contract through a posting on uk.jobs.offerd.

It was a truly excellent way of transacting business . . . no middlemen, no waiting for an interview . . . just e-mail a CV (resume) and fix up a meeting.

Oh, is this a horror story or one of joy?? Absolute joy . . . the place is great, the work excellent, and the people easy going . . . what more could anyone ask for?

Regards,

Andrew Snow

UK

● ●

From: Weston Beal

To: mnemnich@ wiley.csusb.edu

Subject: Re: HORROR STORIES JOBS

When I was in my last year of college, I scanned the job.offered groups every day, looking for anything in RF or microwave. I sent my resume by e-mail to anyone who mentioned RF.

One day I received a phone call from a manager at a Microsystems company who was putting together a group to do signal integrity (RF effects in digital circuits) support for engineering. We talked on the phone. I went to California for an interview, and the next week I got a very good offer from the company. It was my first and last onsite interview.
I took the job.

Regards

● ●

Horror Stories or Warnings

Our respondents also had some gripes about the way things sometimes work out there. There is widespread dissatisfaction with opportunistic headhunters, for example. The feeling abounds that these recruiters will say or do anything to get a client placed, true or not.

There were several messages containing a single word: the name of an organization or company. We cannot reproduce those here, obviously, but we can tell you that there are several companies that try to recruit people to their multilevel marketing or pyramid-type businesses. We even noted a chain letter being advertised in a jobs newsgroup. Respondents were furious that this type of posting should be there, cluttering up a listing of bona fide job offers. Worse, these "scammers," as one job seeker termed them, were found everywhere, in every group.

This has fostered suspicion among job hunters. We received several wary replies to our survey: "What do you need it for?"; "Send me more details so I can tell if you're on the level"; and "I have a story, but I want to know how you're planning to use it." In subsequent replies, we were careful to point out that we were "neither headhunters nor salespeople."

We heard a few times that people were glad "somebody is looking into this." We were also asked to notify the respondents when our work was finished. They were happy to participate to help others avoid or at least recognize similar pitfalls. Here are their stories:

● ●

Subj: Re: Tell us your success/horror story! (New book!)

Date: 96-05-13 06:13:42 EDT

From: (Bobby Holstein)

To: jobnet@aol.com (Jobnet)

Here's one from the other side.

I am president of Fuji Publishing Group. Since 1994, we have had http://www.fuji.com. A monolithic film company petitioned internic to have fuji.com put on hold status (they don't want it, they just don't want anyone else to have it). As a result, we now have fujipub.com as well.

Last October, one guy started sending his resume to postmaster@fuji.com every other week. Looking at his bulk mailing list, he was also sending this to every domain he could think of. He then started putting names in with the email addresses. For fuji.com, he put Fuji Film. Even a cursory examination of our web pages makes it perfectly clear that we have nothing to do with Fuji Film. I pointed this out to him and told him that his sloppiness in marketing himself precluded us from considering him and to remove us from his mailing list. He then started making profane and vociferous comments towards us, which I shared with everyone on his mailing list (most of whom I know quite well).

Bobby Holstein

President

Fuji Publishing Group

● ●

To: mnemnich@wiley.csusb.edu

Subject: I wouldn't go so far as to say....

Date: Tue, 14 May 1996 16:49:12 -0700

this was a horror story.....

But, it sucked nonetheless.

I had sat for hours cruising the "information" super highway, thinking, maybe I could find a job through the web that I could do from home and earn a living, as I was 8 months pregnant and looking at the end of my unemployment insurance. I found a certain location (of which I no longer have the name of the company or the e-mail address, unfortunately) that sounded absolutely perfect! I was really excited about the prospect. Their web page stated that you could find many positions through their company.

What they offered was, for $24.95, they would provide you with a listing of companies that were looking for people to work with their PC from home. The positions available were: data input, database management, e-mail responder (this really turned me on!) Plus, there were more technical positions, and some photographer positions as well. Well, I thought, how awesome....I could work from home, and be an "e-mail responder." Thinking to myself, there must be a "huge" need for this, I mean, come-on, imagine how many people/companies must be literally bombarded with e-mail....

So, I immediately mailed off my $24.95.....fortunately for myself, using a credit card check.....to some address in Florida. You know it's funny too, 'cause I'm normally SO careful, but I was so excited about the prospect.

They even had success stories with other people, including their pictures. So, about a week later...I'm thinking, "Sheesh, I wonder if they've gotten my check yet?" I kept checking my mail, thinking they would have written me...duh! So, (fortunately, again) I had bookmarked their address on the web. So I went to access their web page, and lo-and-behold....it didn't exist anymore! I thought...that's funny... So, then I tried to e-mail them at their address......guess what? My mail came back to me......their address was nonexistent! THAT'S WHEN I GOT (mad!)

I immediately called my credit card company and put a stop payment on the check! So, I didn't lose my money, but I still kept wishing that it had been a legitimate company, I was so looking forward to that opportunity. Oh, well.

That's my story. A "semi" horror story, with a success at the end. I was sorry, however, that I had not written down the name of the company, and the address to which I had mailed it. I would have gone so far as to go the postmaster, and try to get them busted, but alas, I had not......

Hope this helps you in your studies.....

Take care, and have a good day.

Kate

● ●

To: mnemnich@wiley.csusb.edu

Subject: Re: HORROR STORIES JOBS

Horror stories:

1. Folks trying to get free consulting by "interviewing": How would you solve >THIS< network problem?

2. Headhunters illegally excluding folks over 40, determined by "What year did you get your B.S.?"

3. Folks interviewing for jobs already filled but organization says "X" number of people must be interviewed.

● ●

From: Carlos

To: mnemnich@ wiley.csusb.edu(Mary Beth Nemnich)

Subject: Re: HORROR STORIES JOBS

One horror story is that these headhunters say they have plenty of jobs and System Administration personnel, but you find out that they only have 2 or 3 System Admin's and no jobs. I have found that most don't even know the computer business and are only salespeople trying to make $$$.

Carlos

● ●

From: Brian

Subject: (fwd) HORROR STORIES JOBS (fwd)

To: mnemnich@wiley.csusb.edu

The headhunters won't stop!!! They call all day and even nights and weekends. They are like flies around a . . . of . . . .

● ●

• •

From: Paul

To: mnemnich@wiley.csusb.edu

Subject: Re: HORROR STORIES JOBS

O.K. Here is my job seeking problem. I am a senior at Syracuse University, and I have been sending my resume all over the place through e-mail and keep getting calls interested in me "immediately." I clearly put on my resume that I will be graduating in May, but these people responding fail to read it carefully. What can I do about this problem?

• •

From: a Bay Area Employer

To: mnemnich@wiley.csusb.edu (Mary Beth Nemnich)

Subject: Re: HORROR STORIES JOBS

While it is changing daily, a few years ago the majority of people on the net were connected to a university. We posted 3 positions and, being a defense company, were very explicit about citizenship requirements. We were flooded with resumes from students who were citizens of eastern Europe, Russia, or mainland China. It also seemed clear that since it cost nothing for students to access the net, it was easy to send out canned resumes. In some resumes it was apparent that they did not have access to a good word processor.

• •

From: Steve

To: mnemnich@wiley.csusb.edu

Subject: Horror Stories

An addition to your horror/warning story file.

I am a newly graduated human resources specialist who uses the net to look for open recruiting positions. One user of the Delphi service in the states had posted an open invitation for recruiter applications. I e-mailed the guy, outlining my education and experience. I received an enthusiastic response saying I was the kind of person he was looking for. He wanted my address, so he could mail me a video tape that would outline the business and give more details.

The video arrived, and I popped it in my VCR, expecting to hear about a contract recruiting job. The offer was actually to sell weight loss and fitness products door-to-door in my city! It had absolutely nothing to do with recruitment at all. I telephoned the guy and told him not to waste my time, and mailed the video back, postage due.

Because he has my address, I have been receiving more offers about this opportunity about once a week. I have sent every one back postage due.

I am more careful now in applying for net jobs.

Steve Clark

• •

One thing we found to be true time and again is that Internet users are more than happy to help each other. Unlike many other real world venues, these folks will respond to you if you write them. It is the perception that they are all linked by a common interest—some would say passion—in the Internet that makes net users so accessible to each other.

It is also probably because they all inhabit the same "world," a world unlike the outside one. It may be because the Internet world is so different that people don't feel constrained to act in the same ways that they do in the "real" one. Whatever the reason, people are more open to communication with others on the net. They are "there" for each other.

There are many places online where you can meet with other job seekers, get advice, and discuss career issues. Let's take a look at some of them.

Online Forums

America Online has an area devoted to the concerns of job seekers. It is called Real Life. Contained within this area is a message board feature where job seekers may obtain advice and opinions from other job seekers and employers. One forum was called Getting the Pink Slip and dealt with the frustrations and concerns of laid-off workers. Another was called Coping With Job Loss. The "chat" feature in Real Life focuses on investment strategies and financial planning to help you decide how to invest your wages when you're working and plan for periods of unemployment.

CompuServe likewise has a support service for job seekers. It's called Career Management Forum. Here you may access workshops on such things as networking and interviewing strategies. One forum, called Job Search Depression, enables members to vent their feelings about the process of searching for work. In a forum called Support and Success, job seekers share job hunting tips and offer support and encouragement to each other. They also post their success story when they land a job.

Real-Time Chat

In real-time interactive communication, or chat, you actually carry on a live conversation on-screen with another user. The person or people at the other end can see on their screens the words as you type them. The Internet, including commercial online services and BBSs, and the World Wide Web have places for users to meet and discuss career-related issues.

The best known and most interactive tool is Internet Relay Chat (IRC). IRC has many channels of live chat, which anyone can join at any time. To be frank, most IRC use today is recreational and often sophomoric, but we do know people who have made valuable contacts on the IRC.

If your system already has an IRC client installed, it is a simple matter to join an interactive conversation. At the main prompt, just enter **irc** followed by a nickname of your choosing, up to nine letters long. For example,

```
irc mary
```

The first screen on IRC usually contains information about your local client, such as how many channels are active and warnings and advice for its use.

To use IRC, you will need to type your commands at the cursor. All commands on IRC start with / (slash). To get a list of all current IRC channels, type /**list** at the cursor. This will give you a rapidly scrolling list of channels. To get a closer look at them, press the Pause key. Each listing shows the name of the channel, the topic, and the number of users currently online. To choose a channel, enter /**join** and the name of the channel. You can then enter the conversation by typing your comments at the cursor. To change channels, enter /**join** and the name of the new channel.

A very useful command in IRC is /**help**. Use this command to get information on how to use IRC. To quit IRC, the command is /**quit**. If you don't have a local IRC server already installed on your system, you can telnet to a public IRC server.

For questions on IRC, go to the newsgroup `alt.irc.questions`. For a list of IRC servers on the WWW, go to

```
http://www.yahoo.com/computers_and_internet/
internet/chatting/irc/
```

This site will also provide a list of channels plus a FAQ on Internet Relay Chat.

IRC also exists on the WWW. Some include the feature as a part of their home pages. For example, check out the San Antonio Express-News Online (EN Online) forum on the WWW. Go to

```
http://www.express-news.net/chatx.htm
```

Finally, if you find you're spending WAY too much time in IRC, go to the newsgroup `alt.irc.recovery`.

One other interactive tool used for real-time communication is called "talk." With the talk feature, one user may communicate with another one on the same computer system. To use talk, you need to know the other person's userid, and that person needs to be online at the same time as you. For example, when Mary wants to chat with Fred, she simply enters:

```
talk fjandt
```

Fred then enters **talk** followed by Mary's userid. When the real-time conversation begins, you'll see a split screen, with one person talking in the top half, and the other person talking in the bottom half.

Psychological Aspects of Electronic Job Search

Frustration

Frustration is a standard problem with job search in general. It usually results from the just-missed opportunities, the "one that got away." Applicants often wonder who that other "perfect" person is who is taking all the jobs. It is easy to let feelings of inadequacy creep in. Added to this problem is the fact that, in today's labor market, job seekers are constantly playing a numbers game. *So many* people are looking for work.

On the Internet, frustration is a constant companion. After all, the sheer vastness of the system is daunting. How can one possibly find all there is to find? It is easy to begin to feel like an infinitesimal speck in cyberspace, a mosquito smashed on the information superhighway.

Prior to the advent of the World Wide Web, one particularly frustrating problem with job search on the net was "pathing." *Pathing* refers to the different screens you pass through to reach a desired area. This was the problem with gopher because of the way information is arranged in successive menus. Unless you had some record of how you'd gotten to a particular section, it was difficult to find your way back to where you'd been. If you're using gopher on the Internet, it's still a good idea to make a "map" of the route you have taken.

Thanks to the World Wide Web, pathing is not the problem it once was. Most browsers come equipped with a feature that will mark and hold your spot for you to return at any time. This is known as a "Bookmark" in Netscape, "Favorite Places" on America Online and "Personal Favorites" with CompuServe Mosaic. Wherever you are on the Web, you just add the site to your bookmarks, and you can retrieve it later. Also, when you are navigating through a Web site, all you need to do is use the "forward" and "back" features—usually arrows pointing in either direction—to get to where you have been. You can always keep a record of favorite URLs and just enter them at the URL prompt and get taken immediately to the requested area. As with everything else on the Web, pathing is much easier.

Of course, with "information overload," which is often experienced on the Internet, the question is where to look, what to consider, and what to ignore. When it comes to job search, you can control for geographical area, occupation, even wage range. If you are an accountant seeking work in Minnesota, why search for jobs in the West? Similarly, don't waste your time looking at all the accounting clerk postings, which are clearly below your level of expertise. Remember, too, that you don't want to waste an employer's time by "going fishing" in San Diego when you only want to "reel in" a job in Minneapolis. Focus your attention precisely on what you want.

Side-Tracking/Isolation

One peculiar aspect of the Internet culture is that users—particularly new ones—tend to get hooked by the seemingly endless parade of information available. It is not unusual to log on at 6:30 p.m. "just to take a quick look" and find yourself turning off the computer at 2 a.m. Some people get so caught up in the Internet world that they become isolated after a while, spending days at a time online, chatting with this or that newsgroup, or playing some interactive game. BEWARE. You have a job to do. If you go on the net twice a day, make sure that at least one of those times is dedicated to job search. Promise yourself that you won't get sidetracked by some other seductive activity until you have made at least one productive contact or attempt at getting a job. Then, by all means reward yourself.

Go play on the Web. Cruise around some completely frivolous sites. Check out the reviews of the newest movies, read up on your personal passions, download a sound clip of the latest release of your favorite group or spend some time talking to a job seeker's support group. Just never lose sight of your main mission and purpose for using the Internet. Stay on track and get "hooked" on a job.

In Word Only

There are some advantages and disadvantages to the absence of non-verbal cues in electronic communication. Those cues are what your receivers can see and hear when communicating with you face-to-face—such as voice tone and inflection, facial expression, and body language—which influence how they interpret your message. For example, "Nice jacket," said with a snide tone and a roll of the eyes has a meaning altogether different from that of the words by themselves. When you are not there to provide interpretation or any nonverbal clues, your message can be construed a number of ways. Following are some characteristics of the applicant not readily apparent in electronic communication.

- ■ **Gender.** When a return address on a message to an employer says simply, "jsmith," it could be anybody. Many female applicants have chosen this option for the initial stages of application—say an e-mail letter of interest to a company—to give themselves a better shot at jobs in nontraditional occupations (jobs typically held by men). In other cases, the name of the applicant could be either male or female, such as Kelly or Dana or Pat, giving no gender clue to the employer.

By the same token, if no clue is given in the return address of the employer, you also have no idea of the identity of the person on the other end. Say your contact in the company was a woman, though you didn't know it. Michele, who works for a clothing manufacturer, says people responding to her often mistake her name for "Michael."

"When I get messages like, 'I'm looking forward to meeting a manager who takes his interest in fashion design seriously,' I've already formed a negative impression of the candidate." A careless pronoun could cost you a job opportunity.

■ **Age.** E-mail messages are not age-specific. Unless the job seeker says something completely obvious like, "I got my experience in construction starting when I was in the Seabees during the Korean War," there is no way to tell the age of the applicant. Be careful, though. One applicant warned us of unscrupulous recruiters who ask, "When did you get your degree?" or similar questions designed to elicit age without asking for it directly.

■ **Appearance.** Employers reading your message cannot discern your appearance from words on a screen. They don't know if you are totally bald or have a beard to your chest. They can't tell whether you are sitting at your computer in a business suit or in your underwear. (Actually, they try not to think about that!) Ken, an executive search consultant, calls it a "guessing game." "You can't help but form mental pictures of the person writing to you," he says. "Funny thing is, I've only been close to what the real person looks like a couple of times. I think that helps keep the whole business fair." It is precisely because they can't see you that personal preferences and prejudices of employers don't play as prominent a role in electronic communication as face-to-face. This is a major benefit. In electronic communication, the playing field is level. You can truly be judged by the content of what you have to say, not by how you sound or look while saying it.

■ **Anxiety.** A common but troublesome problem with in-person job search is nervousness. With electronic job search, this difficulty is virtually eliminated. There you sit, at a very comfortable distance from the employer, at your own desk, on your own turf. No one is there to accept a sweaty-palmed handshake or hear the quiver in your voice. You are relaxed and confident.

■ **Facial Expression.** For many job seekers, merely making eye contact with the employer is difficult, whether out of shyness or nervousness. For others, smiling does not come naturally with strangers in a "forced" situation. Yet, eye contact and facial expression are critically important in face-to-face interviews. Employers are people, just like you. If you don't look them in the eye, they don't trust you; if you don't smile at them, they don't like you. Electronic job search has an advantage here too. "I just feel like a big phoney, grinning at total strangers," says Albert, a loan processor. "When I 'talk' to them on the Internet, though, I can be friendly in writing. It helps me sort of get to know them before I actually meet them."

- **Speech Patterns.** Employers' prejudicial attitudes toward certain speech patterns can hold otherwise competent applicants back in the selection process. Job seekers who speak in heavily accented English, though they may have excellent credentials otherwise, don't always get a fair shake, usually not making it past the telephone interview. The same is true for individuals with language disabilities who often experience discrimination in the application process.

Dolores, a recruiter with an outplacement firm, told us about one candidate she had difficulty in placing. "He had been an engineer in Cambodia and had found work in a Bay Area firm owned by fellow Cambodians. When the company downsized and he looked for work in other companies, he was faced with major discrimination because of his accent. He worked as a math tutor for the local junior college and his students had no trouble understanding him. We concentrated on his writing skills, had him focus on e-mail applications, and eventually he was placed."

E-mail provides an unbiased forum for these applicants. Here, they may express themselves eloquently in writing, although they may not do as well orally. The employer gets a look at the candidate's credentials, free of prejudice. They are able to judge the applicant based on merit, not on any particular patterns of speech. In electronic job search, everyone sounds the same.

- **Typed vs. Handwritten.** Another definite plus for many Internet users is the keyboard itself. Handwritten correspondence and applications can work against you, whereas all e-mail messages look alike, in terms of writing. Type is type. No judgments there. Additionally, no one is there to watch you laboring over your work application or cover letter. No erasures or unsightly white-out blobs mar your presentation. Your mistakes will never be seen. They will have been conveniently edited out before the employer ever sees them.

All the employers we spoke to were in agreement on one major point: They seemed to feel that the absence of nonverbal cues imposed fairness on the application process and made them better recruiters. Jeannette Daly, a human resources assistant, summed it up, "There is a tremendous advantage to using e-mail for the hiring person because no information about the applicant is evident, other than the individual's qualifications. For example, we can't hear an accent and don't have any idea about how the person looks. We have to judge the individuals on personal merits, as it should be. It eliminates bias."

A Whole New Game

Accessibility

The greatest advantage of electronic job search is probably access. You can "get in" to employers in a way that is often impossible in the real world. All you need is an e-mail address. When you locate a job on the net, the contact name given is the name of the one person in that organization who can help you. You don't have to search all over the company until you find the person you must talk to about the job. The scenario in real-world job search goes like this: You target a company that you think—sometimes it's no more than a vague idea—may have need for a person with your skills. You then either make a phone call or go by in person to inquire.

Receptionist: "May I help you?"

Job Seeker: "Yes, I wonder if I could please speak to the person who does the hiring?"

Receptionist: "We're not hiring."

Job Seeker: "Well, who normally does the hiring for data entry operators?"

Receptionist: "We're not hiring."

Job Seeker: "Then, could I fill out a job application, in case a job opens up?"

Receptionist: "WE'RE NOT HIRING."

Make no mistake, the receptionist or operator or assistant is not necessarily privy to what goes on in terms of hiring for every department. There may very well be a job open about which the receptionist knows nothing, but this person's job is to keep you away from the busy managers. Essentially, the receptionist stands between you and the opportunity.

In electronic job search, no gatekeeper—assistant or secretary—must be gotten through first. This has changed the whole game of job hunting, really. The "invisible shield" between you and the employer has been lowered by this very accessible medium.

Speed

Working along with the accessibility factor is speed. You are not relying on conventional mail delivery or on someone else's dependability to get your message to the employer. Thus, turnaround time can be remarkably fast in electronic job search. Remember, too, that you are not limited to certain hours of the day when you try to contact an employer. There is no locked door with an "Open M-F, 8 a.m.-5 p.m." sign on the Internet. You can send your message any time, any day.

Internet Culture

One last important benefit to this new world of job seeking is that you and the employer are meeting on common ground. You are essentially both members of the same club or community. You have each spent time in the fascinating world of the Internet. However, with entry into this new "global village," you take on certain responsibilities. In the parlance of the net, a "lurker" is someone who sits by and reads postings without ever joining in the discussion. But the Internet experience is participatory. It is incumbent on you to learn all you can about its many uses, and then, jump in! There is room for everyone, and your input is welcome.

You will not find a more helpful community. When we were doing research over the Internet, our requests for assistance were **never** refused. Virtually all users who were asked for information or to render an opinion or to allow us to quote them agreed enthusiastically. We were frequently referred to other people and sources for more help. We also found that hierarchy, so prevalent in real-world interactions, is absent from the Internet. A telephone call to a large corporation seeking comment from a highly placed source would likely result in the query being referred to an underling to be "handled." We had equal access to CEOs and unemployed job seekers alike. **We boldly e-mailed where no phone call had gone before** and were pleasantly surprised at the response. Once you have truly interacted with your fellow citizens of the Internet, you will never again understand the "lurker" mentality. You will begin to relish the opportunity to help someone, repay a favor, or pass on a tip or insight to a kindred job seeker. In short, you will take your place as a participating member of the Internet culture.

As you tackle the grueling job of finding a job, remember that, with electronic job search, it is not the lonely business you have been used to. You are not alone. You now have a support group that numbers in the millions. Now, doesn't that make you feel better?

Preparing Your Electronic Resume

What if you were to receive some 50 to 100 letters per week? Let's say that you already knew the general ideas that were to be covered in each letter and that only the details would vary. How likely would you be to pore over every single one of them? Wouldn't it be more likely that you would skim through them to find the one that looked most interesting and give that letter your full attention first? This scenario adequately describes a weekly task of most human resource professionals: reading resumes.

In the labor market of the '90s, the flood of resumes threatens to bury most human resource managers. Now, thanks to the Internet, there is another source of resumes assailing personnel representatives. Employment bulletin boards, online resume services, and e-mail have added to the crush of paper resumes waiting in the in-basket. Human resource managers look for the most expedient way to get through the "stack" to find the people they want to talk to. This chapter is devoted to getting you into the "keep" pile.

In general, the rules for writing a winning traditional paper resume apply also to electronic resumes. But some special problems do arise when you translate resumes to the electronic medium. These require our close attention. In the following pages, you will learn how to adapt the rules of paper resumes to the electronic medium. Tips on how to make paper resumes attractive and professional will be applied to the electronic variety. Because employers receive hundreds of resumes through e-mail (one service we explored posted more than 1,000 for California alone!), yours must be more competitive than ever.

The Audience

When preparing an electronic resume, a primary thing to keep in mind is the audience—who will read your resume. Of course, you want the readers to be employers. But, remember, the Internet is public—anyone will be able to read your resume.

When using e-mail, always keep in mind that it is not secure. You have no control, for example, over where and to whom your recipient forwards your message.

Technically it is possible that other people could read your mail on its way from your computer to your recipient's. Users concerned with e-mail privacy can use programs such as Privacy Enhanced Mail (PEM). Although these are not in widespread use, they can encrypt and decrypt your mail. Also, anonymous remailers are available that remove your address from your e-mail message.

Now, let's look at the basics of preparing an electronic resume.

Building Your Resume

Any word processing program can be used to create, edit, and update your resume. Unlike the old days of the typewriter, today you can easily make changes to adapt your resume to each job. Some word processing programs come with templates or "wizards" to help you create a resume. Microsoft Works, for example, offers a resume format. You decide how you want it organized and the program presents you with a fill-in-the-blanks template to enter the information. You can use the same program to compose cover letters and follow-up letters, and track prospects and responses. For help creating resumes in WordPerfect, see *Using WordPerfect in Your Job Search,* by David F. Noble (JIST Works, Inc., 1995).

Resume Software

There are software packages available to walk you through the creation of your resume:

WinWay Resume 3.0 CD by WinWay Corp. includes resume and letter writing features and a job-search database. It also includes video career counseling and video simulated interviews. WinWay 3.0 requires an IBM-compatible with Windows 3.1 or Windows 95 and a CD-ROM drive.

ResumeMaker Deluxe CD from Individual Software includes a resume writer, sample letters, interviewing workshop, career planning, and a job-search database. ResumeMaker is also available on floppy disk for MS-DOS and Macintosh but for the basic resume-building tools only.

Perfect Resume by Davidson provides a basic, easy-to-use resume builder. The program also includes a Power Letter feature and a database for tracking contacts, phone calls, and interview notes. Perfect Resume is available on CD-ROM for Windows and Macintosh and on floppy disk only for Windows.

In order to e-mail a resume to an employer, it is necessary to save the resume in an ASCII file. This acronym stands for American Standard Code for Information Interchange. ASCII is a text-only format, meaning that an ASCII file does not contain pictures, special fonts, programs, or any of the other bells and whistles available to you on a word processor. Files typed and saved in ASCII are left-aligned and devoid of special formatting codes. In the next section, we discuss how to create a resume that is attractive and readable, even given the limitations of ASCII.

Resume ABCs

Three basic factors should serve as guiding principles so that you can prepare any resume properly. We call them the "ABCs" of resume preparation. Simply, a resume should be attractive, brief, and clear.

The first factor, *attractiveness*, captures employers' attention and invites them to read on. The second factor, *brevity*, keeps employers interested enough to finish reading. The third, *clarity*, enables employers to conclude whether you have what they want. In this chapter, we examine all three factors and apply them to the electronic resume.

Making Resumes Attractive

In written resumes, one of the most readily apparent indicators of attractiveness is the paper itself. You should give time and thought to selecting paper that is the proper weight and shade. The same is true for choosing the color of ink that will complement your paper choice. For example, a resume printed with burgundy ink on dove (pale gray) paper makes a more distinctive impression than regular black type on white bond paper. Likewise, navy ink on pale blue parchment is elegant and crisp. There are even some new papers that contain artistic borders on one or more sides. Ecru paper, bordered in mahogany marble with brown ink, would surely stand out in a crowd of black-on-whites.

With electronic resumes, however, these appearance factors are eliminated. The "paper" is all the same—a computer screen. Additionally, as a rule, no special fonts or inks are available to you. Thus, you need to concentrate on those aspects of appearance you can control.

Note: If you are submitting your resume to a company that uses resume scanners, you want to make your resume as basic as possible (For more information, see the section, "Preparing Your Resume for Scanning.")

One of these is called the "lie" of the resume. By this, we don't mean that you should stretch the truth of your background! The "lie" of a resume refers to its arrangement on the page, or for our purposes, the screen.

This arrangement is key in getting the employer to read your resume. If a resume is too wordy, covered with print, and has very little screen showing through, an employer will deem it too time-consuming to read. Consider again that this person has many more of these to plow through. The best resumes, then, are spare, with good spacing between the body of the resume and the headings, and with decent margins.

Now, let's look at how to arrange the electronic resume to give it a readable and an attractive "lie."

- ■ **ASCII**. The problem with formatted electronic resumes is that they must be sent in ASCII. Especially problematic for us is that ASCII does not contain the codes to make specially formatted documents. When the resume arrives on the employer's screen, the resume is no longer formatted. Instead, it is totally left-aligned and arranged in a haphazard manner.

  Accordingly, when typing your resume in ASCII, you can't use the "center line" feature, so you need to space everything as you type it and then save it. If you don't, when you upload your resume to send it, it will not look as professional as a properly formatted resume. Furthermore, it will be confusing to read. *Note:* See section titled "The Multimedia Resume" for more on special resume formatting.

- ■ **Headings**. The easiest kind of resume to read has side headings on the left separated by at least five spaces from the body of the resume on the right. Employers like this style of resume because this format is easy to view for information. For example, if an employer is looking specifically for the educational background of an applicant, it is simple to glance at the side headings for "Education" and quickly locate the desired information. Employers appreciate this kind of format in electronic resumes as well.

  Some resumes have the headings centered above the appropriate sections. In paper resumes, which should usually be no more than a page in length, space is at a premium. Without a fair amount of spacing—say at least two expensive lines—between headings and sections, centered headings are more difficult to find and thus more frustrating to employers. (These are people you haven't even met yet. Now is certainly not a good time to frustrate them.) With electronic resumes, space is not such a crucial factor. But it still requires a bit more looking on the part of the employer to find the needed heading if it is centered above the section. It is preferable to set your headings off to the left of the body of the resume.

On paper resumes, headings should be in boldface to make them easier to read. With a variety of fonts available through word processors, the headings can also be in a different size or style than the body. The idea is to make the heading stand out. However, you don't have the luxury of fonts in ASCII. So, the best way to make your headings eye-catching is to put them in all caps.

Making Resumes Brief

All employers have had the unpleasant experience of wading through a resume that is several pages long. On paper, this is simply inexcusable. The general rule is that a resume should not exceed one page in length. Longer resumes are not only daunting to read, but also considered pretentious by most employers. How to fit all of their experience onto one concise page is troubling to many job seekers. This is an area in which the electronic resume has some advantages over the paper resume.

Employers are accustomed to paging through several screens while reading their e-mail. This is quite different from shuffling a sheaf of papers mailed by a job seeker. A full page of type will not fit on a single computer screen. Thus, a resume that fills several screens is not considered as breaking the "one page" rule. You have a bit more latitude in the computer medium. However, even here, you need to be careful. A resume that rambles on for six or seven screens will be as annoying to an employer as a paper resume that goes on for two or three pages.

Craig Bussey, HR head of Hüls, America, Inc., a chemical manufacturing company in New Jersey, adds, "A resume is like a teaser for a movie. You're not supposed to show the whole movie. The idea with a resume is to get an interview. If you give too much information, there's no reason to do one."

So, you will still need to edit your experience. Here are some tips.

- **Prioritize your experience.** Limit your job experiences to those that are most important or relevant to the job for which you are applying. Rank them in order, from most to least important. Focus on those skills that you know will be most significant to the prospective employer.

- **Use bullets.** Full sentences eat up space. It is much more expedient to use *bullets*—short statements that summarize your experience. For example, consider the following excerpt from an auto mechanic's resume:

  I have repaired and rebuilt all types of cars, both foreign and domestic. I can do all phases of auto repair from simple tune-ups right to complete engine rebuilds. I have all my own tools, including both standard and metric. I have all kinds of manuals and my own rollaway. I have had lots of experience in repairing Nissan and Toyota models. I am certified for headlight adjustment and smog inspections and repair.

This bit of experience takes many lines of precious space to communicate. The message is wordy and also breaks another rule of proper resume etiquette: it uses personal pronouns. Bullets, along with the elimination of personal pronouns, would take fewer lines to say the same thing:

■ Full service from simple tune-ups to complete rebuilds on all makes and models, foreign and domestic

■ Full set of tools, standard/metric; manuals; rollaway

■ Nissan and Toyota specialist, including electronic systems; smog and headlamp certified

This applicant could even add two more experience bullets and still use less space than it took in sentences. Additionally, the look is cleaner, and bullets are easier and faster to read.

■ **Limit the scope of previous jobs.** There are two factors to consider here. First, resumes should never go back more than 10 years. Depending on your field, some experience is stale after a mere five years. Employers are simply not interested in ancient history. Second, you should include only work history that is significant to the position for which you are applying. If you are an administrative office assistant, for example, your experience as a house painter during college is simply not relevant to the employer. It is helpful if you title your work history section "Significant Experience," rather than "Experience." This lets the employer know that you plan to concentrate only on those things in your background that relate directly to the desired position.

■ **Never list references on your resume.** Unless you are specifically asked by the employer to provide references, do not list them on your resume. Generally, references are checked only when the employer is interested in hiring you. To add them to an unsolicited resume not only wastes valuable space, but also unnecessarily invades the privacy of your friends and business associates.

Edit ruthlessly, choose judiciously, write frugally. Keep it brief!

Making Resumes Clear

Have you ever known someone who tries to build you a clock whenever you ask them what time it is? The person ends up giving you so much useless information that you practically forget what it was you asked for in the first place. This is a common problem in resume writing. Employers want you to tell them in the clearest, most comprehensible terms what it is you did and exactly what you want. Too many job seekers end up getting bogged down in jargon, acronyms, or vague and inappropriate language. Here are some suggestions on how to clarify your information.

■ **Jargon.** This is in-house, job-related language that people use as a sort of "shorthand" to describe different duties, activities, or responsibilities at work. Bureaucracies are especially good at using jargon, but all companies use it to a certain extent. Some positions or job-related activities occur in various industries but are called by different names. Thus, the jargon used to describe them can vary widely.

Consider this example. A person who checks product quality can be known as a quality control technician, a quality assurance evaluator, a production checker, a quality tech, a process control supervisor, a line inspector, or a quality examiner. Imagine the confusion when you describe yourself as a PCS (production control supervisor) to an employer who uses quality control technicians (QCTs). Just because your former company knew what a PCS was, doesn't mean your future company will.

Even something as mundane as an interoffice memo can become confusing when referred to in company jargon. Memos are known variously as "buck slips," "sheets," even "snow-flakes!" Some companies refer to quality control inspections as "surveillance." However, most people associate surveillance with law enforcement.

Applicants who have served a lengthy period of time in the military have a particularly hard time freeing their resumes of jargon. When, for example, they want to reflect time spent in a temporary assignment, former military personnel often refer to it as "TDY." This acronym stands for temporary duty. When they are moved permanently, they call it "PCS" (permanent change of station). To an employer firmly rooted in the civilian world of employment, it is gobbledygook to read "PCS to Guam" followed by a job description on a resume. These applicants often have difficulty translating military language to civilian terms as well. For instance, people don't in the business world "command" or "lead." They supervise or manage.

It is absolutely essential that you communicate clearly on a resume. Once you have written your job descriptions, have two people completely unfamiliar with your profession read them. If they encounter something that they don't understand, you have most likely fallen into a jargon trap. Is there another term to describe the word you used? Perhaps it can be explained rather than named. Find a way around it. Confused employers everywhere will thank you.

■ **Language.** Keep the language of your resume crisp and professional, but allow your own sense of style to show through. Job seekers frequently believe that resumes should be like the job application, only without lines on the page. The result is a lackluster, dry recitation of facts, with no hint of the applicant as a person. However, the fact is that a resume is meant to be much more than a work history. The primary function of a resume should be to capture the employer's attention. It is often the first look an employer has of an applicant. Consider, then, how you want it to represent you.

When preparing an electronic resume, you want to strike a balance between language that is too rigid and language that is inappropriately informal. Apply the basic rules of proper grammar and spelling. Avoid slang and familiarity. Describe your duties in professional, understandable language, but choose language that is more colorful when describing personal and professional strengths. The busy personnel manager who must read a ton of e-mail resumes will appreciate it.

Next, we'll examine the proper order for organizing the material in an electronic resume.

Organizing Your Resume

When creating a paper resume, there is a certain order in which the information is arranged. Typically, the heading goes first: name, address, and phone number. Next, comes the "Position Objective." This is where you tell the employer in specific terms what you are looking for. Then, some resumes use a "Summary" paragraph, in which you briefly describe your experience.

This is followed by "Experience" and "Education" sections. These two headings can switch places, depending on what you have to offer. For example, if you have recently received your degree in engineering, this is your most valuable asset and should go first. However, if you have 15 years of experience as an engineer, plus a degree, you should lead off with your experience. The areas following experience and education can also vary. Some common headings are "Military Service," "Publications," "Community Service," "Activities," "Specialized Training," and "Awards/Honors." Most resumes conclude with "References furnished on request." This last line is not really necessary because most employers assume that permission to contact references will be given at the appropriate time. You might want to save that space for something more important.

This standard paper format must be manipulated a bit for electronic resumes. Remember that the first few lines on the employer's computer screen will be taken up with the header—your return address, date/time, etc. So, if you begin with your name, address, and phone number, it may be all the employer sees on page one. This is not a strong incentive to read on. Or, the employer may get your heading plus a fragment of what comes next, which doesn't create a professional first impression.

On many of the resumes we looked at on the World Wide Web, we noticed that people left off their address and phone number entirely, opting instead to give an e-mail address only. The problem with this is if an employer is interested, she or he may desire to pick up the phone immediately and call. Some employers don't have e-mail capability within their browser. When you put in an e-mail link, a recruiter without e-mail capability cannot just click and go. They need to write down your e-mail address, exit the browser and call up their e-mail program. Still other applicants left off their e-mail address, choosing to use their name as a hypertext link that, once clicked, gave way to an e-mail screen. If you are reluctant to put your full address, at least indicate your city and state. In the event you are e-mailing your resume, put your name and job title only at the top of the resume as a heading, rather than waste that first screen with header and address. Following the heading, you will write a summary.

With only about 20 lines on the first screen to work with, it is imperative that you make a strong, favorable impression within the first few lines. Therefore, we suggest that you lead off with a summary paragraph immediately following your name and job title. Include your very best skills, abilities, and qualities. Make that employer want to page to the next screen! This summary paragraph sets up the rest of the resume to follow, in much the same way a lead paragraph in a news story previews the report and invites the reader to read on. It also saves the employer some time. Lastly, the summary paragraph should contain the main keywords that describe your skills. Thus, the first part of your resume will look something like this:

J.B. Seeker
Public Relations Specialist

SUMMARY: Talented Public Relations Practitioner with more than 15 years of experience and a proven track record in community and media relations. Excellent writing skills. Facility with desktop publishing, including Pagemaker (6.0), Quark, and Microsoft Publishing. Familiar with MS Word and Windows 95. Motivational speaker. Adept at press relations and creative advertising. MA

This opening can be followed by a traditional resume, beginning with your name and complete address, phone number, and e-mail address. We will provide you with a complete sample of a properly formatted electronic resume later in the chapter.

To get the most out of online resume services, it is necessary that your resume contain certain words that employers are likely to enter as keywords when they are making a candidate search through a resume database. This will be important in getting your resume read by automatic resume tracking devices known as "scanners." In the next section, we show you how to use keywords in your resume so that it gets the maximum number of "hits," or selections by employers.

Preparing Your Resume for Keyword Searches

How can employers deal with all the resumes they receive, much less all those posted on the Internet? Resumes on the World Wide Web are searched by keywords. You need to convert your resume into a keyword resume. First, consider the job titles you use to describe your past positions. Employers are likely to search using job titles from *The Dictionary of Occupational Titles*. For example, if you were employed as a laboratory technician whose responsibilities included drawing blood, an employer's keyword search wouldn't find you unless you used the word *phlebotomist*. (The *Dictionary of Occupational Titles* is available from JIST and may be online at O*NET at `http://www.doleta.gov/programs/onet/onet_hp.htm` (see Chapter 7).

Second, give careful attention to all the words you use. It wasn't too many years ago that job seekers were advised to use active words such as *developed* and *implemented*. No more. Employers don't do keyword searches on these words; they do keyword searches for specific skills. Keyword searches are more likely to be done on nouns such as *finance* and *electrical engineer*. If you don't use the words employers use for keyword searches, your resume may never be seen by human eyes! How do you know what words to use? One way is to study current job listings for the popular keywords.

The idea with resumes with keywords is to make them more "scanner friendly"—that is, to ensure that they get selected when examined by a resume scanner. The following section will explain about scanners and the special considerations they present to online job seekers.

Preparing Your Resume for Scanning

Companies such as AT&T, Ford Motor Co., Hewlett-Packard, and Texas Instruments now use software that makes it possible for them to turn the resumes they receive into a database that can be searched by keywords. Since 1991, Hewlett-Packard has been using software that can handle the 330,000 resumes the company receives yearly.

Let's say you prepared a resume you're proud of, you've had it prepared in an unusual attention-getting typeface, you've used selective underlining to emphasize your skills, and you've had 500 copies printed on a special colored paper. You're ready to use the World Wide Web to find job vacancies, but you'd really rather mail your prefect resume by snail mail.

You still haven't converted to the computer age! When your resume is received, it is likely to be scanned into a computerized database. Your unusual typeface, underlining, and colored paper may not scan. Hard copies of your resume should be printed on white paper in a popular type font such as Helvetica or Courier, which scan the most accurately. You should also use a font that is 12 points or larger because scanners have a difficult time reading smaller type. Don't use italic for the same reason. And be careful not to fold or crease your paper resume, because some scanners can't read into the fold.

Craig Bussey tells us that his company, Hüls America, Inc., receives thousands of resumes every year. He uses Resumix to scan them. He cautions job seekers to stick to basics when writing resumes for scanning. "Don't include graphics or fancy paper or unusual fonts because the scanner won't know what to do with them. It comes down to this: If your resume can't be scanned, it can't be used."

Some companies give instructions about submitting a resume that is suitable for scanning. The following message is posted in the "How To Submit Your Resume" section of the Hughes Space and Communications Web site:

> Resumes received by HSC are scanned into our applicant tracking system. Therefore, resumes must be typed or computer-generated using letter-quality printing. To facilitate our scanning process, please use white or off-white paper and standard typefaces, such as 9-, 10-, or 12-point Times Roman, Courier, or Helvetica. Please avoid using boldface and fancy fonts, underlines, bullets, and italic. Margins must be at least 1/2 inch on each side.

The summary paragraph on a resume is the first thing the scanner will encounter. Therefore, it's important that the summary contain keywords. However, you should remember that, once your resume is scanned and sent to an employer, it will still be read by a human being. Thus, your summary paragraph should be written as a cohesive, organized statement, not just a collection of disjointed words. "The automated resume system is really only a tool and doesn't replace the human thought process," says Craig Bussey.

> (Applicants) are better off structuring some type of summary statement that includes as many key terms as it can, yet still makes sense. Remember that if I like the resume, I'm going to print it and take it to the hiring manager. I am not going to "re-do" a resume. It has to look right and make sense when it arrives at my screen.

Resume tracking software can sell from about $80,000 to more than a million and at this writing is used by over 400 companies. Resumix software contains 10 million terms for specific skills typically linked to a general profession title. For example, Resumix software permits the employer to search not just for *accountant*, but for *general ledger accountant*.

The advantage to the employer of computerized resume databases is that they are able to manage increasing numbers of job applicants with shrinking human resources budgets in automated tracking systems. Hüls America's Craig Bussey took the bottom line firmly into consideration when he decided to use a resume tracking program.

> A company will generally spend between $1,500 and 2,500 on a display ad for a one-day exposure. Let's say it draws 100 resumes. Typically, the company may interview 8 to 10 candidates, narrow that down to 4 or 5 who actually meet the hiring manager. What does the company do with the remaining resumes? Even if they keep them for a year, if they throw them away, at $2,500 for 100 resumes, you're throwing away $25 for every resume you get rid of. My company spent $98,000 on nationwide recruitment advertising in a year. I figure it's more cost-effective to purchase a resume tracking program than to throw away $98,000 in recruitment costs.

The advantage to the job seeker is that the employer will be doing keyword searching through all the resumes submitted, not just those submitted for a particular vacancy, so you'll be automatically considered for all the vacancies the employer has.

The resume posting site Monster Board offers companies with Restrac software to download resumes directly into their databases! Thom Guertin, Creative Director of Monster Board explains:

> RESTRAC is a desktop software solution utilized to index jobs and resumes electronically. Corporate recruiters can keyword search through thousands of jobs and resumes in real-time using the RESTRAC system. The Monster Board/RESTRAC partnership will enable recruiters to load jobs from their desktop computer directly into the Monster Board, as well as access the resumes of thousands of qualified candidates online.

Now that you have the basic tools for creating an electronic resume, let's look at some actual samples from Career Mosaic:

Sample Resume 1 -

Ann Tolliver — Advertising Team Member

ANN L. TOLLIVER
000 S. 00st
Phoenix, Arizona 00000
(000) 000-0000

EMPLOYMENT

Present An Advertising Agency Phoenix, Arizona
     Advertising Team Member/Graphic Artist for full-service advertising agency.
     Design and create computer graphic art for print, broadcast, and the Internet;
     work with team to create advertising concepts, new business names, logos,
     slogans, and copy.

1994-1995   Some Hi-Tech Graphics Company Phoenix, Arizona

Advertising Team Member/Graphic Artist for full-service advertising agency. Involved in concept creation for client campaigns as well as individual advertisements; designed computer graphics for advertising; placed print advertisements; wrote copy.

1993-1994   Portland Photographic Studios Portland, Oregon

Administrative Assistant/Production Support Person for studio of professional automotive photographers. Orchestrated communications, props, travel, transportation, and accommodations for studio and location shoots; managed sales representatives' office; assisted with office expansion and automation upgrade, which involved equipment and software selection, computer program formatting, and training.

EDUCATION

Important State University at Somewhere
1991 Bachelor of Arts degree in Communications, specializing in Advertising

Western State County Community College
Continuing Education
Spring 1994: 175 hours of Management

Another College
Continuing Education
1995: 114 hours of Spanish; 24 hours of French

PROFESSIONAL AFFILIATIONS

Phoenix Advertisers Group - Member since 1995

1995 National Advertising Award (NAA)
Committee Member - local

— —

Sample Resume 2 -

Elizabeth Murphy — Registered Nurse

Elizabeth Murphy
000 Walnut Court
Some City, Somestate 00000
(000) 000-0000

OBJECTIVE:
Discharge Planning/Utilization Review/Case Management

EDUCATION:
Any College, Anytown, Anystate, 1996

Completed 15-week certificate program in HEALTH CLAIMS EXAMINING. Obtained extensive hands-on experience in health claims processing utilizing DPT, ICD-9, HCPCS, and revenue codes. Coursework also covered COB, PPO, Medicare claims handling, and the analysis and computation of contract benefits. Trained in both manual and online adjudication. Attained proficiency in insurance and medical terminology.

Some Other College, Nice Place, Somestate, 1996
Completed nursing Certificate Program in Quality Management. Coursework included Quality Improvement, Utilization Management, Risk Management, Discharge Planning, and Legal Aspects.

A University, Some City, Smallstate
Completed AS Degree in Nursing, i986. Graduated Cum Laude.

SUMMARY OF QUALIFICATIONS:
Registered Nurse since 1986. Specialized in patient teaching and care. Expert in Ostomy care, Diabetes, and AIDS care. Provide home and emotional support. Have strong customer service and supervisory background as well as excellent communication skills.

PROFESSIONAL EXPERIENCE:
Staff Nurse/Charge Nurse, Some Hospital, Newtown, Oldstate (9/88 to Present) Specialized in Medical/Surgical and orthopedic unit and acted as nursing team leader. Duties involved dispensing medicine and reporting any abnormal lab results or changes in patient care to the Physician in charge. Acted as Assistant and Charge Nurse as needed.

Staff Nurse, Well-Known County Hospital, Some City, Somestate (9/87 8/88) Specialized in Medical/Surgical and orthopedic unit. Provided total patient care, monitored recovery, and charted patient progress. Interacted with physicians, provided assistance as requested, and advised of patient progress.

Staff Nurse/Charge Nurse, Village Medical Center, Quiet Town, Somestate (9/86 - 8/87) Worked in both acute care and at skilled nursing facility. Monitored IV's, checked blood sugar levels, dispensed medication, and charted patient progress. Provided updated status reports to physicians.

MISCELLANEOUS:
Available immediately. Prefer Coastal or Bay Areas.

— —

Sample Resume 3 -

Harvey D. Chatwicke — Senior Accountant

Harvey D. Chatwicke
HARVEY-CHATWICKE@mail.booksonline.com

OBJECTIVE
A rewarding and challenging senior accountant position that will fulfill audit requirements towards CPA certification.

SUMMARY

* Solid knowledge of GAAP; passed all four parts of CPA exam; certification pending audit experience.

* Excellent team worker and eager to learn. Seeks responsibility. Organized, thorough, and attentive to detail.

* Strong interest and demonstrated abilities in all aspects of general accounting and controller's areas: A/P, A/R, tax preparation and planning, F/S and P/L preparation and analysis.

* Experienced with IBM PCs and compatibles, Computron, MAS90, MS Office Word and Excel.

EXPERIENCE
Some Communications Co., Inc. Bethesda, Maryland

Senior Accountant
Feb 96 to Present

* Authorize payments, monitor and reconcile prepaid postage. Implemented USPS CTA System for payments, which eliminates payables processing time and shortens funding lead time by up to one month.

* Determine sales and use tax liability, file taxes with jurisdictions, reconcile accrued sales and use tax accounts. Responsible for research of tax assessments. Calculate and file return for commercial rent tax liability.

* Train new staff and temporary accountants effectively.

* Record and reconcile WIP, calculate title unit cost and transfer titles to Finished Goods. Analyze variances in cost, record raw materials transfers and all inventory entries.

* Created procedures and scheme for implementation of new general ledger system and served as member on ledger conversion team. Independently created training materials and trained peers.

Staff Accountant
Dec 95 to Feb 96

* Reconciled bank statements and prepared cash entries.

* Monitored fixed asset acquisition records, assessed and recorded depreciation, and reconciled the fixed asset and accumulated depreciation.

* Reconciled WIP, prepaid postage and determined sales and use tax liability as noted above.

SeniorAccounts Payable Representative
Nov 93 to Dec 95

* Processed invoices related to inventory and capital expenditures; reconciled and analyzed accounts related to capital expenditures at month-end.

* Prepared and posted manual checks and voids, prepared month-end analysis and reconciliations related to same.

* Assisted in sales and use tax audit research.

Reliable Communications Firm

Accounting Clerk
July 91 to Sept 93

* Scheduled, audited, and released payments of up to $500.000 in daily accounts payable.

* Assisted senior accountant in year-end FS preparation and inventory control review.

* Facilitated and expedited collection of $15,000.00 in refunds from vendors through extensive research and communication.

Barton A. Killibrew, PC, Some City, Somestate

Accountant
Nov 90 to May 91

* Audited, coded, and posted ledgers and journals for 30-35 active clients.

* Prepared end-of-period and end-of-year FS, income tax returns, and quarterly sales tax and payroll returns.

EDUCATION
Some College of Somestate at Some City

Bachelor of Science, Accounting

Honors Program Graduate, GPA 3.0

Sample Resume 4 -

Kirby Bixby — 3d Modeler/Animator — (555555555)

KIRBY BIXBY — 3D Modeler/Animator
555 5TH AVENUE, APT. 555
NAPERVILLE, IL 55555
555/555-5555

PROFESSIONAL AVENUE:
Employing my creative ideas and 3D animation experience, building upon my computer skills, and increasing my knowledge of current and upcoming applications and systems

Lightwave 3D 4.0, Imagine 3.0, Turbo Silver, DKB Trace, Pixar's Typestry 2, DPS par Software, Penllo, DCTV, EGS Paint, Image Master, Art Department Professional, Rend 24, Digi-Paint III, Deluxe Paint IV, Painter, GVP's Image FX, Photogenics, Macro Media Director, Adobe Premiere 4.0

7 years PC experience, 7 years Amiga experience,
5 years Macintosh experience, 6 months Silicon Graphics Experience

JOB EXPERIENCE:
Some Company, Some Town, Freelancing high-end 3D animation artist
      -Meeting with company video directors and producers to conceptualize future productions
      -Integrating live video footage with 3D, using Lightwave 3d and a DPS par equipped with a TBC IV
      -Recreating electronic parts and connectors in 3D for use in 3d animation
      -Creating all video backgrounds and still frames for company product videos
      -Developing CG animation and still frames
      -Reproducing company logos for video use
      -Providing the video department with creative hardware/software solutions

COMPUTER ANIMATION & STILL FRAME PROJECTS
      -Created, programmed, and published 3D magazine released monthly on bulletin board systems
      -Actively ran an international 3D/Video bulletin board for 3 years, beginning at age 16
      -Currently producing 2D/3D advertisements for local bulletin boards
      -Conceived local Amiga computer users group

EDUCATION & SEMINARS
      Some University, Some City, Somestate
          Graphic Design Major
          Emphasis on 3D animation
      Another University, Old City, Somestate
          Liberal Studies
      Some High School, Another Town, Samestate
          Emphasis on programming

      Attended Seminars
          College Seminar, Some Town, Somestate
          Media Seminar, Small Town, Somestate
          Film and Video Seminar, New Place, Somestate
          Multimedia Convention, Old Town, Somestate

OTHER INTERESTS AND HOBBIES
      Internet and the World Wide Web
      In-Line Skating

Sample Resume 5 -

Roland Hague — Manager of Marketing
ROLAND W. HAGUE
55 N COUNTY LINE RD.
SOME TOWN, SOMESTATE 00000
Tel or Fax: 000-000-0000
E-mail: X000X@Prodigy.com

QUALIFICATIONS

- Skilled developing sales, markets, products, programs, and distribution channels.
- Skilled creating and meeting strategic planning objectives through teams.
- Proficient identifying opportunities and solving a variety of business problems.

SALES/SALES MANAGEMENT

- Managed sales territories, building relationships, identifying needs, and implementing sales strategy with distributors, retailers, and end users.
- Working with database marketing, tracked data to target customer groups.
- Forecast buying trends and motives, analyze competition, and position products.
- Managed and motivated sales force, increasing sales $15 million, adding 240 dealers.

PRODUCT MANAGEMENT / PRODUCT DEVELOPMENT

- Managed the profit and loss of two consumer product lines through product planning, strategy, marketing new product, introduction, pricing strategies, competitive analysis, advertising, communications, and product team coordination—20% annual growth.
- Identifying market segment, premium value positioned product by improving, naming it TRADENAME, increasing sales 25 million units (52%) in first month.
- Added value to a product, naming the addition TradeName; then packaged addition in special containers, adding $950M in sales.

PLANNING

- Led analysis of market trends and demands, constructed and implemented marketing plans and strategies, guiding the development of products and distribution.
- Strategically positioning sales team as consultants, changed commodity product and price rated supplier to a value-added marketer, by packaging services as products.

MARKET TRENDS AND RESEARCH

- Developed and executed research projects, forecasting buying trends, competitive analysis, identifying markets, and creating positioning strategies. (Methods: direct mail, focus groups, telephone surveys, database analysis, and database marketing).

OPERATION MANAGEMENT/IMPLEMENTATION

- Working with manufacturing, selected unique containers, then set up contract packaging, complementing existing plant filling capabilities.
- Installed computer system, supporting sales using e-mail and electronic forms.
- Designed comprehensive marketing communication network system, linking the field with marketing, which increased customer service, reducing expenses (38%).

TRAINING

- Created product introduction and training on video- developed/published manuals, and end-user seminars.
- Trained dealers to develop sales, marketing, promotion, and advertising plans.

CROSS-FUNCTIONAL WORK TEAMS

- Member of team conceptualizing through opening a franchised business called SOMENAME (restaurant, c-store, fast-food, car care, truck stop—opened 32 stores).
- Led creation and rolled out of home-warranty business and gas subsidiary.
- Developed centralized Ad specialties system, converting it from cost, to profit center.

MARKETING PROGRAM DEVELOPMENT/DESIGN

- Working with top management, developed strategic plans, marketing programs, promotions, and sales direction.
- Constructed strategic tool Customer Relation Survey, positioning the sales force as a business partner.

ADVERTISING / PROMOTION / COMMUNICATIONS

- Produced communications plan, outlining execution and measurement of advertising, promotion, and merchandising of consumer product lines.
- Developed division budgets; managed $2.4 million annual advertising budget.
- Created innovative campaigns, using giant displays, billboards, and novel show exhibits.
- Created marketing newsletter, developing positive relations with consumers.
- Designed customer/market-driven, "pull through," direct-mail flyer program.

1994-	Manager Market Planning Some Company, Some Town, Somestate
1990-94	Sales/Marketing Manager Some Company, Some Place, Somestate
1989-90	Product Development Manager Some Business, Some City, Somestate
1980-89	Marketing Services Mgr., Product Manager Some Company, Some Place, Somestate
1978-80	Sales Rep, Buyer Some Business, Some City, Somestate
1976-77	District Sales Manger Some Company, A City, Somestate
1974-76	Regional Sales Rep. A Company, Some Town, Somestate
EDUCATION	BA Psychology/English A University Emphasis: Behavior Trends and Market Research
ADDITIONAL TRAINING	Direct Marketing, TQM-Facilitator, Marketing Communications, Consumer Behavior

---

Sample Resume 6 -

Thomas Abbott — Regional Sales Manager

Dear Manager:

As a candidate for a Sales Management, Sales position with a progressive consumer products company, I am offering my resume. Revealed in the resume is a proven track record with both large and small consumer product companies. My success in directing regions and divisions, and in managing both direct and indirect sales forces in multitrade environments, demonstrates my ability to produce for you. My background includes specialization in the Grocery, Lawn & Garden, Mass Merchandise, Chain Drug, and Home Center/Hardware Industries.

Let's become acquainted soon to discuss mutually rewarding areas of opportunity.

Sincerely,

RESUME OF:

THOMAS R. ABBOTT
000 Some Street
Some City, Somestate 00000
Phone & Fax: 000-000-0000
E-Mail: tabbott@xxx-xxxxx.net

KEYWORDS:

Sales Management. Sales. Broker Manager. Account Manager. Region Sales Manager. Division Sales Manager. District Sales Manager. 18 Years Sales Management Experience. $32 Million Sales. National Travel. BS Degree. Some City. Somestate.

Direct Sales. Food Brokers. Distributors. Manufacturers Representatives. Supermarkets. Drug Stores. Discount Stores. Home Center Stores. Hardware Stores. Military Sales. Commissaries. Exchanges. XXXX. XXXXX. XXXXXX. XXXX.

OBJECTIVE:

Sales Management position with progressive consumer products company.

QUALIFICATIONS:

Progressively responsible sales and sales management experience, achieved predominantly in managing, planning, and directing the activities of Food Brokers, Distributors, Manufacturers' Reps., and Direct Sales Organizations.

- Consumer product companies background - A Business, A Business Consortium, and A Corporation.
- Team leader positions with 45 direct sales personnel, brokers, and distributor organizations accounting for up to $32 million in annual sales.
- An energetic, ethical professional sales manager experienced in the hiring, training, directing and motivating sales teams and independent business owners and executives.
- Proven ability to develop, implement, and coordinate successful sales and marketing strategies to grow volumes & market share, including major new product introductions.
- A creative sales manager with strong organizational and communication skills, who demonstrates the ability to successfully forecast, plan, and accomplish major budget and profit responsibility.
- Proficient with computer. Excellent working knowledge of DOS, MS Office (Excel, Word), Lotus 1-2-3, WordPerfect, Harvard Graphics, and many additional software applications.

EXPERIENCE:

A Business - Some City, Somestate 1991 - Present
Regional Sales Manager - Northwest
Responsible for the sale of products through brokers and Manufacturers' Representatives organizations.

- Managed broker region of 15 northwestern states - 32 broker firms, plus national sales - XXXX and group - XXXXX and XXXXX.
- Direct sales responsibility includes: Company Name and Business Group, national group - Company Name and major retail group - Company Name.
- Designed and implemented Company's annual sales programs.
- Increased the dollar volumes of various accounts by 280%.

EXPERIENCE:

A Company - Some City, Somestate 1983 - 1991

Divisional Sales Manager - Particular Division responsible for sales of consumer products. Sold through Brokers, Distributors, Manufacturers' Representatives, and a Direct Sales Team.

- Managed broker division in 9 northwestern states - 28 firms. Led company for 3 years: dollar sales increases, market share growth, new distribution gains, and retail bookings.
- Directed division in a 6-state area. Successfully reintroduced a particular brand. Achieved a +64 increase in dollar volume through increased distribution, mass retail displays, and reduced price feature ad support.
- Additional responsibilities: national, international, and chain sales.

EXPERIENCE:

Some Corporation - Some City, Somestate 1966 - 1982

District Sales Manager - Particular Division

Responsible for sales of certain products through brokers in certain northwestern states.

- Successfully introduced certain brands through establishing specific strategies and aggressive plans with product management group and customer service.
- Led the northwestern region in dollar and case sales increases for fiscal year 1980: + 31 , + $3.15 million dollars. All three particular state brokers won honors at a national convention.

Earlier Company Positions:

- Territory Sales Manager
- District Sales Supervisor
- District Account Manager
- District Sales Representative

EDUCATION:

Bachelor of Science - School of XXXXXX - XXXXX and XXX
A College, Some City, Somestate. 1966

Award - President of XXXX & XXXXXXX of the School of XXXXXX

A Fraternity - International XXXXX Fraternity

REFERENCES:

Available upon request.

— —

Sample Resume 7 -

Bennett Hamilton — Painter

BENNETT J. HAMILTON
Some Address
SOME CITY, SOME PROVINCE XXX XXX
(000) 000-0000

FAX: (000)000-0000

ATTRIBUTES AND ATTITUDES

 Customer-oriented, flexible, honest, trustworthy
 Work well without supervision
 Diploma in Consumer Electronics Program
 Good sense of humour
 Eager to work

ELECTRONIC AND MECHANICAL SKILLS

 Worked on many computer programs
 Upgraded and repaired computers
 Setup and troubleshooting on computers
 Replaced worn components on electronic circuit boards
 Soldered and desoldered components
 Worked in college workshop: troubleshooting, cleaning and repairing
  video tape recorders and stereo equipment
 Filled out work orders

MANAGEMENT AND CUSTOMER SERVICE SKILLS

 Opened and locked workplace at beginning and end of day's business
 Reported numbers of customers and sales to company owner
 Took customers' orders in company
 Supervised workers on construction sites
 Cooked hamburgers, French fries, hot dogs, chicken nuggets and other items,
  fast food restaurant
 Operated cash registers, balanced cash, completed credit card transactions
 Worked in client's homes, discussed their needs, responded to questions

MAINTENANCE SKILLS

 Installed electrical wiring in new and existing homes
 Insulated roof with fibreglass batts
 Shingled garage roof
 Hooked up pipes to faucets, removed and installed pipe and fittings
 Installed furnace ducts
 Ran central vacuum pipes from outlets to canister; ran and taped electrical
 Measured and cut drywall, installed and taped drywall
 Painted interior and exterior surfaces using a variety of applications
 Installed kitchen cupboards, countertops
 Cleaned bathrooms, washed floors, cleaned glass windows and doors in
  commercial buildings

EDUCATION

CONSUMER ELECTRONICS DIPLOMA Some University
Graduated 1995   Some City, Some Province

SOME SECONDARY SCHOOL DIPLOMA	Some Secondary School
Graduated 1989	Some City, Some Province

WORK HISTORY

COMPUTER TECHNICIAN	Self-employed
1993 to Present (Casual)	

PAINTER	Some Firm Name
1987 to Present (Casual)	Some City, Some Province

PROJECTIONIST	Some Company
1995 (Summer)	Some City, Some Province

SNACK BAR WORKER	Some Company
1994 & 1995 (Summer)	Some City, Some Province

SERVICE TECHNICIAN	Some Corporation
1993	Some City, Some Province

COOK AND COUNTER PERSON	Some Firm
1989 to 1990	Some City, Some Province

LAWN MAINTENANCE	Self-employed
1986 (Summer)	Some City, Some Province

HOBBIES AND INTERESTS

> Old Cameras
> Refurbishing old cars
> Skiing

REFERENCES AVAILABLE UPON REQUEST

— —

Sample Resume 8 -

Robert W. McLean — Supervisor Assay Data; Graphic Design

Resume for Robert W. McLean

Address: 000 S. Some St. #15	Business Phone: 000-000-0000
Some City, Somestate 00000	CompuServe: 00000,0000
Phone: 000-000-0000	AOL: Xxxxxxx@AOL.com
	Internet: xxxxxxx@xxx.net

Work Experience

Some Business	June 1987 to Present
000 S. Some St. #15, Some City, Somestate 00000	

Activities:

- Maintain LANs, both AppleTalk and EtherNet.
- Give classes in spreadsheet programs, database programs, graphics, animation, and desktop publishing systems.
- Prepare business presentations.
- Install equipment.
- Evaluate and recommend software and hardware.
- Create logos and other artwork.

Some Company	March 1987 to Present
0000 A Street, Some City, Somestate 00000	

Supervisor Assay Data	October 1994 to Present
Duties include:	

- Desktop publishing, data management, and reduction for assayed control insert
- Computer Graphic Artist; Macintosh
- Supervision of clerical personnel

Technical Computer Support   March 1987 to October 1994
Duties included:
- Management of Macintosh-based LAN (AppleTalk)
- Desktop publishing, data management, and reduction for assayed control insert
- Customer telephone service for controls and QCS
- Technical support for XXXXXX software package

A Company   October 1985 to March 1987
00000 Some Place, Some City, Somestate 00000
Technical Service Representative; servicing accounts in northern United States.
Duties included:
- Installation and training for new laboratory computer systems, instrument interfaces, and subsystems
- Routine and special maintenance of existing sites
- Sales support and demonstrations
- Documentation and software troubleshooting

Some Hospital   July 1980 to October 1985
000 E. Some Street, Some City, Somestate 00000
- Trained in Some Medical-Related Occupation
- Chief programmer and system troubleshooter for purchased XXX system
- Supervisor of Certain communication installation and interface with XXX
- Shift Supervisor, supervising four technologists and five laboratory assistants

Another Hospital   July 1978 to June 1980
0000 Some Avenue, Some Town, Somestate 00000
- Summer replacement for the Autopsy Assistant
- Venipuncturist
- Lab Assistant

Academic Background

A State University, Somewhere
        Bachelor of Science degree in Biology, 19XX
A State University, Somewhere Else
        Attended lectures in Medical Technology, 19XX
        Internship in Toxicology and Special Chemistry

19XX Member of County Multimedia User Group, Somestate
Medical Technology Training, Some Hospital

Some University, Some City
Accounting, 19XX
Computer Languages: BASIC, C, COBOL, FORTRAN

Experience with the following programs:
Acius 4th Dimension
Abbott CanOpener
Adobe
        Acrobat 2.0, Reader, Exchange, Distiller
        Illustrator v. 3.0-5.0
        PageMaker v. 4.0
        PageMill
        Photoshop v. 2.5-3.0
        Streamline
Canvas v. 2.0
Caere Omnipage Pro
Claris FileMaker Pro
Equilibrium Tech. DeBabelizer
Farallon SoundEdit
FoxBase Pro
Fractal Design Painter
HyperCard
Lotus 1-2-3 (IBM)
MacroMind Director
MacWrite
Microsoft Excel, Word, PowerPoint
Netscape Navigator
Norton Utilities
Novell Networks
Odesta Double Helix
Olduvai Read-it Pro
Quark XPress

Strata Studio Pro, Vision 3d
Symantec SAM
System 7
Tempo
Timbuktu/Remote
WordStar (IBM)

Experience with the following hardware:
AGFA 9800
Chinon CD ROM
DayStar Accelerators
Dove Fax+
Farallon MacRecorder
Hayes modems
Hitachi CD ROM HP
DeskJet PLUS
HP Laser series
HP ScanJet PLUS
IBM PC through XT
LaserWriter NXT
Macintosh 128K through Quadra
Microtek Scanners
NEC CD-ROM
NEC Silentwriter
Nicon 35mm reader
Procom MO Drive
QMS Colorscript 100
Qume Scripten
Supra Modems

REFERENCES AND EXAMPLES AVAILABLE ON REQUEST

— —

Sample Resume 9 -

Paul Embick — Medical Technologist

PAUL EMBICK
000 E. Some Lane
Some City, Somestate 00000
Telephone: (000) 000-0000
E-mail: xxxxxx@xx.xxxxx.net

HEALTHCARE INFORMATION SYSTEMS

Available to discuss a challenging position that integrates information systems with laboratory
expertise, allowing for future growth within the company and the profession.

SUMMARY OF SKILLS

.... formal education .... 8 years of microbiology laboratory experience .... experienced in
automated laboratory instrument operations and troubleshooting .... Vitek .... Vidas .... Bactec ....
Coulter .... computerized systems .... quality control .... quality assurance .... staff training ....
presentations .... MS-DOS .... Windows 3.1 .... Windows 95 .... databases .... IBM PCs .... software
and hardware installation and troubleshooting research .... DATAWORKS .... dBASE IV .... pride
in quality performance and achievement .... dedicated and reliable professional with initiative, drive,
and the desire to excel ....

PROFESSIONAL HIGHLIGHTS
May 1992 to present
Some University, Some City, Somestate
MEDICAL TECHNOLOGIST - Microbiology Laboratory

* Analyzed ocular and respiratory specimen for the presence of bacteria, viruses,
  acanthamoebas, and fungi. Instructed physicians on proper laboratory procedures and
  techniques necessary to increase the recovery of pathogens from specimens. Inserviced other
  technologists on current laboratory topics. Participated in medical research projects that
  were presented at national conventions. Evaluated new laboratory procedures.

* Accomplishments: Converted the laboratory from a manual filing system to a fully
  computerized filing system. Trained laboratory personnel on the usage of various computer

software, with special emphasis on programs of significance to the department. Provided inservices to personnel concerning computer hardware. Designed and created numerous laboratory forms and labels that are currently in use by the department. Created a dBASE IV database for positive virology endophthalmitis cases.

February 1995 to present
Some Medical Center, Some City, Somestate
MEDICAL TECHNOLOGIST - Microbiology Laboratory

* Established procedures for the bacteriology section of the laboratory. Worked independently to implement quality control and quality assurance programs in accordance with Some State HRS standards. Designed and created numerous laboratory forms for the proper documentation of quality control for media, reagents, procedures, and instrumentation. Trained other technologists in the area of microbiology.

* Accomplishments: Spoke at length with Some State's HRS inspector and supplied appropriate documentation and information, which resulted in an outstanding passing of the state inspection.

October 1989 to May 1992
Some Hospital, Some City, Somestate
MEDICAL TECHNOLOGIST - Microbiology Laboratory

* Analyzed body fluids and materials from human sources. Duties included virology, mycology, serology, parasitology, and occasional supervisory duties.

* Accomplishments : Utilized OCR software to update the laboratory procedure manual.

November 1987 to October 1989
Some Hospital, Some City, Somestate
MEDICAL TECHNOLOGIST - Microbiology Laboratory

* Responsible for the isolation, identification, and susceptibility testing of pathogens in clinical specimens. Duties included urinalysis, parasitology, serology, mycology, and body-fluid cell count.

* Accomplishments: Created and implemented various charts and flow diagrams for laboratory procedures.

EDUCATION

Bachelor of Science in Medical Technology, April 19XX
Some College, Some City, Somestate

PROFESSIONAL LICENSURE AND AFFILIATIONS

State HRS License in the specialties of microbiology, serology, clinical chemistry, hematology, and immunohematology. Member of the American Society for Microbiologists, and the American Society of Clinical Pathologists.

STRENGTHS

Fast learner, enthusiastic and positive, with patience, care, and the ability to exercise prudent judgment in decision making. Creative and energetic, capable of the sustained effort necessary to see a project through from conception to completion.

REFERENCES

Available upon request.

The next samples are from USENET newsgroups. Notice that they are all exceedingly long and wordy. That makes each resume tedious to read. The first applicant originally prepared his resume for the World Wide Web and has left all the HTML codes within his resume! The result is a confusing hodgepodge of strange symbols mixed in with the text.

Sample Resume 10 -

```
Subject:         Resume: Human Resources/personnel/accounting/
                 investigations
From:    etaylorxxx@xx.xxxxxx.com (Edward Taylor (via JobCenter))
Date:    00 May 19XX 00:00:00 GMT
Message-ID:      <0xxxx0xx$0xO@xxx0.xxx.xxxxxx.net>


Name:            Edward Taylor
Company:         Name of a Company
E-mail:          etaylorxxx@xx.xxxxxx.com
Phone:           000-000-0000
Location:        Some City

<html><head><title>Edward Taylor's Resume</title></head>
<body bgcolor=#e9c2a6>
<TABLE>
<TR><TD>
<Hl><CENTER><img src=http://user.aol.com/xxxxxxx/etaylor.jpg> </
center>
</Hl></TR><TD>
<center><FONT SIZE=+2><b>Edward Taylor<br>
000 Some Street<br>
Some City, Somestate 00000-0000<br>
(000)   000-0000 Home<br>
(000)   000-0000 Pager<br></font>
E-Mail:<a href="Mailto:etaylorxxx@xx.xxxxxx.com">
xxxxxx@xx.xxxxxx.com</a></center>
</TD></TABLE><hr>
<font size=+2>Multitalented, communication skills, leadership
qualities and self-motivated.
Seeking employment in accounting, compliance, computers, personnel,
investigations or public relations in Berkeley, Oakland or San
Francisco, CA.,</font><P><hr>
<center><b>EDUCATION</center><br>
09/75 - 06/80<p>        Some University; Some City,
Somestate<p>
        Bachelor of Science degree with a
major in Business Administration and a specialization in
Accounting.</b><hr>
<center><b>EXPERIENCE</center><br>
06/80 - Present<p>      Self-Employed<p>
Some Company,          Some City, Somestate.<p>
Home-based retail business, selling gift and group merchandise to
individuals and organizations in
person and at conventions throughout Somestate.  Purchase
merchandise, maintain inventory
and the income and expense records.  Prepare the company's annual
sales and business reports.  Also
a Licensed Private Investigator conducting a variety of
investigations and a consultant providing
guidance to assist individuals so that they will be in compliance
in the
```

preparation of their annual
reports.
<p>
01/77 - 05/94<p>
Investigator<p>
Some Government Office, Some City, Somestate.<p> Conducted a
variety of types of personnel security and suitability
investigations, for approximately fifty
federal agencies, on individuals occupying Public Trust Positions
and individuals handling highly
sensitive government information. Interviewed, under sworn oath,
individuals under investigation as
well as sources knowledgeable of the individual under
investigation. Prepared sworn affidavits and
reviewed a variety of documents including residential, educational,
employment, arrest, bankruptcy,
liens, divorce, civil and criminal records. Also conducted
criminal investigations involving
impersonation in taking federal examinations for employment, theft
of government examinations and
fraudulent receipt of retirement funds. Trained newly employed
investigators in the skill of
investigations.
<p>
10/80 - 09/85<p>
10/75 - 09/76<p>
Equal Employment Opportunity Counselor<p>
Some Government Service<p> Counseled employees regarding what
constitutes discrimination. Explained the process for filing
discrimination complaints. Prepared narratives of counseling
sessions outlining the basis of the alleged
discrimination. Interviewed alleged discrimination official and
attempted to resolve issues. Provided
guidance to supervisors and management regarding their role in
providing equal employment
opportunities.
<p>
09/74 - 01/77<p>
Auditor<p>
Some Government Service, Some City, Somestate, California<p> Pre-
audit analysis of reports to determine issues. Audited individual
and business reports to
determine compliance with the U.S. Government Codes. Reviewed
appropriate ledgers and
other pertinent documents provided by citizens including bank
statements, checkbooks, ledgers,
receipts, etc. Conducted follow-up record searches at financial
institutions to verify sources.<p> 10/75 - 01/77<p>
Career Counselor and High School Program Coordinator<p>

Some Government Service<p>
Counseled employees on career opportunities and methods of growth
leading towards higher career
ladder positions with the federal government. Lectured at
surrounding High Schools to eleventh and
twelfth graders regarding career opportunities within the
Government Service and educational requirements.
</b><hr>
<center><b>COMPUTERS</center>
<p>
<b>While I have not worked as a computer professional, but I have
used computers
for a variety of reasons
<ul><li>databases for membership and mailing labels
<li>spreadsheets for statistical and audit analysis.
<li>word processing for meeting notices, convention minutes,
quarterly board meeting
minutes, etc.
</ul><p>
I am learning to make web pages for the internet and have created
this page as well as:
<ul><li><a href=xxxxxxxxx.html">Personal Xxxxxxxxxx</a>
<li><a href="xxxxxxxx.html">Information regarding Some Group in
Somestate and Someotherstate</a>
<li><a href="xxxxxxxxxx.html">Some Group</a>
<li><a href="xxxxx.html">Some Source</a>
</ul><p>
I Started with a 8088 PC, 128K RAM, 5-1/4 DD using MS-DOS, upgraded
to 640K RAM,
a second 5-1/4 DD, 20MB HD and 2400 data modem.<p>
Currently using a DX2-66Mhz, 16MB RAM, 3-1/2 HD, 5-1/4HD, 2X CD-
ROM,
Tape Backup, 420MB HD, 14.4 Data/Fax Modem operating under
Windows95.<p>
Knowledge of AmiPro, WordPerfect, WordStar, Q & A, MultiMate,
Lotus, MSWorks
95, MS Office Pro
95, MS Money, MS Publisher, PageMaker, PROCOMM PLUS, Xtree ,
Netscape Navigator, Netcom NetCruiser and HTML Writer</b><p><hr>
<center>ORGANIZATIONS</center>
<p>
<UL><LI><b>09/77 - 06/80 ... Blacks in Business and Economics, Some
College
Held a position and was responsible for obtaining guest speakers to
speak on the reality of
the job market upon completion of college.<p>
<Ul><LI>02/80 - Present ... Some Fraternity Incorporated</ul><p>
Founder of Some undergraduate chapter at Some College and
reactivator of some
undergraduate chapter at the College as Some City,
Somestate and Past Officer
and Past Different Officer of Some Fraternity graduate chapter in
Some City,
Somestate. Prepared annual

```
budget and created community-based programs geared to youth and
senior
citizens.<p>
<Ul>
<li>06/80 - Present ... Some Division, Some Organization
<li>01/84 - Present ... Some Division, Somestate and Someotherstate
Jurisdiction
<li>01/84 - Present ... Some Group (Group Officers)
<li>04/84 - Present ... Some Division, Some Group
<li>11/84 - Present ... Some Site, Some Group
</ul><p>Some Position, Past Position, and Past Leader of a Group;
Some Position, Some Site
Some Group, Some Position, Some Past Position, Another Past
Position
Position and Past Position of a Division of a Group; Position of a
Group; Committee Chairman
and Past Officer of a Group; Position and Past Position of a Group
and
Honorary Position of a Group.  Responsible for keeping membership
up-to-date on current
events.  Established and promoted several community programs with a
special emphasis on youth and
senior citizens.  Member of the audit and budget committees of
several organizations.  Responsible for the accounting of income
and expenses while on the Group staff.</b>
<hr><center><font size=+2><A HREF="homepage.html">
RETURN TO HOMEPAGE</a></center><hr></pre></body><html>

——————————————————————————————————JobCenter Makes Recruiting Easier
Recognized by the Internet Business Network (October '95) as one of
the top 25 employment related sites on the internet (over 500
evaluated).  Voted "Best in Class" of those sites offering matching
services.  Rated by Point Communications as a "Top 5%" web site
(December '95).

JobCenter offers:

  * Free corporate profile web page
  * Free searching of our resume database
  * Free unlimited online job ad updating
  * Free customized USENET newsfeed distribution
  * Daily e-mail notification of resume matches
  * The ability for you to offer JobCenter services at your site


            5-17-1996    America Online:Jobnet    Page 4
```

Sample Resume 11 -

```
  Subject:      Resume: Highly skilled C Programmer
From:   XXXX00X@prodigy.com (Henry G. Trevell (via JobCenter))
Date:   17 May 1996 15:16:58 GMT
Message-ID:    <0xx00x$0xO@xxxx.xxx.xxxxxx.net>

Name:          Henry G. Trevell
Company:       (none specified)
E-mail:        XXXX00X@prodigy.com
Phone:         000-000-0000
Location:      Somestate


Henry G. Trevell
000 Some Avenue    (000) 000-0000
Some City, Somestate 00000-0000

Experience:

Some Company, Inc.         Some City, Somestate
Systems Engineer           Apr 1988 to May 1995
Design and development of numerous applications utilizing handheld
computers in both batch and client/server environments.
Design and development of communications software utilizing
standard and custom protocols including TCP/IP.
Develop specifications in cooperation with customers for both
handheld and host applications.
Install, debug, and maintain custom applications including problem
support and troubleshooting through pilot/beta testing.

Another Company, Inc.      Some City, Somestate
Owner/Consultant           Feb 1979 to Apr 1988
Design and development of software for hospitals and physicians
including medical billing, medical staff management, audiology, and
pathology.
Design and development of COBOL runtime package for proprietary
operating system.  Maintenance and enhancement of COBOL compiler.
Design and development of operator console subsystem for
proprietary operating system. (XXXXXXXX, Inc.)
Design and development of medical history analysis system including
the design and development of text formatting package with
sophisticated data base capabilities. (XXXX, Inc.)
Design and development of various handheld computer applications
for field service and retail marketplaces. (XXXXXXX, Inc.)

Some Corporation           Some City, Somestate
Supervising Programmer     Jan 1979 to Aug 1982
Project leader on project to develop native code COBOL compiler for
next generation processor.
Member of Some Group to develop overall software strategy for
minicomputer product line.

          5-17-1996    America Online:Jobnet    Page 1
```

Member of a Group to design a common, device independent I/O
programming interface.
Matrix supervisor for all commercial software development for next
generation processor.
Project leader for FORTRAN 77 compiler project.
Project leader for COBOL compiler project.

Some Company, Inc.   Some City, Somestate
Senior Systems Programmer   Nov 1977 to Jan 1979
Design, development, and maintenance of online audit processor for
an electronics fund transfer network used by A Bank.

Another Company, Inc.   Some City, Somestate
Owner/Consultant   Nov 1974 to Jan 1979
Develop check printing system utilizing two printers serially.
Develop air quality monitoring system for an urban area.
Develop smoke stack monitoring system for a Company in Somestate.

Some Hospital   Some City, Somestate
Senior Systems Programmer   Jun 1972 to Nov 1977
Design and develop multicomputer operating system using
minicomputers to support an online medical record system.
Develop a customized BASIC language for applications development in
multicomputer operating system.
Design and develop multistation cardiac stress monitoring system
utilizing A/D and D/A devices.
Design and develop patient accounts receivables package for
multicomputer environment.

Education:
Some College, Some City, Somestate
B.A., Biology, June, 1972

Technical Skills:
Programming Language Experience:

C, C++, FORTRAN, COBOL, BASIC (various), MASM, miscellaneous
assemblers and proprietary languages.

Operating Systems Experience:

DOS, Windows, UNIX, XENIX, VAX/VMS, OS/2, Data General RTOS & RDOS,
Alpha Micro AMOS, Sperry Univac VORTEX, and miscellaneous custom
operating systems.

Professional Affiliations:
Member of XXXXXXXXX.

JobCenter Makes Recruiting Easier

Recognized by the Internet Business Network (October '95) as one of
the top 25 employment related sites on the internet (over 500
evaluated). Voted "Best in Class" of those sites offering matching
services. Rated by Point Communications as a "Top 5%" web site
(December '95).

JobCenter offers:

    * Free corporate profile web page
    * Free searching of our resume database
    * Free unlimited online job ad updating
    * Free customized USENET newsfeed distribution
    * Daily e-mail notification of resume matches
    * The ability for you to offer JobCenter services at your site

        5-17-1996   America Online:Jobnet   Page 3

— —

Sample Resume 12 -

```
    Subject:      Resume: Motivated, Experienced Contract Negotiator
From:   kgruenfeld@xxxxx.net (Klara A. Gruenfeld (via JobCenter))
Date:   17 May 1996 15:20:03 GMT
Message-ID:      <0xx0x0$0x0@xxxxx.xxx.xxxxxx.net>

Name:         Klara Anna Gruenfeld
Company:      (none specified)
E-mail:       kgruenfeld@xxxxx.net
Phone:        (000) 000-0000
Location:     U.S.A. or Germany
```

PROFESSIONAL EXPERIENCE

A Company. Some City, Somestate. March 1994 to May 1996.
Government Contract Compliance Analyst. The position required
extensive working knowledge
of the Federal Acquisition Regulation, Cost Accounting Standards,
Social Security Act,
Medicare statutes and regulations, as well as the Department of
Health and Human Services
Acquisition Regulation Supplement. Additionally, the position
required the highest degree
of professionalism, organization, and efficiency since all projects
and work product are
delivered to members of Senior Management.

. Coauthored Legal and Contractual Requirements for Subcontracting
Under Federal
Contracts - an authoritative discussion of a Federal Contractor's
responsibilities when
purchasing goods or services to be used in the performance of a
Federal Contract
. Advised and led cost-proposal team in the successful bid for a
particular Program,
$1.7 Billion contract
Codesigned a State compliance program
. Codesigned a State purchasing system
and
policies and procedures
. Performed detailed Internal and Management Controls for all
financial and support
areas to ensure compliance with the Federal Manager's Financial
Integrity Act
. Authored supplement to a State manual that
detailed the appropriate means by which costs should be charged to
Federal Contracts

. Performed training sessions for buyers and Purchasing Management regarding compliant
and special purchasing
. Researched, authored, and presented detailed analysis of Contract Novations to the
Chief Operating Officer
. Prepared and submitted financial reports to the Federal Government

Military Command. Some City, Somestate. June 1991 to February 1994. Contract Specialist. Responsible for all aspects of procurements for a particular missile. Duties included: "cradle -to-grave" acquisition planning, preparing and documenting solicitations and source selection procedures, conducting discussions with offerors, awarding contracts, post-award contract administration, negotiating sole-source and follow on contracts, and performing
detailed cost analysis of contractor's proposals. Position required outstanding
analytical skills, negotiation techniques, organizational skills.

. Designed, developed and implemented a missile repair contract that resulted in
a 50 percent per unit cost savings to the Government. Was cited as an exemplary worker in 19XX
. Administered contracts totaling $0.0 Billion
. Performed complex negotiations and competitive procurements to $000 Million

Some Military Command. Some City, Somestate. June 1989 to May 1991. Contract Specialist. Senior Contract Specialist for a particular Program. Responsible for day-to-day contract administration and providing business advice to the Program Manager.

. Renegotiated the schedule, price, and Statement of Work on a $0.0 Billion contract
. Competitively awarded $000 Million contract for Trainers
. Negotiated and performed detailed cost analysis on numerous Engineering
Change Proposals
. Established a correspondence tracking system

EDUCATION

Some University. Some City, Somestate. April 1989. Bachelor of Arts in Economics and German. Cumulative Grade Point Average: 3.X.

CERTIFICATIONS AND RELATED COURSE WORK

. Military Career Contracting Internship Program. Graduated June
19XX
. Defense Acquisition Workforce Improvement Act Certification,
Procurement Level II.
October 19XX

1994 to Present

. Some College: Techniques for Effective Compliance Programs
. Federal Resources. Seminars: Federal Health Care Contracting
. A Corporation. Seminars: Compliance for Health Care Contractors
. A Firm: Hi-tech Negotiations

Federal Government Training Classes - 1989 to 1994

. Management of Acquisition Contracts - Basic
. Cost and Price Analysis
. Negotiation Workshop
. Quantitative Techniques for Cost and Price Analysis (QMT)
. Management of Acquisition Contracts - Advanced
. Government Contract Law
. Contracting and Subcontracting with Small and
Small Disadvantaged Businesses
. Fundamentals of Incentive Contracting
. Prevention of Sexual Harassment
. XXX Workshop
. Total Quality Leadership

REFERENCES

Available upon request

JobCenter Makes Recruiting Easier

Recognized by the Internet Business Network (October '95) as one of
the top 25 employment related sites on the internet (over 500
evaluated). Voted "Best in Class" of those sites offering matching
services. Rated by Point Communications as a "Top 5%" web site
(December '95).

JobCenter offers:

  * Free corporate profile web page
  * Free searching of our resume database
  * Free unlimited online job ad updating
  * Free customized USENET newsfeed distribution
  * Daily e-mail notification of resume matches
  * The ability for you to offer JobCenter services at your site

             5-17-1996   America Online:Jobnet   page 3

The Multimedia Resume

You can take advantage of the what the World Wide Web makes possible, by building photos, sound, video, and links to other Web sites into your resume. HTML resumes, as they are called (after **H**ypertext **M**arkup **L**anguage), present some unique methods for designing your resume. Some of these new techniques, though fun and interesting, may not really serve you in the job search process. Some, in fact, fly in the face of conventional advice. Before we discuss the preparation of HTML resumes, let's take a look at some of the pitfalls.

For many years, job seekers have been warned not to include a photo of themselves on a resume. The one exception to this rule has been for people in the arts, such as actors and singers. The reason for omitting personal photographs is that you don't want to include anything that may prejudice the employer *in any way*. Visual cues are powerful. Decisions may be made, rightly or wrongly, about you based on your facial expression, your mode of dress, even your hairstyle in the picture. In conventional recruiting, before the advent of the Internet, it had never been considered a good idea to take the gamble of putting a photograph on a resume.

Then, along comes the World Wide Web, and job seekers feel duty-bound to take advantage of all the capabilities. The very first thing they think of is to include a photo, sometimes not only of themselves, but of the spouse, the kids, and even the family pet!

Photos of yourself and others are just not appropriate on a resume. Even in the electronic labor market of today, they can be risky. If the photograph is unprofessional or, as so many are, of poor quality, it can actually harm your chances. Some computer-generated images are so muddy that you can end up looking as if you suffer from chronic insomnia or just got released from the penitentiary. Furthermore, you would hardly drag the kids and family dog along to a job interview (one would hope!) This online resume is the very first look the employer has of you and your capabilities. Putting pictures of loved ones or animals on it is akin to bringing your crowd right into the employer's place of business.

Hüls America's Bussey puts it very bluntly: "Putting your picture on a resume is stupid. It will tend to disqualify you because it sends the wrong message. I'm not looking for a 'pretty face,' I'm looking for a skill. What you look like is not a skill."

Using links to other sites also might not be in your best interest. While you can add links to the university you attended and to your former employers, remember that links take the reader away from your resume. The employer may get sidetracked and never return! Or you may have included links that the employer may find offensive or not in line with the interests of the company. For example, if you are sending a resume to UPS (United Parcel Service) and you plug in a link to the home page of your former employer, who happens to be Federal Express, it might not sit well with the UPS representative reading your resume.

Here are some ideas for links:

E-Mail Address: This is a fast, no-hassle way for the employer to get to you directly. This is the one link we highly recommend.

Publications: If you've been mentioned favorably in a Web site, consider a link to that. If you have been published, consider a link to a review of that work. The same would apply to designs, compositions, and art work.

Notable People and Organizations: If you have worked for or with someone who is a known public figure, link to an informational site about that person. Consider carefully, though, an employer's reactions to political and religiously affiliated people.

Colleges and Universities: Boola-boola and all that network stuff, but remember some college and university sites may also have other graduates' resumes.

Scholastic Societies: Phi Beta Kappa, Phi Kappa Phi, etc.

Awards: If you mention an award you have received, an employer might be interested in learning more about it.

Your Home Page: If you are one of the millions of people worldwide who now have a home page, you may want to link to it. *Caution:* Think carefully first about what appears on that page. Most home pages are much more informal than what would be appropriate to show an employer.

Remember to keep links to a minimum. We wouldn't recommend more than *1 or 2 at the most.* Keep that employer interested in your resume: it should be the destination, not a link to take the employer away from you.

One final note. If you are seeking work in another country and you speak the language, prepare a separate resume in that language and then put a link to it within the English-language resume. We noted several resumes in other languages. There was one in German that looked appealing but, though Fred has some facility with the language, we couldn't translate fully. It would have been helpful to have found a link in English to a version in English. Remember that the Web is international. Write for that audience.

When you create an HTML resume, you will have several choices. Besides headings and fonts and graphics choices, you are also given a choice of background. Be careful in choosing one. A background that is too busy or dark may obscure parts of your text. We had to squint to read a link on one resume we saw. The background was a variegated purple and black, and the link—her e-mail address, a vital piece of information!—was nearly impossible to see.

If you choose to use a graphic on your resume, make sure it is appropriate. Avoid cartoons or outlandish artwork. Keep it as simple as possible. One reason for this is that you don't want to "lock" an employer on your page, waiting and waiting for your page to finish loading. They won't. They'll hit the "stop" icon and move on to the next one. Another reason to keep graphics simple and tasteful is that you want everything about your resume to reflect on you as a professional. Remember, too, that not all artwork is in the public domain. You don't want to put a cartoon on your resume that is protected by copyright. Software packages for building Web pages usually include clip art that is available for public use.

You don't have to be a computer genius to build an HTML resume. There is help available to you. For example, Microsoft's *Internet Assistant for Microsoft Word* allows you to create your own home page on the World Wide Web. You can even download the tools you need to do this from Microsoft's Web site. You save your document in HTML format, and it's ready to be posted on the Web.

There are several sites right on the Web where you can learn about making an HTML document. Try *The Idiot's Guide to Creating a Home Page* by Bruce Simpson. It's a simple step-by-step online tutorial. You can access it at

> `http://www.voyager.co.nz/~bsimpson/html.htm`

There are also some publications available that are very helpful. You may want to look at these:

> *Teach Yourself Web Publishing with HTML in a Week* (Sams) Laura Lemay
>
> *10 Minute Guide to HTML* (Que) Tim Evans
>
> *Creating Cool Web Pages with HTML* (IDG Books) Dave Taylor
>
> *HTML - The Definitive Guide* (O'Reilly and Associates) Chuck Musciano and Bill Kennedy

For a comprehensive list, go to

> `http://wwwiz.com/books/html.html`

or

> `http://www.webreference.com/books/html.html`

Let's check out some sample HTML resumes from the World Wide Web:

Sample Resume 13 -

<u>Marya M. Mason</u>
000 Some Street
P.O. Box 000
Some City, Somestate 00000
Tel.: (000) 000-0000

Career Objective To become a very experienced nurse.

Education

1987-1991

A Particular High School
Some City, Somestate

Graduated in 1991 after honors program. Member of the National Honor Society 1990-1991. Grade point average: 3.20 of possible 4.00. High school expenses paid for by part-time job and parental help.

1991-Present

A Particular University
Some City, Somestate

Bachelors Degree in Nursing, June 1996 Grade point average: 2.56 of possible 4.00. All college expenses paid for by part-time job and parental help. During my stay at Some University, I have completed four clinical rotations(OLF, Medical Surgical Nursing, Pediatrics/Obstetrics, and Psychiatric and Community). I am currently in senior Medical Surgical Nursing clinical. We, as nursing students, get a wide variety of education, such as IV administration, oral administration, dressing changes, and teaching the client with a variety of health problems. Examples are cancer, AIDS, stroke, cardiac and respiratory disease. These rotations give us a basis on which to start our nursing career.

Employment

1990-1991

A Grocery Store of Some City, Somestate

Beginning as a bagger and then advancing to cashier. My responsibilities were cash handling and employee supervision.

Summer 1994

A Business of Some City, Somestate

Beginning as a cashier and then advancing to the service desk where my responsibilities were cash handling, returns, cash refunds, and employee supervision.

1995-Present

A Care Facility of Some City, Somestate

Assuming responsibilities as a certified nurses aid where my duties included patient care and completion of patient's daily health activities.

1995-Present

Science & Engineering Center of Some City, Somestate

Assuming responsibilities as a tutor for nursing and general biology classes.

Personal

Awards/Special Skills

CPR certified from 1992-present. CPI certified as of November 1, 1995. National Honor Society 19901991. Assistant editor of the yearbook. Senior board member for A Club. Achieved high academic grade point average (Fall, 95) and was placed on Dean's list.

Activities

Intramural volleyball team. Environmental Club 1990-1991. Raising money for Service Club through the local chapter. In College, student board member on the academic advisory committee January 1995 to present. Member of the Student Nurses Association. AIDS peer counselor. Tutor for nursing classes as well as general biology classes.

Interests

Reading, animals, the beach, and volleyball.

Send any comments or questions to:
X0000XXX(@Xxxxxx).xxxx

— — — — — — — — — — — — — — — — — — — —

Sample Resume 14 -

James Peterson — Composer, Musician, Audio Engineer

James Peterson
714 Prospect Blvd.
Pasadena, CA 91103 USA
818-792-1005

Education	Bachelor of Arts in Music University of California at Los Angeles
Special Skills	- Computer literate: - Macintosh, Windows 95 and Atari - Microsoft Word, PowerPoint, Excel, Cubase and others - Professional composer and musician - Substitute Teaching Credential - Extensive knowledge of audio equipment, mixing, consoles, synthesizers - Highly motivated - Customer-oriented

Experience

Film and Television Composer   1990 - present
Freelance
Clients have included:

AT&T: Composed musical underscore for over 35 foreign market AT&T television commercial campaigns including True World Savings, True Voice, Business Advantage, Special Country Plan, and World on Sale. Worked closely with CPG Production Company, AMKO Advertising creative directors, and AT&T's commercial division to determine the creative direction and musical style of each campaign.

California Lottery: Composed musical underscore for Keno and Scratchers campaigns. Developed theme music for the California Lottery's "Bouncing Ball" commercial.

Bank of America: Developed an arrangement of the "Banking on America" theme for the foreign market. Worked with translators to develop versions of the theme in Mandarin, Cantonese, Korean and Vietnamese. Composed and arranged music for radio and television commercials using traditional Chinese instruments and authentic playing techniques. Collaborated with members of the Peking Opera while composing and recording this music.

NBC: Composed "Feature Story" and "Special Interest" themes. Composed music for a news special on Bay Area hospitals and trauma centers called "When Seconds Count."

ABC: Composed music for "American Dance Honors," an ABC special program honoring dance and dancers from American Ballet Theater to Paula Abdul.

Customer Service Representative   1992 - 1993
Dave's Video and Laser Disc
Supervised rental department. Organized library of over 10, 000 video titles. Worked with production companies and pulled titles for broadcast and compilation.

Substitute Teacher   1990 - 1992
Los Angeles Unified School District
Taught junior high and high school English, Social Science, and Music.

_ _

Sample Resume 15 -

ARTHUR B. MERIWETHER

To receive contact information, request it from: xxxxxx#x#xxx@xxx.xx.xxx.com

PROFILE:

1. Accountant with years of experience in accounts payable, general accounting, and program accounting,

2. Extensive financial background including account reconciliations, variance reporting, and preparation of monthly financial reports.

3. Self-motivated, organized, and team-oriented.

EXPERIENCE:

Some Company, Some City, Somestate 1974-1995
Specialist - Accounts Payable

❑ Maintained monthly cycle file to help resolve price and quantity variances, thus expediting vendor payments.

❑ Resolved receiving issues on invoice quantities versus ordered quantities to expedite vendor payments.

❑ Worked with buyers to amend purchase orders when additional materials were received and the material requester chose to keep the overshipment.

❑ Established and implemented new vendor codes by verifying with Dunn & Bradstreet vendor's validity.

❑ Interfaced with vendors daily to resolve payment problems.

Accounts Payable Clerk

❑ Prepared blanket order invoices for payment by verifying that P.O. # was correct, invoiced quantities were received, price was correctly billed, and enough funds were left on the purchase order to allow payment.

❑ Worked closely with the Purchasing Department to amend the P.O.'s when the dollar limits were exceeded, when quantities were increased or decreased, and when prices were incorrect, thus expediting prompt payment to vendors.

❑ Interfaced with Managers responsible for purchase orders to issue needed amendments to the P.O.'s in a timely manner to allow payment to vendors without interruption.

EDUCATION:

A Company's Financial Management Program graduate
A.A.S. Accounting, Some University, Some City, Somestate

Additional Courses:

Advanced Lotus
Microsoft Excel for Windows
OfficeWriter I and 11
Advanced Contract Law
Principles of Government Contracting
Contract Management Strategies

To receive contact information, request it from: `xxxxxx#x#xxx@xxx.xx.xxx.com`

— —

Sample Resume 16 -
Willi Grünwald
- Freier Journalist -

Baumstrasse 00 / 00000 Köln / Tcl. (0000) 000000 / Fax (0000) 000000

Werdegang

Wie die Meisten habe ich schon zu Schulzeiten mir meine Noten damit versaut, dass ich
lieber eine Schülerzeitung aufgebaut habe, als nur den Unterrichtsstoff zu pauken.
Als ich 990 anfing, MA Anglistik (dementsprechend bin ich fliessend in Englisch
spoken and written)- einigermassen beherrsche ich Niederländisch - maar ik ben og op de weg!),
Soziologie und Politologie zu studieren, übernahm ich die Leitung der hiesigen
Uni-Zeitung, Zeitgleich fing ich an, für einen örtlichen adiosender zu arbeiten.
Seit 1992 ernährt mich der Hörfunk in der ARD, vor llem der Westdeutsche Rundfunk
und der NDR. Dort arbeite ich hauptsächlich ktuell. 1995 führte mich mein
Weg für einen Monat zum NDR nach Schwerin. Neues Programmumfeld,
neue Menschen und neue Mentalitäten sind schliesslich keine Bedrohung,
sondern eine Herausforderung. Mein Haupttätigkeitsgebiet ind zur
Zeit aktuelle Magazinprogramme. Fitbin ich (ob meines Alters - 25 ahre!)
auch in der Formulierung für Jugendprogramme. Dann und wann arbeite ch auch
für Print (Ruhrgebietsmagazine und "Autozeitung").

Motto:

(Auch wenn's naseweis klingt - meiner Ansicht nach wird's viel zu selten beachtet:)

"Jeder Beitrag oder Artikel muss dem Hörer oder Leser die Frage beantworten: Was hat das mit mir
zu tun? Im Zweifelsfall ist ein "Thema" eben KEIN Thema!"

"Spezialgebiete":

❏ Wirtschaft und Kommunalpolitik Ruhrgebiet

❑ Bildung und Universitäten

❑ Jugend und Gesellschaft

❑ Buntes (immer mal wieder gern genommen!)

❑ und (natürlich - sonst hätte ich hier keine Homepage) EDV / Computer / Online

Wenn Sie Interesse an einer Zusammenarheit haben, dann rufen Sie mich bitte an oder faxen Sie. Bei entsprechend grossen Projekten bin ich natürlich bereit, im Vorfeld Textproben oder Demo-Cassetten zu verschicken. In Zukunft werden auch hier "Pröbchen" aufrufbar sein.

... oder klicken Sie HIER, um mir eine E-Mail zu schicken

!!! Auch Volo-Angebote werden immer mal wieder gern genommen (Grins) !!!

Sample Resume 17 -

MICHAEL TIDMUS

RÉSUMÉ AND PORTFOLIO

2117 Avon Street, Los Angeles, California, 90026-1905
Telephone: (213) 665-9456, Facsimile: (213) 665-1739
Electronic Mail: mtidmus@smtp. anomtec. com

❑ Photo Illustration
❑ Typographic Design
❑ Freelance Experience
❑ Technical Expertise
❑ Additional Expertise
❑ Exhibition History
❑ Select Publications
❑ Select Collections
❑ Lectures and Panels
❑ Academic Experience

MICHAEL TIDMUS

PHOTO ILLUSTRATION

My work combining computers and photography began over ten years ago with a 128K Apple Macintosh and a dot-matrix printer, which *doubled* as a *scanner.* When I couldn't find a photo-processing house in Los Angeles willing to make simple, archival-quality, black and white prints from Linotronic film negatives, I gerry-rigged a darkroom and taught myself basic darkroom technique. This piqued my interest in photography as a medium. Six months later I had my first gallery show as *a photographer* alongside such noted photographers as Irving Penn, Horst, Bruce Weber, Herb Ritts and Joel Peter-Witkin.

As available hardware and software have progressed, so has the experimental potential of this medium. The examples included below are from among hundreds of images created simply *by playing* with cameras and computers.

Click on any image above for a closer view and notes on the photographic source material and process.

SUMMARY PAGE   ○

The following sample will give you an idea of how to arrange an electronic resume. This has been prepared for transmission via e-mail. It will also work for the World Wide Web, where you might consider adding a graphic. Remember, though, that scanner-friendly resumes do not include asterisks, graphics, special fonts, or pictures.

```
****************************
          J.B. Seeker
   Public Relations Specialist

****************************
```

SUMMARY: Talented Public Relations Practitioner with more
                 than 15 years of experience and a proven track
                 record in community and media relations. Excellent
                 writing skills. Facility with desktop publishing,
                 including Pagemaker, Quark and Microsoft Publishing.
                 Familiar with MS Word and Windows 95. Motivational
                 speaker. Adept at press relations and creative
                 advertising. MA

                 J. B. Seeker
                 4231 Success Lane
                 Excell, CA 91116
                 (909) 555-4285
                 jseeker@igc.apc.org

OBJECTIVE: Challenging position as PR director for a progres
                 sive company with an eye on the future.

SIGNIFICANT
EXPERIENCE:

1987-Present   PUBLIC RELATIONS MANAGER

                 The Westbrook Group, Palm Springs, CA

                 * Managed staff of PR and Advertising
                   professionals, developing PR program that in-
                   creased visibility and acceptance of
                   company programs.

                 * Directed advertising dept. Wrote and
                   edited copy, designed advertising campaigns.

                 * Interfaced with television, radio,
                   and print media, building strong contacts
                   and positive relations.

                 * Represented company as featured speaker
                   and ambassador at various community and
                   charitable functions.

1983-87   PUBLIC RELATIONS REPRESENTATIVE

                 Eagle Manufacturing, San Francisco, CA

                 * Designed successful PR campaigns
                   for company products and services.

                 * Acted as media liason. Offical spokesperson
                   during labor crisis.

                 * Promoted good will as company
                   representative through community
                   contacts.

                 * Developed in-house training programs.

                 * Designed company brochure and point-
                   of-purchase materials.

EDUCATION: Master of Arts, Public Relations
                 University of San Francisco

                 Bachelor of Arts, Communication Studies
                 University of California, San Diego

PERSONAL
STATEMENT: Creative and innovative. Cutting-edge
                 approach to public relations. Energetic and loyal
                 company advocate with a healthy understanding of
                 the bottom line.

This resume, prepared and formatted in ASCII, took a total of five screens to transmit via e-mail as follows:

Fig. 9.1. First screen of resume, displaying name and complete summary.

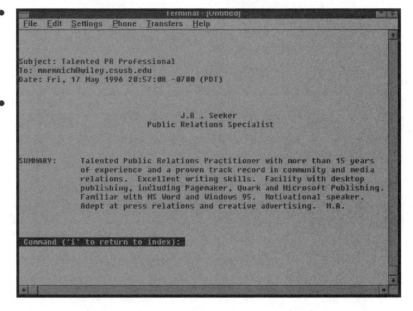

```
Subject: Talented PR Professional
To: mnemnich@wiley.csusb.edu
Date: Fri, 17 May 1996 20:57:08 -0700 (PDT)


                         J.B . Seeker
                    Public Relations Specialist


SUMMARY:      Talented Public Relations Practitioner with more than 15 years
              of experience and a proven track record in community and media
              relations.  Excellent writing skills.  Facility with desktop
              publishing, including Pagemaker, Quark and Microsoft Publishing.
              Familiar with MS Word and Windows 95.  Motivational speaker.
              Adept at press relations and creative advertising.  M.A.



Command ('i' to return to index):
```

```
                    J. B. Seeker
                    4231 Success Lane
                    Excell, CA 91116
                    (909) 555-4285
                    jseeker@igc.apc.org

OBJECTIVE:      Challenging position as PR director for a
                progressive company with an eye on the future.

SIGNIFICANT
EXPERIENCE:

1987-Present    PUBLIC RELATIONS MANAGER
                The Westbrook Group, Palm Springs, CA

                * Managed staff of PR and Advertising
                  professionals, developing PR program
                  that increased visibility and acceptance of

44 lines more (52%). Press <space> for more, 'I' to return.
Alt-Z FOR HELP3 VT100 3 FDX 3 19200 N81 3 LOG CLOSED 3 PRINT OFF 3 ON-LINE
```

```
                    increased visibility and acceptance of
                    company programs

                *  Directed advertising dept. Wrote and edited
                   copy, designed advertising campaigns

                *  Interfaced with television, radio and print
                   media, building strong contacts and positive
                   relations

                *  Represented company as featured speaker and
                   ambassador at various community and
                   charitable functions

1983-87         PUBLIC RELATIONS REPRESENTATIVE

                Eagle Manufacturing, San Francisco, CA

                *  Designed successful PR campaigns for company
                   products and services

24 lines more (73%). Press <space> for more, 'i' to return.
Alt-Z FOR HELP3 VT1003 FDX 3 19200 N81 3 LOG CLOSED 3 PRINT OFF 3 ON-LINE
```

```
                *  Acted as media liaison. Offical spokesperson
                   during labor crisis

                *  Promoted good will as company representative
                   through community contacts

                *  Developed in-house training programs

                *  Designed company brochure and point-of-
                   purchase materials

EDUCATION:      Master of Arts, Public Relations
                University of San Francisco

                Bachelor of Arts, Communication Studies
                University of California, San Diego

PERSONAL
STATEMENT:      Creative and innovative. Cutting-edge

4 lines more (95%). Press <space> for more, 'i' to return.
Alt-Z FOR HELP3 VT100 3 FDX 3 19200 N81 3 LOG CLOSED 3 PRINT OFF 3 ON-LINE
```

```
STATEMENT:      Creative and innovative. Cutting-edge
                approach to public relations. Energetic and
                loyal company advocate with a healthy
                understanding of the bottom line.




Command ('i' to return to index):
Alt-Z FOR HELP3 VT100 3 FDX 3 19200 N81 3 LOG CLOSED 3 PRINT OFF 3 ON-LINE
```

Now, let's look at a complete sample of an electronic resume format:

```
************************
            Name
          Job Title
************************
```

Summary:
* Strong, short opening paragraph, summarizing your best skills/strengths
* Identify your profession
* Highlight 4-5 of your job strengths. Think in terms of keywords, nouns, rather than verbs
* Invite the employer to read on

Name
Address
City, State, Zip,
Phone (H) Phone (msg)

POSITION OBJECTIVE:
State a specific goal. Gives resume direction.

SIGNIFICANT EXPERIENCE:

(Dates go here)
List jobs that support Objective.
Position Title
Name & Location of Company
* Put each job description in "bullet" form to save space.
* Work in reverse order.
* List most important duties.
* Do not use personal pronouns.

EDUCATION:
Name & Location of College/University
Type of Degree and Major
Honors, if appropriate.
Certain, applicable coursework, if required.

Optional Headings:

MILITARY SERVICE
Branch. Dates. Rank/Job.

SPECIALIZED TRAINING
Job-related, not covered in Education.

PUBLICATIONS
Name of publication. Title. Date.

HONORS/AWARDS
Job-related most helpful.

PERSONAL STATEMENT:
* List personal qualities that reflect fitness for employment.

* Make an assertive statement of your job-related strengths.

REFERENCES:
This information is optional; employers assume references will be supplied. Never list reference information on resume.

Name
E-Mail Address

Now that your resume is ready, you need only find where to send it. In the next chapter, we show you how and where to submit your electronic resume.

Submitting Your Electronic Resume

There are many ways to get your resume on the Internet. In this chapter, we'll discuss how you submit your resume and provide locations where it can be posted.

Submitting Your Resume

When submitting your resume to a site, you should consider the manner in which the document will be presented. For example, on a USENET newsgroup, resumes are grouped together but not organized in any usable way. Each resume is given a subject line, and the employer selects the line to open the resume. A resume submitted to an online recruiter will be scanned and made accessible to employers by keywording. An independent posting of your resume on the World Wide Web gives you lots of freedom in creating it but poses some problems in getting it accessed by employers.

Your Own Site on the WWW

The main problem with posting a resume independently—that is, without going through an online service—is how the employer will find you. Bear in mind that thousands of employers access online services every day. They go where they expect to find job seekers in numbers. When you're out there all alone, you need to keep in mind that most employers will just "stumble" over you.

One way they can find you is by using a search engine, such as AltaVista, and typing in a few keywords, such as *photographer resume*. This will yield, in some cases, tens of thousands of "hits"; and if your resume is not in the top 30 or so, it's very unlikely they will find you. Some job seekers post a message on USENET Newsgroups directing the employer to their Web site. Ward Christman of Online Opportunities regards this as a disturbing and decidedly unprofessional "trend" in online job search.

> We sometimes pull resumes off newsgroups, and I've noticed a sort of trend by job seekers to post one or two lines telling employers to check out their URL to see a cool resume. What they don't realize is that employers are not likely to surf around the Web looking for them. The employer will just bypass them and go on to the next posting. The more an employer has to work to do something, the less likely they are to do it.

To post only a URL to a newsgroup that is meant for the posting of resumes is also to misuse the group.

If you want to make your URL known through a newsgroup, add the URL to the end of a traditional resume. If employers are interested in you—and they won't know whether they are until they have read your resume!—they may want to access your Web resume later.

Submitting Your Resume by E-Mail

E-mail is perhaps the most common means of submitting a resume electronically. When employers request a resume via e-mail, they assume you know the basics of ASCII (see Chapter 9) and that you will transmit a resume that is coherent and reasonably professional-looking. Typos and misspellings are deadly in a resume, let alone in e-mail messages to employers in general. Build your resume in your word processor, using proper format and keeping it concise. When it has been spell-checked and constructed properly, save it in an ASCII file. Then, if you have Microsoft Windows, you can simply copy it and paste it into your e-mail program. Otherwise, you may upload it into e-mail by using the upload feature of whatever communications program you use (PROCOMM, for example).

A real bonus in sending resumes by e-mail is the all-important, but frequently overlooked, subject line. Too many applicants throw an opportunity away by writing "Resume," "Resume for registered nurse," or something equally mundane for the subject. When an employer scans hundreds of resumes listed by subject line, the catchy ones get looked at first.

Submitting Your Resume Through a Newsgroup

The resumes we've seen on USENET newsgroups are often very long and full of mistakes. You should apply the same principles of submitting your resume by e-mail to posting it to a newsgroup. After you have properly formatted, proofread, and saved your resume in ASCII, you may upload it through your communications program the same way you did in e-mail. In newsgroups, where there are thousands of other job seekers and nothing is arranged in any particular order, a subject line is also very important. Many of them make little sense. It's as though the job seeker decides to throw down a few words that are related to their particular field. This is just not wise. You want to somehow distinguish yourself from the rest of the throng, and at the same time give the employer a reason to want to access your resume instead of all the others there.

You can do a few things with the subject line to catch an employer's attention. One idea is to put your subject in capital letters or surround it with asterisks. You could also use angle brackets (> <) as arrows pointing to your subject line. Use adjectives. Put spaces and back slash marks between titles or terms. Be bold! Use attention-getting words such as "talented," "innovative," "ambitious," and "creative."

Look at some of these examples:

```
WRITER / MANAGER / ANALYST / V. QUALIFIED / CURIOUS _
TALENTED, GIFTED, AMBITIOUS COMPUTER SCIENTIST
============TOP SALES POSITION WANTED=============
******>>>>CREATIVE FREELANCE PHOTOGRAPHER<<<<******

INNOVATIVE P.R. PROFESSIONAL>>>>PROVEN TRACK RECORD

Compare those with these:

entry-level psych research position

Systems/software

Management

proj. 1dr/rdbms/client-server/imaging
(whatever that means!)
```

A creative subject line grabs the employer's attention and invites the individual to look at your resume. Use it with flair! Become a standout in that endless field of boring one-liners. You'll get noticed. But, be careful–nothing too funny, and never off-color.

Now that you know the general rules submitting your resume, let's explore some places where you may go to post your resume.

Internet Resume Sites

E-Span's Interactive Employment Network accepts resumes. It can be reached at

> http://www.espan.com

Internet Executive Professionals (IEP) located in Palmyra, New York, converts your resume into HTML, creating your own unique Web address for your resume. They're located at

> http://www.webcom.com/resumes

You send them your resume on paper, by e-mail, or on floppy disk. For a $25 charge, they convert your resume into HTML. For an additional $10 charge, you can include a photograph. The company will then post it on the World Wide Web. Your resume will have its own unique URL or Web address.

Here are some well-known, large, resume databases.

Online Career Center

Online Career Center is funded by employers and maintains a resume database. The center is located at http://www.occ.com. Complete access to the resumes on the OCC is limited to its member companies.

On adjoining page are the guidelines for submitting your resume on OCC:

Online Career Center now creates home pages for job seekers. For a fee of about $40, you get up to three pages of text, two graphic images, and two links to other Web sites.

And, by the way, OCC will take your resume on paper!

How To Enter Resumes   http://www.occ.coM/occ/HowToEnterResumes.html

(**FAQ**) (**OCC** Home) (Join OCC) (Jobs) (Resumes) (Recruiters Office) (Career Assistance) (On Campus) (Help)

 ## How To Enter Resumes

Make your resume available to employers worldwide through OCC on Internet. The resume database may be accessed by any Online Career Center subscriber.

There are no charges to applicants who enter their own resume online.

Email your resume to: ocg-resumes@.occ.com
Your resume must be in plain text (ASCII) format.
The email "SUBJECT:" line serves as your resume "TITLE"—and will be the first information seen by employers when viewing your resume.
HTML Resumes Only
Instructions for submitting HTML resumes.
"HyperResumes" will create your RTML resume for a fee.
If you DO NOT have Internet access, you way mail your typed resume (cover letter optional) to:
Online Resume Service - (US and other countries)
CV Online - (European countries)
You may, at no cost, enter your full-text resume into the OCC Internet database.
Your resume will stay in the OCC database for 90 days. To extend your resume beyond 90 days, you may re-enter it at any time.
Each email account number is permitted only one resume at any given time. Therefore, the most recent resume uploaded will be displayed.
To change or update your resume, simply re-enter it, and the previous one will be deleted.
To remove your resume, please send an email message to; occ100@.occ.com

FAQ | Home | Occ | Jobs | Resumes | Recruiter's Office | Career Assistance | On Campus | Help

Online Career Center, occ@.occ.com

Copyright(c) 1995 - **Online Career Center LP – All Rights Reserved**

CareerMosaic

CareerMosaic posts resumes for free. It's located at `http://www.careermosaic.com`. CareerMosaic allows you to create your resume either online or offline. The online resume builder is a form on which you enter your resume information into the boxes provided. If you have an ASCII resume, you have the option of copying and pasting it into the boxes.

You resume stays in the CareerMosaic database for 90 days. In order to keep it current beyond that date, you must repost it. CareerMosaic issues you an ID number that you may use if you want to delete your resume.

No confidentiality or security is offered by CareerMosaic. Your resume is accessible to read by anyone with an Internet account.

Monster Board

Monster Board offers some unique features with its resume database. The Monster Board is located at

> `http://www.monster.com`

Monster Board will post your resume online for free. What's unique is that your name and contact information will not be released until an employer's search matches your qualifications. Also, Monster Board allows you to develop your resume online and update it.

From the Monster Board home page, select Resume On-Line. You will arrive at Monster Board's resume area, which is known as Resume City.

Fig. 10.1. Monster Board's on-line resume builder.

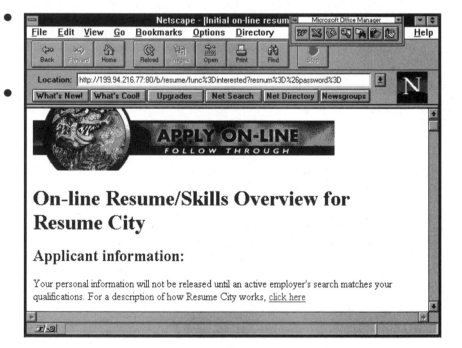

Using a fill-in-the-blanks format, you enter information into a series of areas to build your resume. There is a separate area for writing a brief cover letter to an employer. You can detail both technical and nontechnical skills. Then, there are the traditional resume sections for work history, education, areas of interest, and even an optional salary requirement.

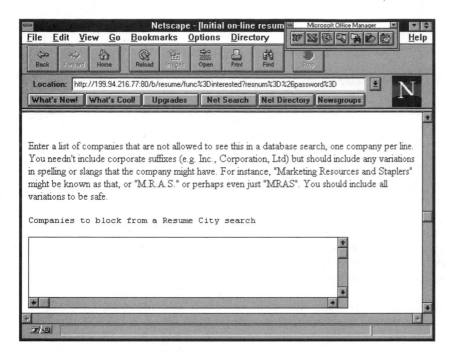

Fig. 10.2. *Area for blocking employers you choose to deny access.*

Of particular interest is the area where you may block certain companies from accessing your resume (see fig. 10.2).

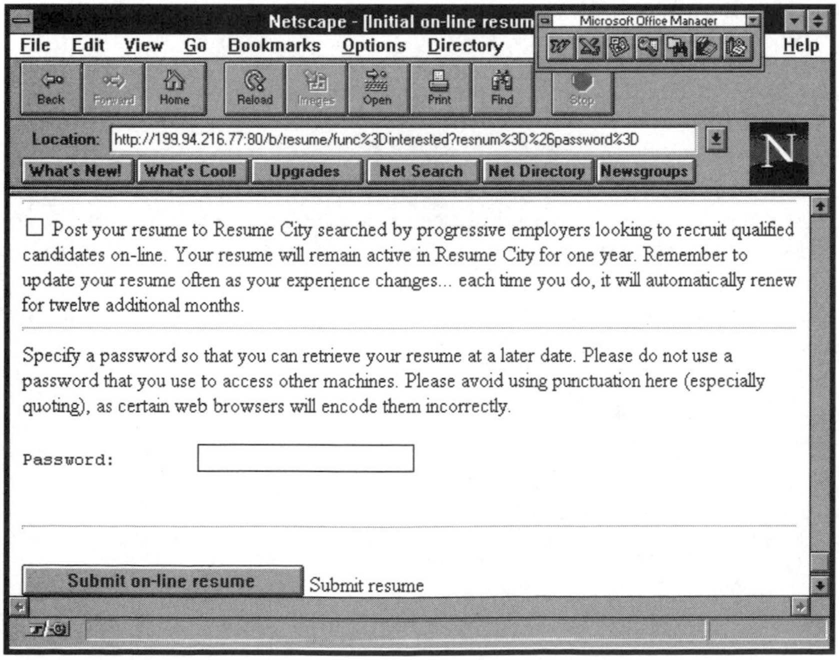

Fig. 10.3. *Submit Resume screen.*

When you have finished making your entries, you click the **Submit on-line resume** button.

Monster Board will also allow you to update your resume as needed. In fact, such updating is recommended!

IntelliMatch

IntelliMatch Online Job Center also has some unique features. This site is located at

> `http://www.intellimatch.com/`

IntelliMatch utilizes a system in which employers and job seekers are matched by a database of "structured resumes." The free online resume creation tool is known as WATSON (Where Applicants Turn Skills into Opportunities Nationwide). Employers use a search engine known as HOLMES (Hiring Through On-Line Matching of Employment Specifications)to do a "structured job query" of applicants. HOLMES software searches the WATSON database and presents the top-ranked candidates to the employer.

The WATSON Structured Resume Builder leads the job seeker through a series of questions that yields a detailed applicant profile. This allows a more precise match between employer and candidate. WATSON also permits you to rate your skills and abilities, from "familiar" to "expert." In addition, you may specify preferences for location, employment type (full-time, salaried, contract) and job function.

IntelliMatch allows you to control who may access your resume. You may block a certain employer, such as your current one, or you can specify that your contact information be withheld from all employers until you give your consent to release it.

The WATSON Structured Resume builder is very easy to use. You simply follow a series of prompts for information, filling in the blanks with requested information. "The text goes into the IntelliMatch database as you type it," said Doug Kryzan, Director of Marketing for IntelliMatch. "As soon as you start typing, a profile is created for you. Once you have entered a resume, you can come back and update it as often as you like."

Here's a look at WATSON from IntelliMatch:

From IntelliMatch's Welcome page, select WATSON.

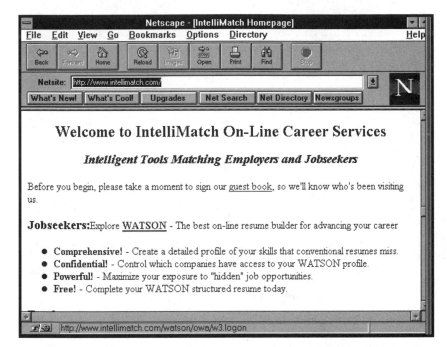

● ● ● ● ● ● ● ● ●
***Fig. 10.4.** IntelliMatch Welcome page.*
● ● ● ● ● ● ● ● ●

To log on to WATSON resume builder, you must enter a name and password (see fig. 10.5). You are asked to enter the password twice.

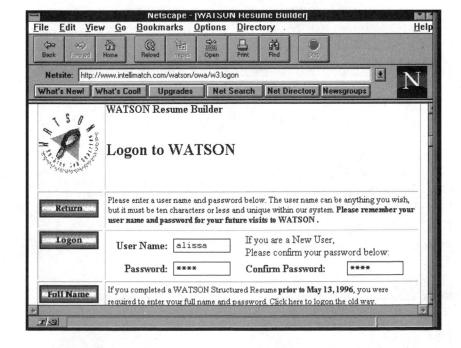

● ● ● ● ● ● ● ● ●
***Fig. 10.5.** WATSON Logon screen with Userid and Password.*
● ● ● ● ● ● ● ● ●

You will see a menu of resume headings/areas (see fig. 10.6):

● ● ● ● ● ● ● ● ● ●

***Fig. 10.6.** WATSON resume data options.*

● ● ● ● ● ● ● ● ● ●

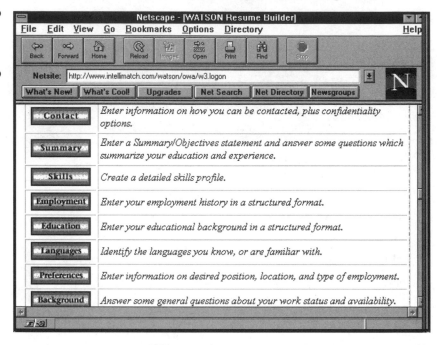

You will enter your data in detail in each area. This is the Employment Detail section:

● ● ● ● ● ● ● ● ● ●

***Fig. 10.7.** Employment Detail section of WATSON.*

● ● ● ● ● ● ● ● ● ●

When complete, your resume will be added to the IntelliMatch database.

Specialized Databases

Some resume databases specialize in one area. Here are some examples:

Engineering and computer science:

One-Stop Job Services features a questionnaire for job seekers with a minimum of one year of experience in engineering and computer science. Resumes are accepted by e-mail, fax, and snail mail. There's no charge to the job seeker. This resume database is viewed by over 200 recruiters who can search the database by keywords. It's located at

```
http://www.telalink.net/~shack/tsearch/
tsearch.html
```

A FAQ is located at

```
http://www.telalink.net/~shack/tsearch/
tsintro.html
```

Television:

Resumes from people in television are posted for a small charge by tvjobs, located at `http://www.tvjobs.com`. There are other locations on the World Wide Web where you can post your resume. You can use a WWW search engine to find others. Search on the word *resumes,* and you'll find others.

Now that you have submitted your resume, it remains only for you to get that job interview. There are some special rules at work in the world of online job search. In the next chapter, we give you some tips on how to conduct yourself as you find your way to a job.

Internet Job–Hunting Netiquette

CHAPTER 11

Most job seekers wouldn't dream of dropping in unannounced on an employer in the middle of a business day and expect an audience. Yet, through the miracle of e-mail, such casual interfaces are now entirely possible. When employers access the "new mail" message and find your resume there, you have effectively "gotten in" to see them. If you were fortunate enough to get a busy employer's undivided attention you would not take liberties with this important person. You would be extremely mindful of your behavior during your interview. However, when electronic job seeking in the unique culture of the Internet, people often make mistakes in etiquette and conduct that they might not otherwise make in person.

Conversation on the net, "chat" if you will, is highly informal. People use nicknames and feel free to speak very candidly to others "out there" in cyberspace. This is due largely to anonymity in computer-mediated communication. The thinking is "They can't see me, they don't know me, and they can't find me." There is something remarkably freeing in knowing that. So, people tend to let down their guard and say and do things they wouldn't ordinarily say or do in face-to-face conversation. Be aware, though, that the same rules of etiquette governing face-to-face job hunting also apply in the electronic labor market. Remember that the employer is evaluating you from the first word on your subject line to the last statement on your resume. You are not there to give those all-important nonverbal cues to the employer. All they have of you is written words on a screen. Those words, in effect, become you. So, you would do well to give some serious thought to how you want them to represent you.

Suppose a total stranger approached you on the street, slapped you on the back, and called you by your name as though he or she had known you intimately for years. Then, this same person proceeded to ask you for a big favor involving money. This person finished by saying he or she would be calling you soon. Language directed to employers that is too informal is a serious breach of job-hunting etiquette. It is akin to slapping an employer on the back when you don't even know him or her. Employers don't like it one bit.

General Rules

In the real world of work, manners are expected. If an applicant is too familiar, the employer will be turned off. Such behavior is presumptuous. Even though you may think that the dynamics of your relationship with an employer are different by virtue of your contact taking place in cyberspace, you must remember that the basic power structure remains the same. Certain behavior is expected of you. Here are some rules of etiquette for electronic job seeking:

- Never address the employer by first name. "Ms. Jones:" or "Dear Mr. Brown:" is appropriate. *Never* "Hi, Joan."

- Always use your full name when signing correspondence. Using only your first name presumes intimacy.

- Watch return addresses. A few of the net resumes we checked out had "clever" names. We found a "Smart Guy" and a "Wise Guy," for example. Consider the effect these nicknames have on employers. They are being provided with a first impression based on these seemingly insignificant "clues." They wonder, "Is this guy maybe too 'smart' for our organization?" It is a risk better not taken. Use your own name.

- Never e-mail a resume "for a friend." We noted several subject notations that said this very thing. This is the same thing as taking a friend along to an interview or calling a company for someone else "just for information"–practices employers loathe. If you must send resumes or correspondence by someone else's access, have that person forward it for you. Your name and identifying information will appear on the resume or letter itself. The employer will figure out that this is where you can be reached.

  Along these same lines, if you accessed your employer through a resume service that the employer paid for, do not share this referral with other job seekers. Employers pay for the privilege of having the service screen for them. You have been approved and are expected. Your friend has not and is not.

- Avoid slang expressions. "I'll get back to you" is rude. "I will contact you again at the end of next week" is more appropriate.

- Forget about using "smileys," or "emoticons," those facial expressions made by using punctuation marks :-). They are used to add expression, emotion, and feeling to written statements. If an employer sends one to you, that's an invitation to be more informal. Otherwise, they are inappropriately casual.

Write in complete sentences. People communicating electronically tend to use a type of verbal shorthand, such as, "Available after next week. Thanks for attention." Take the bit of extra time and keystrokes it takes to respond properly.

Never presume on the employer's time. Always ask if what you propose is convenient. "I would like to arrange an interview at your earliest convenience," not "Give me a buzz so we can talk" or "I'll be expecting your call."

Don't make demands. For example, don't tell employers to respond to you by a certain date. "I haven't even met this person yet, and they're ordering me around," says Kimberly, a human resource interviewer with a national retail chain. "It is better to make polite requests, rather than aggressive demands. Manners really count in e-mail messages." Let employers set the agenda. It's their call.

Never assume employers are waiting breathlessly for you to come along and "save" their company. A little humility goes much further than a lot of bravado.

Don't inundate the employer with a string of messages. Once you have sent your resume, you may follow up at well-paced intervals–about every three to five days. Remember, this person is receiving hundreds of these things. Give the individual a little time to get back to you.

Don't assume that the employer will remember you. In subsequent messages, it will be necessary to reference your prior correspondence, the kind of work you do, and any communication or instructions the employer may have sent you. Julie, a supervisor in a large HMO says, "I get these message fragments and have a hard time trying to figure out what the person is referencing, what we had previously discussed. It really helps if I have a copy of at least part of our prior message. That way, I can put our conversation and the applicant in context." And always identify yourself clearly, with both names, in every message.

Check your e-mail several times a day, every day. If you let your messages sit for several days, you may risk losing a job opportunity or alienating a potential employer. Things move pretty fast in the Internet world. You need to keep pace.

Never keep employers waiting. Answer your e-mail messages promptly. You know how it feels to watch for that "new mail" message. Most people wouldn't dream of ignoring a phone call from an employer; they answer it right away. Yet they tend to let their e-mail in-basket pile up. Or, they read their messages and don't answer them until later. Keep on top of your mail. It's only polite.

- Be polite and observe proper manners. "Thank-you" is a completely legitimate phrase. The time it takes an employer to read an e-mail message and respond is just as valuable as any face-to-face encounter.

- Be friendly, but not too familiar. Adopt a professional, yet cordial writing style. These people are human beings just like you. They are interested in you. Be careful, though, about crossing the line. Don't ask personal questions, and never volunteer personal information about yourself.

- You need to strike the right balance. Be assertive . . . but not aggressive. Enthusiastic . . . but not pushy. Professional . . . but not stiff. Agreeable . . . but not a doormat. Knowledgeable . . . but not a know-it-all. Persistent . . . but not annoying. Above all, be respectful. Don't forget: This person may be your future boss.

Newsgroup Fundamentals

Sometimes you will job search by use of newsgroups. These are conferences devoted to employment-related topics. Some are support groups, where weary job seekers can air their gripes and frustrations about the crummy labor market. But many others are places for actual job and resume postings. Following are some tips for proper behavior on and use of newsgroups.

Follow the Employer's Instructions

READ! Sounds simple, doesn't it? But, when you spot a "perfect job," you may be in such a rush to respond that you miss the all-important message which says, "Please fax or mail resumes." or "No e-mail except messages!!!!!!" (We counted the exclamation points on that one—there were six. Think the employer means business?) If you ignored or missed that message, your resume would not be considered, regardless of your qualifications. The employer reasonably deduces that, if you can't follow simple instructions in the application process, you certainly won't be able to do so on the job. Furthermore, it just plain ticks employers off!

Several announcements said, "Local applicants only," meaning that people outside a specific geographical area would not be considered. The employers probably wanted to avoid relocation expenses. Sometimes the reason is that they want people familiar with the local sales or labor market. One posting said only in-house applicants would be considered. In this case, the company was a large, international firm with a staff of thousands. Their employees all over the world could read this message and respond to it, but no outsiders should. When you respond inappropriately, it inconveniences the employer and disappoints you. Read the instructions carefully and follow them!

Follow Newsgroup Usage Instructions

Established newsgroups, such as those that post jobs, frequently have rules governing their use. Often, they will post frequently asked questions (FAQs) that help new users learn the ropes. Don't be the kid in class who raises a hand to ask a question the teacher answered yesterday. Take the initiative and read the "about the (newsgroup name)" section carefully. Then, play by the rules of the group. If you don't find a FAQ list, post a short note asking for one. People who have been utilizing the newsgroup for a while get tired of seeing the same questions posted again and again.

Networking

Oops! There's that word. All too often overused in the world of work and job hunting, the networking concept was made for the Internet. While perusing a new newsgroup, that computer whiz you were chatting with last night on the conference sees a posting for a software designer which fits exactly with your qualifications. A quick e-mail and you've accessed a position that you may have missed before. Or you respond to a job posting, and the employer tells you thanks, but you're not the right one. By all means, ask for a referral. So often, these people know each other or have heard of other openings within the industry. If they know of something, they'll usually pass it on.

Choose Your Group

Maybe you've been spending all your time in a sort of generic "jobs" group when a different newsgroup exists that serves your particular career or field of interest. Special conferences exist where participants discuss issues pertinent to their specialized discipline or sphere of work. In these exclusive newsgroups, users forward information they have found at other sites on the Internet. Of course this information includes job postings. Here, you will find only those jobs that are relevant and appropriate to your field. We spotted Wayne Greenwood's resume posting for "Human Interface Designer" in the Online Career Center. We sent him a message inquiring about responses to his somewhat unusual resume. He replied: "I did end up finding a job through the Net, but my new employer didn't find me the same way you did. I replied to a posting in the Internet newsgroup comp.human-factors, which is where the snarly interface designer types hang out. . . interviewed with them a couple of times and landed the job."

Surf the net and find your own niche. It's just like moving into a new neighborhood. You have to get out there and make friends—contacts who can help you move forward in your new community. By the same token, if you come across something that isn't suitable for you, pass it on. In the unique culture of the Internet, individual users are, in a sense, part of a "neighborhood," a community linked together by avid interest in this remarkable form of communication. Much like people in a real-world community, net users watch out for one another. They have to do their "community service." If you help your electronic neighbor "raise a barn" today, the same community will rally round to help you raise yours tomorrow.

Postings Are Public

Remember that what you write is likely to be viewed by many, many people. These can be people who know you or the employer you are trying to target. Keep your postings professional and never publish private e-mail messages.

Writing Tips

In the world of face-to-face interviews, the applicant's appearance— grooming and facial expression—is all important in a chance at the job. Some employers rate appearance as high as 75 percent in determining whether the applicant is selected. Appearance is easily controlled through intelligent, pertinent grooming choices. In electronic job search, however, your entire appearance is limited to what is written on the screen. Let's take a careful look at how to write on the Internet.

The problem with the written word is that it is static. Once it's on the page and you hit the Send key, it's there forever. Someone wise once said, "Never put anything in writing!" What lies behind this extreme caveat is the fear that what is written will forever have the potential to come back again and the writer will be held to its content. There is also the fear that, with the written word, no opportunity exists for mediation of the message by the writer. In other words, however the receiver interprets it is how it will be received. We are reminded of the quotation: "I am sure you believe that you understand what you think I said. But I'm not sure you realize that what you heard is not what I meant."

Messages on the net are especially vulnerable to misinterpretation. The receiver can't hear the inflection of voice or discern a chuckle from a sneer. They can't see the raised eyebrow or a roll of the eyes. There is not even handwriting to be analyzed! All that is there are words.

So you must be thoughtful and cautious when constructing your messages. Here are some ideas:

- **Don't e-mail mistakes!** Be sure that you write your messages in complete sentences, using proper grammar, punctuation, and spelling. If writing is not your forte, you might consider com- posing all messages in your word processor first, where you can spell-check them and, in some cases, even style-check them before uploading them into e-mail. Some mail systems on the net already have processing functions like these built in.

- **If you don't know, don't guess**. Just as your messages have the potential to be misunderstood by employers, you also can misunderstand theirs. If something comes to you that you just don't "get," query and ask for clarification. Don't try to bluff your way through a response. Chances are you'll get it wrong and end up looking bad.

■ **Avoid being "funny."** A "clever" remark on your end can arrive as impudence on the other. Better to play it straight, unless and until you have established some kind of relationship with the employer through several messages and have a sense of his or her brand of humor.

■ **Watch line length**. It is a good idea to limit the length of your sentences to approximately 60 spaces rather than going all the way to the side of your screen. The reason is that your message can be somewhat indented when it arrives at the other end. Different systems "read" sentence length differently, so your neatly composed message can reach its destination looking sloppy. Deliberately press enter at the end of each sentence, allowing for a neat right margin and no line extension to the end of your screen.

■ **Don't use Caps Lock**. In the language of electronic communication, capitalized words are read as shouting. The only place caps are permissible is in your subject line. Don't forget, there is no way to add emphasis, such as underlining or italicizing yet. Your written sentence must convey meaning by itself. And remember: NO SMILEYS.

■ **Watch your tone**. Don't whine or gripe. Employers get plenty of messages that read, in part, "Haven't you come to a decision yet? I have been out of work for more than six months, the bills are due, the car's broken down, the dog's sick . . . " Or, "This is my third message. When are you going to get back to me?" This is not the way to win a job.

■ **Write for several readers**. Often the receiver is not the only person who reads your message. The human resources manager may forward it to the department supervisor who then gives it to the line supervisor. These people can be different genders, ages, and ethnicities. At the very least, they are all individual personalities. Each has a different frame of reference on the job. Your message should be generic enough to be read, understood, and appreciated by all of them.

■ **Stick to the point**. You're here to do business. Get to it. Don't meander all over with irrelevant chat. If you want to insert a personal note, fine. Just stay focused on your stated purpose— finding a job.

The issue of netiquette has been written about extensively on the net. Articles are frequently excerpted and posted to various newsgroups, forums, and BBSs. The reason is simple: When many people are sharing the same arena, occasional misunderstandings, conflicts, and mistakes are bound to occur. Chuq Von Rospach has been involved with USENET and the Internet since 1978. He works for Apple on various projects, including Internet tools. We selected an excerpt from an article he wrote, "A Primer on How to Work with the USENET Community," to sum up the importance of netiquette (reprinted by permission).

A Primer on How to Work with the USENET Community

by Chuq Von Rospach

USENET is a large collection of computers that share data with each other. It is the people on these computers that make USENET worth the effort to read and maintain, and for USENET to function properly those people must be able to interact in productive ways. This document is intended as a guide to using the net in ways that will be pleasant and productive for everyone.

This document is not intended to teach you how to use USENET. Instead, it is a guide to using it politely, effectively, and efficiently.

The easiest way to learn how to use USENET is to watch how others use it. Start reading the news and try to figure out what people are doing and why. After a couple of weeks you will start understanding why certain things are done and what things shouldn't be done. There are documents available describing the technical details of how to use the software. These are different depending on which programs you use to access the news. You can get copies of these from your system administrator. If you do not know who that person is, he or she can be contacted on most systems by mailing to account "usenet."

Never Forget That the Person on the Other Side Is Human

Because your interaction with the network is through a computer, it is easy to forget that there are *people* out there. Situations arise in which emotions erupt into a verbal free-for-all that can lead to hurt feelings.

Please remember that people all over the world are reading your words. Do not attack people if you cannot persuade them with your presentation of the facts. Screaming, cursing, and abusing others only serves to make people think less of you and be less willing to help you when you need it.

If you are upset at something or someone, wait until you have had a chance to calm down and think about it. A cup of (decaf!) coffee or a good night's sleep works wonders on your perspective. Hasty words create more problems than they solve. Try not to say anything to others you would not say to them in person in a room full of people.

Don't Blame System Admins for Their Users' Behavior

Sometimes, you may find it necessary to write to a system administrator about something concerning his or her site. Maybe it is a case of the software not working, or an escaped control message, or maybe one of the users at that site has done something you feel requires comment. No matter how steamed you may be, be polite to the sysadmin. He or she may not have any idea what you are going to say, and may not have any part in the incidents involved. By being civil and temperate, you are more likely to obtain his or her courteous attention and assistance.

Be Careful What You Say About Others

Please remember: you read netnews; so do (millions of) other people. This group quite possibly includes your boss, your friend's boss, your girlfriend's brother's best friend, and one of your father's beer buddies. Information posted on the net can come back to haunt you or the person you are talking about. Think twice before you post personal information about yourself or others.

Be Brief

Never say in 10 words what you can say in five. Say it succinctly, and it will have a greater impact. Remember the longer you make your article, the fewer people will bother to read it.

Your Postings Reflect on You—Be Proud of Them

Most people on USENET will know you only by what you say and how well you say it. They may someday be your coworkers or friends. Take some time to make sure each posting is something that will not embarrass you later. Minimize your spelling errors and make sure that the article is easy to read and understand. Writing is an art, and to do it well requires practice. Because much of how people judge you on the net is based on your writing, such time is well spent.

Use Descriptive Titles

The subject line of an article is there to enable a person with a limited amount of time to decide whether or not to read your article. Tell people what the article is about before they read it. A title like "Car for Sale" to rec.autos does not help as much as "66 MG Midget for sale: Beaverton, OR." Don't expect people to read your article to find out what it is about because many of them won't bother. Some sites truncate the length of the subject line to 40 characters, so keep your subjects short and to the point.

Think About Your Audience

When you post an article, think about the people you are trying to reach. Asking UNIX questions on rec.autos will not reach as many people as you want to reach as if you asked them on comp.unix.questions or comp.unix.internals. Try to get the most appropriate audience for your message, not the widest. If your message is of interest to a limited geographic area–apartments, car sales, meetings, concerts, etc.–restrict the distribution of the message to your local area. Some areas have special newsgroups with geographical limitations, and the recent versions of the news software allow you to limit the distribution of material sent to world-wide newsgroups. Check with your system administrator to see what newsgroups are available and how to use them.

Be familiar with the group you are posting to before you post! You shouldn't post to groups you do not read or groups from which you've only read a few articles–you may not be familiar with the ongoing conventions and themes of the group. One normally does not join a conversation by just walking up and talking. Instead, you listen first and join in if you have something pertinent to contribute.

Be Careful with Humor and Sarcasm

Without the voice inflections and body language of face-to-face communication, it is easy for a remark meant to be funny to be misinterpreted. Subtle humor tends to get lost, so take steps to make sure that people realize you are trying to be funny.

Only Post a Message Once

Avoid posting messages to more than one newsgroup unless you are sure it is appropriate. If you do post to multiple newsgroups, do not post to each group separately. Instead, specify all the groups on a single copy of the message. This reduces network overhead and lets people who subscribe to more than one group see the message only once instead of having to wade through each copy.

Summarize What You Are Following Up

When you are following up someone's article, summarize the parts of the article to which you are responding. This allows readers to appreciate your comments without trying to remember what the original article said. It is also possible for your response to get to some sites before the original article. Summarization is best done by including appropriate quotes from the original article. Do not include the entire article because it will irritate the people who have already seen it. Even if you are responding to the entire article, summarize only the major points you are discussing. When summarizing, summarize!

Use Mail, Don't Post a Follow-Up

One of the biggest problems we have on the network is that when someone asks a question, many people send out identical answers. When this happens, dozens of identical answers pour through the net. Mail your answer to the person and suggest that they summarize to the network. This way the net will only see a single copy of the answers, no matter how many people answer the question. If you post a question, remind people to send you the answers by mail and at least offer to summarize them to the network.

Read All Follow-Ups and Don't Repeat What Has Already Been Said

Before you submit a follow-up to a message, read the rest of the messages in the newsgroup to see whether someone has already said what you want to say. If someone has, don't repeat it.

Be Careful About Copyrights and Licenses

Once something is posted on the network, it is probably in the public domain unless you own the appropriate rights (most notably, if you wrote the thing yourself) and you post it with a valid copyright notice; a court would have to decide the specifics, and there are arguments for both sides of the issue. Now that the United States has ratified the Berne convention, the issue is even murkier. For all practical purposes, though, assume that you effectively give up the copyright if you don't put in a notice. Of course, the information becomes public, so you mustn't post trade secrets that way. When posting material to the network, keep in mind that UNIX-related material may be restricted by the license you or your company signed with AT&T and be careful not to violate it. You should also be aware that posting movie reviews, song lyrics, or anything else published under copyright could cause you, your company, or members of the net community to be held liable for damages, so we highly recommend caution when using this material.

Cite Appropriate References
If you are using facts to support a cause, state where they came from. Don't take someone else's ideas and use them as your own. You don't want someone pretending that your ideas are theirs; show them the same respect.

Mark or Rotate Answers and Spoilers
When you post something which might spoil a surprise for other people–such as a movie review that discusses a detail of the plot–mark it with a warning so that others can skip the message. Another alternative would be to use the "rot13" protocol to encrypt the message so it cannot be read accidentally. When you post a message with a spoiler in it, make sure the word *spoiler* is part of the subject line.

Spelling Flames Are Considered Harmful
Every few months a plague descends on USENET called the *spelling flame*. It starts out when someone posts an article correcting the spelling or grammar in another article. The immediate result seems to be for everyone on the net to turn into a sixth-grade English teacher and pick apart each other's postings for a few weeks. This is not productive and tends to cause people who are friends to get angry with each other. It is important to remember that we all make mistakes, and that many users on the net use English as a second language. There are also a number of people who suffer from dyslexia and who have difficulty noticing their spelling mistakes. If you feel that you must make a comment on the quality of a posting, do so by mail, not on the network.

Don't Overdo Signatures
Signatures are the identifying information you put at the end of an e-mail message. They can become quite elaborate, with all of your addresses and even a favorite quotation. Signatures are nice, and many people have a signature added to their postings automatically by placing it in a file called $HOME/.signature. Don't overdo it. Signatures can tell the world something about you, but keep them short. A signature that is longer than the message itself is considered to be in

bad taste. The main purpose of a signature is to help people locate you, not to tell your life story. Every signature should include at least your return address relative to a major, known site on the network and a proper domain-format address. Your system administrator can give this to you. Some news posters attempt to enforce a four line limit on signature files—an amount that should be more than sufficient to provide a return address and attribution.

Limit Line Length and Avoid Control Characters

Try to keep your text in a generic format. Many (if not most) of the people reading USENET do so from 80-column terminals or from workstations with 80-column terminal windows. Try to keep your lines of text to less than 80 characters for optimal readability. If people quote part of your article in a follow-up, short lines will probably show up better too. Also realize that there are many different forms of terminals in use. If you enter special control characters in your message, it may result in your message being unreadable on some terminal types. For instance, a character sequence that causes inverse video on your screen may result in a keyboard lock and graphics mode on someone else's. You should also try to avoid the use of tabs because they can also be interpreted differently on other terminals.

Summary of Things to Remember:

- Never forget that the person on the other side is human.
- Don't blame system administrators for their users' behavior.
- Be careful what you say about others.
- Be brief.
- Be proud of your postings; they reflect on you.
- Use descriptive titles.
- Think about your audience.
- Be careful with humor and sarcasm.
- Post a message only once.
- Rotate material with questionable content.
- Summarize what you are following-up.
- Use mail, don't post a follow-up.
- Read all follow-ups and don't repeat what has already been said.
- Double-check follow-up newsgroups and distributions.
- Be careful about copyrights and licenses.
- Cite appropriate references.
- When summarizing, summarize.
- Mark or rotate answers or spoilers.
- Avoid spelling flames; they are considered harmful.
- Don't overdo signatures.
- Limit line length and avoid control characters.

Just as in any flourishing community, observance of civilities and appropriate behavior keep peaceful coexistence a reality. Practice good manners.

World Wide Web Netiquette

As with every other area of the Internet, whether e-mail or newsgroups, there are certain forms and rules of behavior that users of the World Wide Web observe. These are still emerging, as the Web is still in development. When you access the Web, you will begin to see almost immediately how some types of behavior can range from vaguely annoying to downright rude. These few tips are offered to help make you a good neighbor in the community of the World Wide Web.

Keep Your Page Simple

Most visitors to Web sites have had the exasperating experience of getting "locked" on a page that takes forever to load. If you use large pictures and complicated graphics, you are going to waste other people's time and just beg for them to hit the "stop" icon and get out. Using smaller graphics will speed up the load time and give your visitors the option of clicking on them to enlarge them.

Limit Your Links

Too many links to boring or redundant sites discourage perusal of your own site. Sometimes, you'll visit a page where seemingly every other word is highlighted. This is clearly not necessary. Furthermore, a smorgasbord of unrelated links just confuses people. They figure, "There's far too much to see here," and they get tired and leave. Only include those that truly have some meaning to you or to your visitors.

Respect the "Low-Tech"

Remember that not everyone has a graphical browser. Some folks can still access only text on the World Wide Web. If you use an imagemap—that is, a graphic containing links embedded in the pictures them-selves—for your links, not everyone will be able to use it. Be sure to include text links in your pages.

Include Your E-Mail Address

Let your readers know whom to contact if they have questions about your documents. Your e-mail address should appear at the bottom of every page.

Send Them Home

After you've had visitors, you should show them the way home. It's only polite. Therefore, put a link back to the top of your home page at the bottom of the document. It saves a tiresome scroll-back.

Update Your Page

Do a little maintenance every so often. Make sure that all your links are still "live" and the information you have included is current. Put the date of the latest revision on the page.

The Net: User Guidelines and Netiquette is a publication by Arlene Rinaldi containing excellent advice on appropriate behavior both on the Internet and the World Wide Web. Rinaldi is Senior Computer Programmer/Analyst with Florida Atlantic University. Among other things, she advises people not only to limit the size of their graphics, but to put a file size (such as 2MB or 10KB) in the description when you are putting sound or video files in your document. This way, users will know how long it will take to download your file. URLs themselves can also be problematic. Rinaldi suggests keeping them simple, with few changes in case (upper- and lowercase letters) as some sites are case-sensitive. She further advises users to include their URL within the document itself so that if a visitor wants to print the page, the URL will be handy for future reference.

You can access Arlene Rinaldi's publication on the World Wide Web at
`http://www.sun.ac.za/outside/netiquette`

or

`http://www.upei.ca/~compserv/netiquet/web.htm`.

Be Respectful of Others

Remember that all sorts of people with all sorts of opinions and points of view will be able to access your documents. Obscenity, profanity, bigotry, and other breaches of civility have no place in any community. You risk not only insulting untold numbers of people, but possible prosecution under various laws. Present yourself in a dignified and appropriate manner. You're putting up a "window on the world." Let others look in without shame or embarrassment.

The Internet Interview

CHAPTER 12

A certain amount of self-analysis is essential to interview preparation, whether it's face-to-face or electronic. Besides a firm idea of the kind of work you want to do, you should have an "ideal" profile in mind of the sort of company for which you want to work. Additionally, you should be well-acquainted with the "product" you will be marketing at the interview, namely, you. Here are some questions you should try to answer about yourself prior to the interview:

- What are my short-term goals? Long-term?

- Am I willing to relocate? Commute? Travel?

- How do my hobbies and outside interests make me a better candidate for this job?

- What factors from my previous job(s) can I use as evidence of my fitness for this job?

- What are my own personal traits that apply to the position in question? (For example, preferences for working alone versus with the public, detail work, supervision, physical work versus cerebral work, need for creativity, structure, firm guidelines, etc.)

- What are my intentions toward this job? Do I plan to stay here and forge a career, or use this as a stepping stone in my career path?

■ Is the corporate philosophy of this company in line with my own philosophy? (*Note:* This question relates not only to how you perceive the nature of the working relationship of employer to employee but may also involve ethical considerations. For example, Claudia turned down a lucrative career position with an oil company because it had caused an environmental accident.)

■ What are my chances for advancement?

■ Is there a good match between my skills, knowledge, interests, abilities, and the challenges of this position?

In interviewing, as with other practices in job hunting, Internet communication once again differs markedly from face-to-face communication. In the usual sequence of events, your paper resume is received by mail and, if the employer is interested in you, you are contacted and an interview is scheduled. One or two clarifying questions may be asked over the phone at the time your interview appointment is set, but, for the most part, any in-depth questions are held off until the face-to-face interview itself. Let's compare this standard practice with the Internet process.

With electronic interviewing, the sequence is largely the same; that is, you respond to a job opening, submit a resume, and are interviewed. What differs is the manner in which the process takes place. First of all, you will have found the job opening through a newsgroup or online placement service on the World Wide Web rather than in a newspaper ad or at an employment agency. Second, your resume will be the electronic variety, sent by e-mail to the employer. Finally, you can expect to be interviewed, at least initially, over e-mail. In fact, there will probably be several preliminary interviews by e-mail before you get a face-to-face interview with the employer. Unlike conventional interviewing, there is almost always a preliminary interview with electronic interviewing.

This chapter examines the electronic interview and helps you prepare for dealing with it effectively. You also are given pointers on telephone interviewing, also a part of the electronic interview. Bear in mind, though, that electronic interviews never supersede the face-to-face kind. Not entirely. You still need to be proficient at answering questions and thinking on your feet when you meet the employer in person. Therefore, the last section in this chapter helps you prepare for that all-important face-to-face meeting with the employer, based on the context of each situation. Now, let's take a look at the e-mail interview.

Electronic Interviewing

When an employer receives your e-mail resume over the Internet, it is screened for basic qualifications. Then, if it is found satisfactory, you will be contacted first by e-mail, before you are called in to interview.

Employers do not proceed directly to the interview from the resume because e-mail provides the perfect means for preinterview inquiry. Preinterview screening is almost never done in the world of face-to-face job seeking. The result is that, for many employers, the interview process is long and can involve some disappointing "surprises"–things the employer didn't discover about the applicant until the actual interview.

The Internet preinterview is conducted through a series of e-mail messages between the employer and applicant. Much of the correspondence is for clarification purposes, but a lot of information is gathered about the applicant during these exchanges. For example, suppose you respond to a posting for an administrative assistant position. You e-mail the employer a resume outlining your experiences related to the job. Let's say, however, that the employer is looking for a specific type of desktop publishing experience and you haven't listed it on your resume. It is a fairly simple matter to send you an e-mail asking for clarification. The employer may also decide to ask you for a bit more detail about that last position you held in the university public affairs office. You respond with the requested desktop publishing information and also flesh out your job duties at the university. Additionally, you detail the way in which you used the desktop publishing program to compile the monthly newsletter and student profiles for the student-of-the-quarter awards.

This give-and-take is exactly what happens in the face-to-face interview. The employer starts with the framework of the resume, and then the applicant fills in the details when he or she arrives for the interview. E-mail interviews provide opportunities for you to give more detail than was previously possible *before* the interview, possibly increasing your chances of getting the position. Electronic interviewing can assist both the employer and the job seeker in the recruitment process. For employers, it saves valuable downtime that would be spent in clarification of details before the "meat" of the interview. They also find out whether the applicant is indeed suited for the position in question before going to the expense of bringing the applicant in for a face-to-face interview. For applicants, they know beforehand if the position in question is a good match for their skills and whether they are interested in the company or the job.

Exchanges Can Be Conversational and Friendly

Even though e-mail interviews are written (see the section, "Voice E-Mail," later in this chapter), with delays between questions and answers, they are still very much conversational and often informal. Thus, employers and job seekers frequently find out other enlightening things about one another besides job-related information. For instance, if an applicant inquires about child care centers available in the employer's area, the employer assumes the applicant has a family.

Sometimes an inquiry about area museums or galleries can spark a discussion of mutual interest between the employer and applicant. Or, if the employer suggests that bass fishing in Minnesota is great around the time your interview is scheduled, you'd have to be pretty dense not to figure out that fishing is an enjoyable hobby for the employer.

A common exchange between job seekers and employers pertains to the medium in which they are meeting. E-mail conversations frequently involve discussions about the types of computers and software being used, preference for one program over another, hobbies involving the computer, experiences of the Internet, even computer games. Remember, the employer talking to you is computer savvy. He or she relies on the medium for recruitment and no doubt uses it extensively in other applications. Chances are very good that the employer has a personal computer at home. This is a good opportunity to demonstrate your knowledge and expertise as well as your genuine interest in the world of computers and the Internet.

One of the most obvious things employers can discern about you through e-mail interviews is your writing skills. This can be tricky, especially if you are not the best writer. It's a good idea to compose responses in your word processor first and then upload them into e-mail. Make sure they are spell-checked and grammar-proofed before you send them. Be sure also to save them in ASCII first. And remember: Once you choose "send," They're irretrievable. Read everything over at least twice before you e-mail; it's hard to take back written words.

Keep your general attitude positive. Just as with face-to-face interviewing, you should never interject negative statements into your messages. Keep references to former employers positive. Be assertive in discussing your capabilities. Focus on what you have to offer, rather than on any shortcomings you have.

Be unfailingly polite. Keep in mind that this *is* an interview. The employer may have initiated more informal conversation, but you don't want to cross the line between friendly informality and impudence. You're building a first impression here. Present yourself in a courteous, dignified manner.

Declining a Position

Suppose you decide that, after having gotten a more detailed look at the company, this job is not for you. After all, this often happens with employers who decide against calling an applicant in for an interview after several e-mail contacts. You should certainly notify the employer that you have decided to decline the position. Just walking away from your "conversation" is rude and unprofessional. And word does get around in business. E-mail the employer a polite thank-you for considering you and decline any further interviews.

Tips on E-Mail Interviewing

Through e-mail interviews employers get a look at your general manner, writing skills, even your philosophy and attitude toward work and their organization. True, it is all taking place on a computer screen, but make no mistake, you are being interviewed. Many of the same rules that apply to face-to-face interviews apply here. Following are some tips for electronic interviews.

- **Be concise.** Do not give vague answers to direct questions. Help the employer understand fully what it is you do and how hiring you will benefit the organization.

- **Give detail.** It is intensely frustrating to get one-word responses to questions and then be faced with "pulling" information out of the applicant. The employer has contacted you in order to get more detail on some aspect alluded to in your resume. Elaborate. By the same token, you need to be aware when the employer is asking you closed-ended questions, such as "Have you worked with Windows applications?" This question calls for a yes/no response. Answer it as though it had been asked as an open-ended question–that is, "What types of word processing packages have you worked with?" Expand on it.

- **One thing at a time.** Sometimes, interviewers will write one question that is dovetailed with another question–for example, "Did you leave your last position to go back to school?" Here, there are really two questions: "Why did you leave your last job?" and "Have you returned to school?" It is up to you to respond to each of these questions individually.

- **Give just enough.** There is really no need to tell the whole story in an e-mail message. Remember, the idea here is to get invited to a face-to-face interview. So, state highlights and always offer to give more information when you meet the employer. **Note:** When it comes to questions of a technical nature, however, in which the employer is asking you to demonstrate knowledge of a particular skill needed to perform the duties of the position, be explicit. If you don't provide this information in the e-mail interview, you won't be invited to a face-to-face one.

- **Give examples.** "The proof of the pudding is in the eating." The best way to convince an employer that you have the needed skills, knowledge, and ability is to cite examples from past job performance demonstrating your experience and qualifications.

The employers we spoke with were enthusiastic about e-mail interviews. They view them as a real boon to the application process. They spoke of a sense of getting a better handle on the applicant through a series of Internet "conversations." Jeannette Daly of Care Management Science Corp. put it this way:

> We use Internet messages to delve a little deeper than the resume, to get a better "feel" for the applicant. We ask things like, "Do you have this specific experience? When did you work with this or that? Please clarify." By the time we're at the interview stage (face-to-face), we feel we already know the applicant and have a better understanding of his or her background.

Ms. Daly noted that most of the correspondence she receives is polite and professional, a point of view echoed by several employers. Andy Ballantyne, Ballantyne Computer Services, added that the tone of the exchange is also important. He, like most employers, is put off by "overconfidence and people who appear to have real ego problems." Sometimes applicants exaggerate in the hopes of making a good impression and beating out the competition. Unfortunately, this is a mistake that can backfire badly. Says Ballantyne, "Don't overblow it and try to make more out of your experience than you really have. The same goes for bragging. Don't do it. Just discuss your background honestly."

E-mail messages also are a more expedient way to stay directly in contact with an employer. Most job seekers have had the unpleasant experience of writing a follow-up letter to an employer, only to never hear a word from that company again. Or, an employer will simply say, "We'll get back to you in a couple weeks." Craig Bussey of Hüls America, Inc. says,

> When a hiring manager says we'll get back to you in 2 weeks, don't believe it. It always takes longer because of the day-to-day things that go on in a company. Unscheduled phone calls from applicants can also be a problem because of the amount of time they consume. If (an applicant) takes the time to write me a letter, I should take the time to answer it. The problem, again is the lapse of time.

> But, e-mail is unobtrusive. I can read and answer e-mail at my own leisure. I don't have to go to a secretary to compose a letter for me. I can do it in my own words. I can be a lot more responsive in e-mail. It's just much easier on hiring managers.

Some companies use interactive multimedia programs to conduct their preinterviews. Great Western Bank uses such technology in its recruitments. In its preinterview process, you can be tested electronically for your fitness for a job in banking. This test, which is performed on an interactive CD-ROM, even includes a transaction where you interact with a "virtual customer" on a computer screen! This is a new twist on the hypothetical interview question: "What would you do if . . . ?" Mary spoke with Michael Dorn, manager of program development in the training department of Great Western, about the company's electronic prescreening procedures.

MN: Where does your interactive CD-ROM fit into your recruitment process?

MD: We use our "applicant assessment aid," as we call it, to accomplish our initial screening for tellers. Usually, an applicant will have filled out an application and undergone a telephone interview prior to assessment. Telephone interviews are very important because bank employees, especially tellers, need good phone skills to field phone calls and assist customers. This initial interview weeds out the bottom 10-15 percent. After that, we call the applicant in to do the interactive program.

MN: How does the program work?

MD: It takes about 20 minutes to complete and covers several important areas. First, there is a math and money section that evaluates basic math skills and the ability to count cash. Applicants respond to questions on screen by use of a touch-screen monitor or a mouse.

Next, there is a voice response section where the applicant "speaks" to customers on a computer screen. This part records the applicant's voice and measures sensitivity to customer service. Then, the applicant's voice is recorded again while making a customer sales presentation in which he or she offers other financial services available at the bank.

Lastly, there is the noninteractive section where the applicant hears three employees describing what the job of teller actually entails. It gives the applicant a realistic expectation and understanding of what the job is really like.

MN: How is this preemployment evaluation scored?

MD: Scoring is based on a five-point criteria system. What we have done is to try to remove some of the subjectivity from the selection process. It can often be scored while the applicant waits. There is a recommended score and if the applicant doesn't score above that, it's unlikely he or she will be called back.

MN: What has this electronic capability done to the interview process for your company?

MD: It has really freed up our managers' time because they only need to spend time interviewing those candidates who are most appropriate for the job. You know, there are those who say that there is no human contact anymore — that the interview process has become depersonalized due to advances like these. But the truth is the applicant still has to meet one-on-one with the interviewer to get the job. That has not changed.

Mr. Dorn mentioned the importance of the telephone interview when hiring bank employees. However, the phone interview is a standard part of the electronic interview process for getting **any** type of job. In the following section, you receive advice on how to succeed in this significant part of the preinterview phase.

The Telephone Interview

Following the e-mail interview stage, a telephone call to the applicant is invariably placed for further clarification. This is not standard procedure in traditional hiring practice. It is much more common with the Internet because the applicant is often remote to the employer. This is a function of the "global marketplace" feature of the Internet, where job seekers can browse for jobs anywhere in the world. So, it is frequently not practical, for the employer or the applicant, to hold face-to-face interviews. Thus, employers make a phone call first.

Telephone interviews present some new problems for job seekers. In this instance, the employer doesn't have nonverbal cues, such as facial expression, body language, or appearance of the applicant. What they do have is your voice, words, and, maybe most importantly, your presentation. The following suggestions may help you succeed in the telephone interview.

Be Prepared

A major problem with phone interviews is that they are rarely scheduled. You can be taken by surprise at any time and be expected to perform well. The solution is to try to prepare in advance for them.

Keep a notebook with job-related information in it near the phone. This should include a current copy of your resume, a list of references, data on the company, and copies of all prior e-mail correspondence with this employer. Mary recommends to all her clients that they keep a file—whether in a loose-leaf binder or file box—of all pertinent job search information, including contacts, dates, notes, and a follow-up suspense file. And KEEP IT UP-TO-DATE.

Take notes as you talk with the employer. It will help with both the current phone call and future reference.

Practice answering questions. Rehearse a couple of different responses to pat questions. Make some notes of questions you might want to ask employers.

Brush up on your phone manners. Answer by saying "Hello," not "Yeah," or by just barking your name into the receiver.

Involve the family and roommates. It is annoying to have children answer the phone and then demand to know, "Who is this?" Teach them to say simply, "Just a moment, please" and get you immediately. Explain to everyone how important it is that you receive all messages if you are not there. Teach everyone how to take a proper message, including the name of the person, company name, and a complete phone number. Leave a message pad and pencil next to the phone.

Put a Professional Message on Your Answering Machine

Skip the tinny background music. No celebrity impersonators. Nothing cute. Say your name or phone number clearly so that employers will know they have reached you and not a wrong number.

If you have voice mail on your computer, put your name first. The employer won't have to wait through a long list of instructions before leaving you a message. You might consider stating, "Please leave your name, phone or fax number, or e-mail address" in your message. It is also a good idea to warn employers to be expecting either voice mail or answering machine on your phone. When you call the employer back, follow these tips:

■ **Modulate your voice.** Try to sound enthusiastic. Speak distinctly. Visualize yourself sitting in front of the person to whom you are speaking. You will find yourself sitting up straight, being more focused, and even smiling into the phone.

■ **Ask for a face-to-face appointment.** Everyone is better in person than on the phone. If the employer appears ready to end the conversation and hasn't yet scheduled an interview, ask if it might be convenient for you to meet with them in person in the near future.

There is no doubt that the Internet will revolutionize the job-finding process. Jobs are easier than ever to access. All you need to know is where to look. Once you find the opening, you have only to contact the employer electronically to get your foot in the door. Then, e-mail smoothes the way by providing important preinterview glimpses of both the employer and the applicant. But, in the final analysis, it all comes down to two people communicating face-to-face in the interview. David Davidowicz, owner of a Boston online placement service called Job Finders, had this observation: "The process really hasn't changed all that much. The job seeker still has to sell him or herself to the employer. It still comes down to the employer and applicant, one-on-one in the interview. The Internet just provides more options."

With that in mind, we need to take a careful look at the traditional, face-to-face interview.

VoiceE-Mail

Just when you thought you were safe and anonymous at your terminal, along comes the latest element in electronic interviewing: your voice. As this book is being written, a new service is being made available on several e-mail programs—voice e-mail. VoiceE-Mail 3.0 may be installed on current versions of CompuServe WinCIM, America Online, Microsoft Mail, Microsoft Exchange, Eudora, and Netscape. For an additional fee, you can add voice e-mail capability to your e-mail account, allowing you to send audio messages of your own voice speaking your message.

VoiceE-Mail 3.0 compresses your message to transmit it over the Internet. To get started, you download VoiceE-Mail 3.0 by following walk-through instructions from your e-mail service. You will need a sound card and microphone, Windows 3.1, Windows 95, Windows for Workgroups 3.11, or Windows NT, plus 4MB of RAM, and 2MB of free disk space. Then, you plug your microphone into your computer and talk away.

At the other end, to receive a voice e-mail message, you need a sound card to play it. Bonzi, the company that makes VoiceE-Mail 3.0, says that a "freely distributable" version of the VoiceE-Mail player will allow you to open, uncompress, and play back messages. For more information, you can e-mail Bonzi at `info@bonzi.com`.

With VoiceE-Mail, you may also send pictures and photographs. However, there is yet another advancement that allows the transmission of your message via video. It is called *desktop videoconferencing*.

Desktop Videoconferencing

With the capability of the Internet job search has come a global applicant pool. Thanks to the Internet and World Wide Web, employers can now expect to receive applications from around the country and around the world. However, it is just not cost-effective to fly in every applicant for an interview. Desktop videoconferencing makes it possible for employers to interview candidates right on their computer screens.

CU-SeeMe is a videoconferencing program developed at Cornell University. It was originally written for the Macintosh by Tim Dorcey under the sponsorship of Richard Cogger of Advanced Technology group in the Network Resources division of the Information Technology Department at Cornell. CU-SeeMe was conceived initially for distance learning. However, it has found application throughout the business community as a conferencing tool and can be used with either Mac or PC platforms.

To use CU-SeeMe, receivers need a connection to the Internet, a Windows sound board like Sound Blaster, and a 256-color (8 bit) video driver. You should also have a 28,800 modem. The sender needs all the above, plus a Connectix QuickCam.

CU-SeeMe can be used for one-to-one or many-to-many conferences. The transmission is accomplished by use of "reflectors," sort of "traffic controllers" for videoconferencing sessions. Everyone connects to the same reflector to take part in the conference.

Desktop videoconferencing poses some special considerations for job seekers. The visual element is there, but the image and sound are not always the best. It is difficult for even a seasoned television pro to come across well on video, so take some time in preparation for your videoconference. Pay special attention to your grooming. Even use powder to keep your complexion from shining. Answer questions directly. Smile, even though the absence of a person may make you feel somewhat awkward. Be aware of pronunciation. Try to "put yourself in the room" with the interviewers, who may be across the country. This is an interview, so conduct yourself professionally. Affect a friendly manner, but be respectful and careful in constructing your answers. Prepare answers to questions in advance. And relax! Not having all those people in the room with you kind of takes the pressure off.

Some employers conduct video conferences by use of a satellite, rather than a program like CU-SeeMe. The means are different, but the effect is the same: You are in a room in one part of the country, and your interviewer(s) are in another. You will probably be called in along with several other job seekers, as employers tend to do all of their video interviews at one time to save costs. If you find yourself in a waiting room with various other candidates, don't let it throw you. Just think of it as the employer's "lobby." Be cordial and professional.

The Face-to-Face Interview

This is it. The big moment is at hand. You have navigated the vast highway of cyberspace and located a job. You've managed to make it past a sea of other applicants with a resume that opened the door to an opportunity. Subsequent e-mail interviews with the employer opened the door wider. And now you wait confidently to walk through that door the next morning at the face-to-face interview. Well, perhaps "nervously" better describes your frame of mind as you contemplate the coming appointment. What will the interviewer ask? How will you respond? Have you made the right grooming choices? How will you handle that all-important salary discussion? You wonder what the interviewer will be like, how heavy traffic will be on the way there, and whether this is really the company for you. At least, we hope that is what's going through your mind before an interview. You should be trying to think ahead, to prepare for every eventuality. Sadly, many job seekers fail to prepare adequately for their interviews. The result is that they fail to get the job or end up in a job that is less than satisfactory. For a successful job interview, preparation is key.

On the other hand, there are those applicants who "overtrain"—read all the books, attend every seminar, and spend so much time in preparation that there remains no spontaneity at all in the interview. These job seekers run the risk of failure because they end up giving rote, canned responses that turn interviewers off. Consider the following scenario: "Tell me," the interviewer asks, "what would you say is your greatest strength?" As the job applicant launches confidently into a response, the interviewer listens with a sigh. This is her sixth interview today and this is the third time she has heard the same response. Not *just about* the same, *exactly* the same. She wonders how she will get past the rote, automaton-like answers to the real person across the desk from her. In fact, she has almost begun to reject applicants on the basis of such a canned response to her questions. Have all job seekers read the same book, gone to the same class, or what? she wonders.

The experience of this interviewer is hardly unique. So many self-help guides are available on interviewing that applicants have begun to take on an "assembly line" appearance. For the most part, the advice is good advice; that is, it would work, in a sterile, generic type of interview. The problem is that no interview fits that pattern. All interviews are individual. Each possesses its own character and tone. Thus, a single, prepared answer can't possibly work for every interview. What is missing is any consideration of the context of each individual interview.

In the following pages, we will take a situational approach to the employment process. You will be encouraged to analyze the context of the particular situation and to weigh the factors evident in each interview before making a decision on how best to respond to questions. Context will also help you realize how to best handle the other components of the employment process, such as grooming.

Context Clues

Any number of factors, or clues, can help you assess the interview context. Some are quite obvious and readily observable in the setting itself. Others require some advance preparation and forethought on your part. The three most helpful components to evaluating the interview situation are these:

1. Researching the company;

2. "Reading" the surroundings; and

3. "Sizing up" the interviewer.

We now examine each of these variables to get a clear "fix" on the interview context.

Researching the Company

An excellent way to research a potential employer is to talk directly to the people who work there. This can be accomplished through an informational interview or simply by chatting with members of the organization. The purpose here is to find out about the workings of the company—its corporate philosophy, the general working environment, even the salary and benefits structure.

Here are some general areas to consider for formulating questions appropriate for an informational interview:

- Description of the kind of work performed—outline of positions within the organization

- Types of background necessary to apply. Include degrees, certificates, etc., besides work experience

   Personality traits desirable in employees

- Available career paths and training options

   Most rewarding aspects of the job

   Most frustrating or difficult aspects of the job

   Best way to do well and advance in the organization

   Organization's main competition

   Organization's salary/benefits structure

   Organization's mission statement

The last item is valuable in forming a picture of the company's philosophical base and is essential to gauging the context of the interview.

Face-to-face informational interviews are set up with either the personnel director or the head of the particular department that interests you. They are scheduled, structured periods, usually about 15-20 minutes in length. That's a big chunk out of a busy human resources person's day.

Consequently, job seekers often have difficulty in getting an appointment. With the Internet, you can e-mail a brief message to the employer, outlining your purpose and questions. These "interviews" are much more favorably regarded because of the time factor. Also, the threat that the applicant will press for a job, contrary to the stated purpose of gathering information, is nonexistent. Consequently, interviewers feel more comfortable discussing the company from the safe distance the Internet provides.

In your message, make the employer aware that the purpose of the "interview" is *only* to derive information about the company. You must also remember that the aim here is not to ask for a job, but to find out everything possible about the organization in order to make yourself the best competitor for the job. Employers regard these queries as an expedient means of getting a look at what's "out there" in terms of applicants and also as an inexpensive way of getting good P.R., always a priority with businesses.

The other way to go about informational interviews is with the line staff themselves. If the staff actually serve the public directly, it is a simple matter to approach them as a customer and informally ask what it is like to work for that company. You should make no secret of the fact that you're looking for work and may be considering their organization or a similar one. In fact, you should talk to everyone. Many an opening has been found through networking and passing the word. For example, if someone has a friend with a brother who works for the company of interest to you, that's one way of getting an informational interview with a staff member. Sometimes a phone call to any department in the organization, but preferably to the one that interests you, is sufficient. Just remember to be honest. If you don't state the real reason for the interview up front, such behavior will be remembered later.

Reading the Surroundings

Want to know the lay of the land before the actual interview? Then, by all means, pay a visit to the site. Most companies have an open door to the public. One can drop in as a consumer or curious passerby. Of course, an excellent time to pay a call is at the informational interview itself. However, if you haven't had time to do so beforehand, a brief visit to the site before the scheduled interview time, just to look around, is essential.

Of course, once in the interview itself, an applicant has a chance to really get a feel for the corporation. If one is astute, clues can be picked up that reveal a great deal about the context. Consider the physical layout of the interviewer's office. Is it very orderly, neat as a pin? Somber? Professionally decorated? Poorly lit? A total mess? These factors all dictate behavior based on context. Let's consider some other environmental clues:

Are the offices discrete rooms with doors or are they separated by low, uniform dividers?

What is the pace of the visible staff? Brisk? Relaxed? Calm? Frenetic?

Is there music? What kind?

What is the decor, such as furniture, paintings on the walls, carpeting? Is there any decor to speak of?

Are there constant interruptions, or is the interview room cloistered?

How are the employees dressed?

Look at the parking lot. Are there separate, marked spaces for management and supervisers?

What is the breakroom like? Are there comfortable chairs or tables? Is it neat or cluttered? Clean? Are there magazines or music or some other form of entertainment? What about a bulletin board? If there is one, what sort of information is posted there?

Is there a time clock?

Do phones ring constantly or rarely?

Is there conversation among employees?

Is there noise, or can you hear the clock ticking?

Some of these clues give rather obvious information. If, for example, the phones ring constantly and the employees tend to run rather than walk, you could fairly surmise that the atmosphere is harried and probably stressful. But, it may require some thought to put these factors together to come up with a more or less cohesive and accurate picture of the organization. For example, the use of uniform height dividers for offices rather than walls generally denotes a company with a "team" philosophy, where all employee input is valued and hierarchy is downplayed. Work spaces are similar to encourage interaction by management and staff. On the other hand, a parking lot with clearly delineated spaces for management and supervision might be indicative of a tight hierarchy within the corporate structure, where supervision is favored and workers know their place. Sometimes an office with a hopelessly anal-retentive demand for order and structure may stifle an individual with a strong need for flexibility and creativity. If, on the other hand, such order appeals to you, you would be well-advised to point out your penchant for the orderly.

So far, we have laid some crucial groundwork in trying to discover the context of an interview situation. It remains for us now to get a handle on that all-important person across the desk as the final piece of the context equation.

Sizing Up the Interviewer

It is intrinsic to human nature to take the measure of the people we meet. We do it all the time, automatically. We develop an instinctive way of reading others that is sometimes the saving of us and at other times can prove to be our undoing. It is this instinct that makes us form instant, lifelong relationships with some people or causes us to give a wide berth to others because we get a "funny" feeling about them. With some careful consideration and planning, though, these "feelings" can be honed into a useful tool for gauging the personality and character of interviewers and, by extension, their expectations of potential employees. Let's examine some clues.

- **Their e-mail.** You can tell a lot about your interviewer by his or her e-mail messages. Some interviewers are very warm, writing in a conversational style, addressing you by your first name. Others are witty, mixing little jokes and humorous remarks in with job-related questions. Still others get right down to business—no chit-chat or informality. Before you ever meet the interviewer, you begin to form certain "pictures" of the person, based on his or her approach and style. But it still remains for you to check him or her out face-to-face.

- **Their office.** Let's begin with the physical setting of interviewers' offices. Some put a desk the size of a 747 between themselves and you. This is a clear message to you to keep your distance. A straight-backed, rigid chair for the applicant says, "O.K. Let's get down to business, and then you leave so I can get back to mine." Here, you would be advised to adopt a crisp, businesslike style, with brief, professional answers. And, for heaven's sake, **don't touch that desk!**

  Then, there is the homey, comfortable environment—kids' pictures on the desk, executive "toys" around, soft chairs, and a sofa. There may not even be a desk between the applicant and the interviewer, but rather two chairs grouped around a coffee table. This environment invites more intimacy. It says, "Be yourself. Tell me about who you are so I can get to know you." Here, your manner, though still professional, should be relaxed and open, more personable. It would be a mistake with this employer to sit ramrod straight and give cool, truncated responses to the questions.

- **The Interviewers.** Then, of course, you must evaluate the interviewers themselves. As a job applicant, you should be like a sensory sponge, drinking in every detail of the interviewers, processing them in order to figure them out. How is the interviewer dressed? What is his or her hairstyle? What is his or her body language saying? Consider the following suggestions about what to look for in an interviewer:

- What items has he or she chosen to display on the desks or walls? Certificates, pictures, personal memorabilia, awards?

■ What does the interviewer do between questions while you are speaking? Look directly at you? Fiddle with items on the desk? Take notes or stare out the window?

■ Are shoes shiny, buttons all in place? Or is hair messy, clothing rumpled?

■ Does the interviewer smile and make eye contact or does he or she tend to look away and maintain a sober, noncommittal expression?

■ Does the interviewer make "chit-chat" or stick strictly to business with rapid fire, closed-ended questions?

■ Are you invited to call the interviewer by his or her first name?

■ Are you invited to sit down or offered a handshake?

Sometimes, a room is designated the "interview room" and is not the personal work space of the interviewer, so it may not always be possible to draw conclusions about the person based on working environment alone. But you must always be alert to the personal clues visible on the interviewer. Look for personal style, manner of speech, eye contact, and facial expression. All should help dictate the applicant's behavior. All of them reveal the context of the interview.

Hypothetical Interview Situations

Now, using what we have learned so far, let's set up some hypothetical contexts based on our observations and think about what sort of interview situations they might dictate.

Situation I

Through research, you find that this company was founded by a single individual on a shoestring. The company has grown dramatically and is now a national, public enterprise. The founder and CEO, who is still very much a viable presence in the organization, maintains a hands-on style of leadership. Company perks are many, with employee bonuses given for exceptional performance.

The office building is fairly new, the offices decorated in contemporary style and colors. The working spaces are separated by low, uniform dividers. There is an air of subdued energy, with the employees engaged in busy but not frantic activity. You observe some conversation but no music. Personal accoutrements in the work spaces are limited to one or two pictures and some plants, but otherwise, desks and areas are more or less uniform. There are two designated parking spaces in the lot—one for the office manager and one for the employee of the month.

In the informational interview, you learned that this company offers flex-time, an on-site gymnasium, child care assistance, and an incentive program for employees wishing to take college courses. An open door policy exists for every supervisor and manager, all the way to the top of the organization.

The interview is held in a comfortable office which, it is explained, is the office of the interviewer. There are lamps rather than overhead lighting, plants, a desk in the center of the room, and two club chairs and a coffee table near the window. A full-length mirror hangs on the back of the door, which has been closed for privacy. The interviewer is a woman, extremely well-groomed in a fashionable red business suit. She greets you with a warm smile and handshake, asks you to address her by her first name, and ushers you to the chairs by the window.

Contextual Conclusions

These factors point to a context in which you must make particular choices. To begin with, knowing that the company was started by a self-made entrepreneur, you should emphasize your strengths as a motivated self-starter. The tone of the office suggests that energy, enthusiasm, and ambition must be stressed as personal qualities you possess. It would help tremendously if you could point to examples of outstanding job performance, such as an instance where your efforts resulted in a monetary savings to your former employer, because it has already been determined that this company rewards excellence. Of course, interest in physical fitness would be nice, but what is called for here is a more general sense that you are the sort of person who strives for a "personal best."

Lastly, your grooming should be first-rate. This interviewer takes personal appearance so seriously she has a mirror in the office for periodic checks. Note, however, that the color of suit chosen is far from somber or serious. This is a cue to the applicant that some latitude for personal style and sense of individualism is afforded by this company. (Although you must beware of mirrors placed directly behind the interviewer. This is a "trick" to see if the applicant is easily distracted or self-absorbed. Avoid glancing at your reflection, primping, or looking at your image as you answer questions. Yes, some applicants actually do that! Keep your attention focused on the interviewer.) Next, let's examine a different interview context for comparison.

Situation II

In this case, your research revealed that the company is a well-established local accounting firm with two branch offices in the same county. A company-supplied brochure emphasizes the firm's stability and reputation. Nothing is said of profit or growth except in very general terms, as the pamphlet is merely an introductory statement to prospective clients. The company president has been appointed by a family board of directors and handles the interviewing himself.

The offices are located in the same building they have occupied for more than 25 years. Colors are dark and carpeting is neutral and worn. Several formal paintings decorate the walls, but no personal effects are visible on any of the employee desks or in their work spaces. There is very little noise, except for the sound of computers, typewriters, and telephones. Office chatter is minimal and conducted in hushed tones. The pace of the workers is subdued.

The interviewer is a man in a dark blue suit and plain navy tie. His clothes are conservative and appear a bit dated. His office contains a large desk, a painting on one wall, and several certificates from community agencies and a business license on the other. His desk holds no personal items. The applicant sits across the desk in a straight-backed mahogany chair, which has been placed about two feet from the interviewer's desk. The employer previously declined your request for an informational interview, so you have spoken to one secretary and the security guard. They tell you that there is very good job security with the company, but it takes a long time to move up. On the way to the interviewer's office, you note that the breakroom is really nothing more than a partitioned area furnished with commercial tables and gray chairs. State labor law regulations and notices of upcoming meetings are posted on the bulletin board. There is a time clock just inside the door.

Contextual Conclusions

Clearly, this data represents a completely different context from the previous interview situation. Free-form answers emphasizing creative thinking ability and ambition are not called for here. What should be stressed is the applicant's desire for long-term employment and company stability. Respect for authority and chain of command plus the personal qualities of dependability and loyalty would be prized in this organization. Because this company has a time clock, punctuality should also be offered as a strength. Answers should be pointed and brief. Grooming called for here is conservative and simple. And don't touch that desk!

Questions in Context

Of course, the interview questions themselves must always be evaluated in terms of the context of an interview. Some of the more commonly asked questions should ideally yield somewhat different responses, depending on the circumstances of each interview. We will look at a few commonly asked interview questions and decide on appropriate answers based on knowledge of self and context.

What is your greatest strength?
Answers to this question require a bit of tailoring from one situation to the next. No pat answer will work every time. With this particular question, the interviewer is looking for two things in

your answer. The strength in question could be either **professional** or **personal.** Thus, in formulating a response to this question, you must weigh not only the interview situation itself, but also the type of job being discussed and your own real strengths. Let's consider a couple possibilities for answers.

Professional: In the case of an interview for a highly technical position, a job-related strength—demonstrating expertise in a particular skill—would be the best choice of response. An auto mechanic might say, "Besides being able to do a complete engine rebuild, I can machine valves and do milling to specifications. I am also very strong in electrical systems diagnosis." Here, the applicant has focused on strengths as they relate to performance of the job. Similarly, a bank teller would focus on his or her ability to balance consistently and correctly. A machinist should emphasize the ability to work to tolerance. All of these job-related strengths tell an employer that the applicant isn't just talking. Referring to specific skills not only demonstrates competence but also knowledge of what the position entails. However, there is still the second component of this answer to consider—your personal strengths.

Personal: If an employer were hiring a machine to do the job, a simple recitation of professional strengths would suffice in this answer. But, the fact is, employers hire people, and people come equipped with different strengths as well as weaknesses. It is essential, therefore, that the interviewer reveal the person, not just what that person can do. If you misunderstand this fundamental concept of interviewing and hiring, the game is lost.

Put another way, you may have heard or even said yourself, "Employers hire friends. It's not what you know, it's who you know." Quite right. They do not hire people they don't like or trust, essentially, people they don't "know." Your primary job during the interview, then, is to communicate to the employer who you are. You do this by emphasizing personal qualities that make you a desirable candidate for the job.

One way to understand the importance of your personal qualities as an applicant is to put yourself in the position of the employer. Let's say you wanted to hire someone to clean your house. What if you had to go out on a public street, stop the first person you saw, and ask that person to clean your house. You would give him or her some money and the keys to your home, and send your new employee off. You're thinking, "No way!" Yet, that's exactly what employers do every time they hire someone. They "give the keys" to a stranger and offer that person money to do a job. Just as your first concern would be with the *kind* of person you were sending into your home (letting the cleaning ability take a back seat), so employers are acutely interested in you as a person, not just in what you can do.

Know Your Strengths and How to Communicate Them

The "strengths" question requires some self-knowledge on your part as well as the ability to communicate this to the employer. The auto mechanic in our first example, then, should point out to the interviewer that he or she is not only a competent mechanic but a dependable employee who can be counted on to be at work as scheduled. The bank teller would be wise to emphasize cash-handling ability as well as strong interpersonal skills because tellers are in the public eye. A secretary could stress discretion and the ability to handle multiple tasks. These qualities are all crucial to an employer but are not evident on the surface of things.

Self-awareness and consistency are both important in considering answers to tough questions and interview context. A secretary who stresses neatness as a strength but has a button missing has clearly made a blunder. You should always be sure that your answers reflect reality. In other words, it is better to be honest when listing your personal qualities to an employer.

Be acutely aware of the dynamics at work in the whole process. Let's again consider the applicant at the interview where the phones ring off the hook, harried people bustle around, and the interviewer is continuously interrupted by work. Offering punctuality, say, or interpersonal skills as strengths wouldn't score nearly as many points at that particular interview as offering the ability to work well under pressure.

So, you must be able to select a strength from a whole host of possibilities and then make sure it really applies to you and fits the context of the interview. Here are some suggestions for personal strengths that employers find appealing:

☐ dependable	■ detail-oriented
☐ motivated	■ flexible
☐ good listener	■ punctual
☐ self-starter	■ organized
☐ discreet	■ loyal
☐ personable	

Plus, the ability to:

☐ work independently

☐ think creatively

☐ work well under pressure

☐ make decisions

■ shoulder/delegate responsibility

■ work effectively with people at all different levels (*Note:* Never say, "I like to work with people!" Not only is this a cliche, the unspoken response of many employers is "What else would you be working with, aardvarks?")

Remember to evaluate yourself fairly and honestly, and choose your representative qualities wisely. No employer likes to be conned. Now let's look at another common interview question.

What did you like most about your last job?

This question practically directs you to think about the context of the interview. Yet, the answers many applicants give no longer warrant them for consideration by the employer. Some common answers given here are, "Oh, I just loved the people I worked with!" or "I really liked my boss." or "They had good benefits." The first two answers tell the interviewer that the applicant's last company was a neat place to work, so why is he or she here? The last answer indicates that this applicant is out for what he or she can get from the company. Neither answer shows any thoughtfulness in relation to the current context.

Again, it is incumbent on you to think about the company to which you are applying and what the conditions might be like on the job in question. You must then evaluate the components of your last job to see if there is a correlation with this one. Consider the following examples:

On her last job, Debra, as division secretary, was responsible for putting together a departmental newsletter that told about current events as well as outlined unit goals and accomplishments. She now finds herself in an interview for administrative assistant to a department manager. Knowing that she will be responsible for generating and editing a great deal of correspondence, wouldn't she be wise to volunteer that she liked the newsletter aspect of her last job?

Claudia worked for a small operation with only a few people on staff. The employees did virtually everything in the operation. Consequently, Claudia had different assignments every day. She is currently interviewing with an organization that has many departments and a diversified product line. Explaining that she liked the varied job responsibilities and prided herself on being flexible in her last job can only help her secure this new one.

Negotiating a Salary

People seek out particular companies and careers for many different reasons. We hope that you find a job that fulfills you both personally and professionally and that you actually look forward to going to work every day. However, the reality is that most people go to work to *make money.* Accordingly, you should know something about the process of negotiating a salary. In his book, *Win-Win Negotiating*, Fred Jandt offers the following advice:

We can't provide you a complete negotiator's manual in this text. What we can provide you are some guidelines to keep in mind when you're offered a job and want to negotiate salary or conditions of employment.

You need to determine whether negotiation is even appropriate. Some organizations make a non-negotiable offer. You're asked to "take it or leave it." Others make a non-negotiable salary offer, but do negotiate certain conditions of employment such as benefits, moving expenses, commuting expenses or telecommuting options, office space, and any other possibility—except salary. And, of course, there are others who are open to negotiating any aspect. How do you find out? Don't assume; do your research. Ask current and former employees.

With this knowledge but before you respond to a job offer, you must first do an honest assessment of your position. First, you need to evaluate your options. Negotiators often speak of one's BATANA or Best Alternative to a Negotiated Agreement. By this they mean that anyone involved in a negotiation MUST understand the consequences of NOT settling. Another way to say this is "What options do you have?" This must be an honest assessment. This evaluation should help you determine how you negotiate with the employer. The weakest position, of course, is to have no money, no other offers, no other applications being considered elsewhere, and no leads. Be realistic. You want to get fair compensation, but you can't afford to have the employer withdraw the offer. On the other hand, the strongest position is to have another job offer. If you do have another offer in hand or are very sure that one is forthcoming, you can afford to take a stronger stand. Actually if that other offer is completely acceptable to you, you should tell the truth—that is, tell the employer that you have another offer. Caution: All professional negotiators will tell you, never lie! If you bluff, you may lose. If you lie, you will be found out eventually, and we don't think that you would want your new employer to discover that you can't be trusted.

Second, you need to set realistic objectives. Professional negotiators know that having carefully researched and determined their objectives results in better outcomes than trying to negotiate for the "best deal you can get." The negotiator who is prepared knows the range and average salary for the position and knows what others doing the same work in the organization receive. How do you find this out? By now you know to expect us to say to search the World Wide Web for salary information. Before you negotiate, you must have first done your research and set realistic objectives.

You need to determine the authority and expectations of the person you are negotiating with. Does the person have the authority to negotiate salary and conditions of employment or are they limited in their authority? We recommend a simple but effective approach: Ask, but of course ask politely. You don't want to come off as a potential employee who is going to be difficult to deal with. Second, you need to determine the other party's expectations about negotiation. Do they typically make a low first offer expecting the applicant to ask for more? Or, do they typically make a mid-range offer and expect to discuss it with you but not negotiate it with you? Or, do they typically make what they believe to be a fair offer and resent someone who expects to negotiate? You must find out. So far you've seen that most of the work of negotiation occurs before one word is spoken.

Negotiations can be divided into single issue and multiple issue types. Single issue negotiations are about one issue only such as salary. Multiple issue negotiations offer more opportunities for mutually satisfying outcomes because they offer more ways to construct the outcome.

Let's be direct: Single issue negotiations are most often settled by compromise. If the employer offers to pay $10 an hour and you've asked for $13, if both the employer's offer and your demand are reasonable, and if both of you expect to negotiate and settle, it's probable that you'll walk away with $11.50—the average of $10 and $13.

Knowing this, you know how to be successful in this type of negotiation: 1. The employer expects to negotiate. 2. Both of you have made realistic offers and demands. 3. You have made your demand more than your objective, which permits you to compromise and still reach your objective. Ideally, you need to determine what the employer typically offers so that you can calculate and set your demand at a point that makes it possible for you to compromise at your objective.

Most negotiators prefer to deal with multiple issues. Having multiple issues on the table makes it possible for the parties to link movement on one issue in exchange for movement on another issue. In multiple-issue negotiation, for example, if you are concerned about commuting in heavy traffic, you can offer to drop your demand for flexible hours if the employer agrees to include you in company-sponsored vanpools.

Notice in the preceding example that not only are you trading movement on one issue in exchange for movement on another issue, you've reached an outcome that is in both your interests. You don't have to drive in heavy traffic, and the employer may receive incentives or recognition for encouraging mass transit. This should tell you something about multiple-issue negotiation. Not only do you make trade-offs, you attempt to reach an agreement that benefits both parties. This type of negotiation is called win-win negotiation. Not only do you both "win," you begin to establish a working relationship that can continue to benefit both parties in the future. This style of negotiation puts equal emphasis on the relationship as it does on the outcome itself.

Remember negotiating for a salary should be the beginning of a long-term relationship.

What are the other issues that can be relevant to salary negotiation? Almost anything, but here's a list of the obvious ones:

- Bonuses and profit sharing
- Computer and other home office equipment
- Company car and other commuting options
- Flex time
- Holidays
- Insurance
- Job search assistance for family members
- Medical, dental, and eyecare health programs
- Moving expenses
- Profit sharing
- Retirement programs
- Scholarships and tuition programs for family members
- Uniforms and other special clothing
- Vacation time
- Working conditions such as office size and location

To make multiple-issue negotiation work, then, you need to set more than salary as your objective, and you need to be able to drop issues and to trade off movements on one issue in exchange for movement on another issue. How does this work? Most professional negotiators use what are called "what if" questions. Think about a question like this: "What if I were able to put aside my concern about the cost of commuting, are there ways for me to control my own hours somewhat so that if traffic is heavy I'm not penalized for being late?" The "what if" question has many advantages: It clearly communicates that you are not inflexible in demands. It communicates that you want to work with the employer to solve what can become a shared problem. And it communicates your desire to be a reliable employee.

Other skills you need to develop to make multiple-issue negotiation work are listening, asking questions, and paraphrasing what you've heard the employer say. Many people assume a skilled negotiator is a skilled "talker." If anything, it's the opposite. A skilled negotiator is a skilled listener. Listen carefully to what the employer says. Ask permission to take notes. Ask questions to clarify what you don't understand. To be sure you understand what the employer said, paraphrase in your own words and ask if your understanding is correct. Remember, the agreement is what the *employer* thinks it is—not what you think it is.

That should alert you to remember that any agreement you reach is, as negotiators say, "not real until it's in writing." Don't sell your house and move on a verbal understanding that a job is waiting for you. The employer may have understood your agreement to be that you'll be hired for the next available opening—whenever that is. You may have understood the agreement to be you're hired now.

We all want our employers to be fair and honest. Employers expect the same of their employees. That relationship is often established in salary negotiations. The Golden Rule really does apply here: Treat the employer as you want to be treated as an employee. Remember, too, that salary negotiations reveal how the employer will be treating you. If you feel you're not being treated fairly in salary negotiations, what reason do you have to believe you'll be treated fairly on the job in the months ahead?

Evaluating Yourself

A truly fair and honest assessment of yourself, coupled with an understanding of the context of each interview, will result in an encounter with the employer that will be beneficial and satisfying to both of you. By all means, read all the information you can get on interviewing. Take seminars and find out the common questions and responses. Just remember that, like you, each interview is unique and deserving of individual attention as well as respect. All that is left for you now is to:

Get Serious: Apply yourself to this process in a thoughtful and thorough manner.

Get Started: Lay the necessary groundwork. Research the company. Find out all you can.

Get Ready: Dress for the part. Practice. BE PREPARED!

Get Control: Know the territory. Discover the context.

And, above all,

Get That Job!

Advice for College Students

CHAPTER 13

A rich resource of information is available on the Internet and World Wide Web for college students and recent graduates. Where you look depends on what your career plans are. Perhaps you have decided to stay in education and are searching for jobs at colleges and universities. Maybe you want information on positions for research assistants and teaching assistants. The Web has listings for both of these. Some graduates look for work in specific geographical locations. Still others want to confine their job search to a certain discipline—for example, math or science. It is possible to search only those areas. Or maybe you are still an undergrad and need help focusing on a particular career field.

There are areas on the Web that can help you access all this information.

Places to Look

This section gives you some specific sites and directions for online job search, especially for college students. (See Chapter 4, "The World Wide Web Classifieds," for general job leads.) This list is only a representative sample. Bear in mind that there are many more sites you can mine for jobs.

Entry-Level Jobs

The Student Search System posts entry-level jobs and internships for college students. It posts openings in the computer-related, manufacturing, mechanical engineering, business, and electrical fields, plus offers a listing of temporary positions. Its URL is

```
http://www.studentsearch.com/
```

A database called 4Work also posts internships for students. You can reach it at

```
http://www.4work.com
```

You may also want to check the USENET newsgroup **misc.jobs.offered.entry** for jobs requiring 0 to 3 years experience.

Jobs in Education

For students who decide they just can't get enough ivy, several sites exist for jobs with colleges and universities.

The Chronicle of Higher Education publishes its list of job openings in the Web site ACADEME THIS WEEK. This comprehensive listing gives jobs in colleges and universities both in the United States and overseas. The listing is updated with every publication and appears on the Internet the day before it goes to press. Access this Web site at

```
http://www.chronicle.merit.edu
```

The *Chronicle* can be searched by geographic location, keywords, or a list of terms provided by the *Chronicle.*

Another listing of jobs in education is available through the Academic Position Network (APN). Listings are included for positions at all levels, not just faculty but staff and administrative as well. As with the *Chronicle*, there is no charge to browse the jobs at APN. Access this Web site at

```
http://www.acm.org/member_services/career/
career/apn.html
```

This links you to their gopher site at

```
gopher://wcni.cis.umn.edu:11111
```

You can search APN by entering keywords separated by *and* and *or.* You can also search by geographic location and college or university.

Jobs by Discipline

You may have spent years in college becoming a specialist in one particular field. Searching jobs on the Web by discipline is a relatively simple matter. The easiest way to search is to use a search engine such as AltaVista and key in the discipline and the word *jobs* or *employment* (for example, *Mathematics jobs*). Try different combinations, using *employment* or *job opportunities.* Here are a few sites that concentrate on a specific discipline:

Math: American Mathematical Society

```
http://www.ams.org
```

Go to section called Employment Information and Services.

> **Science:** National Science Foundation
>
> `http://www.nsf.gov/`

Access the area called News of Interest and go to Job Vacancies.

> **Biology/Ecology:**
>
> `http://www.biomednet.com/jobs/htm`
>
> **Physics:** Jobs in Atomic and Plasma Physics
>
> `http://www.plasma_gate.weizmann.ac.il/jobs-com.html`
>
> **Journalism:** National Diversity Journalism Job Bank
>
> `http://www.newsjobs.com`
>
> **Sports:** Online Sports Career Center
>
> `http://www.onlinesports.com/pages/careercenter.html`

JobTrak

JobTrak is a daily posting of jobs available in many college career centers. In order to access JobTrak jobs, you must be a student or alum at that campus. JobTrak has over 2,000 new job postings daily and also provides job search and resume tips, supplies graduate school info, and provides direct links to companies' career centers. Access this site at

> `http://www.jobtrak.com`

Online Career Center (OCC)

Online Career Center is an extensive, free listing of jobs available nationwide with some international jobs posted as well. Various universities and colleges make OCC available to their students. You may search the database by geographical location or keywords. Jobs are in the private and public sector with openings in all areas, including health care, manufacturing, education, industry, and government. Companies pay a fee to list their jobs and search resumes. Access this Web site at

> `http://www.occ.com`

Note: See Chapter 10 for OCC's guidelines on submitting resumes.

Online College Placement Offices

Your campus career center is a wonderful resource for doing job search in general. Such a center provides not only on-campus recruitments and student job opportunities, but career guidance and testing. And now, many campuses nationwide offer free Internet job search for their students and alumni. Campuses differ in how they offer services. Some offer unlimited perusal of their databases. Others are limited to currently enrolled students only. Some offer campus placement services to alumni for a fee. Let's look at two college placement offices.

University of California, Irvine

The Graduate School of Management at U.C. Irvine is one of 10 business schools in the country with a five-star Web site. The site is well maintained and updated frequently. UCI's MBA students and alumni can enter their resumes into a database that is searchable by employers around the country. The Director of Career Services can even set up videoconferences for remote employers wanting to interview candidates. Of course, the database contains job postings too. To look at UCI's online career placement and resume service, access the site at

`http://www.gsm.uci.edu`

On UCI's home page, employers may access resumes simply by clicking on Resume Search Engine (see fig. 13.1).

Fig. 13.1. UCI Graduate School of Management's home page with Resume Search Engine button.

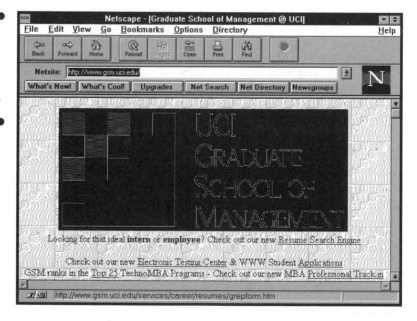

Ball State University

The Career Services center of Ball State is available online to students and alumni of the university and to employers. The site offers a range of services from career planning to employment listings. Students access campus job vacancies through a campus network service called View Jobs. Figure 13.2 shows Ball State University's home page.

Fig. 13.2. Ball State University's home page.

In the Career Services section, students are given a menu of services from which to choose (see fig. 13.3):

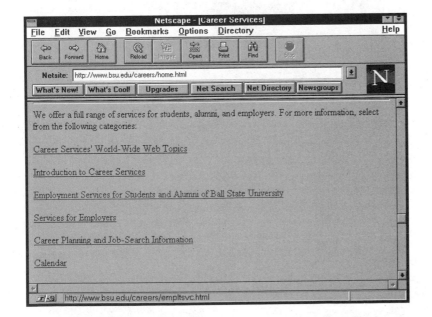

Fig. 13.3. Ball State Career Services menu.

You can access Ball State's Career Services at

> `http://www.bsu.edu/careers/home.html`

You have spent perhaps years at your school, attending classes and preparing to graduate. You have probably been in every building on campus. Yet, most students don't start to look for the career center until very late in the game—sometimes too late. The outcome of a good education is often a good job. By all means, take advantage of the placement services available to you right on campus.

College Grad Job Hunter

A database is available that caters to college students and recent grads. The College Grad Job Hunter posts entry-level jobs and includes information on resumes, interviewing, offer negotiation, and more. Figure 13.4 provides a look at its Web site.

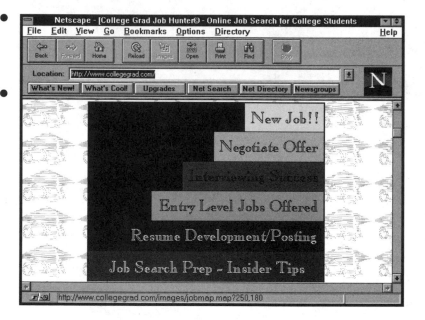

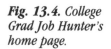
Fig. 13.4. College Grad Job Hunter's home page.

Click on Entry Level Jobs Offered and you access an area searchable by keywords (see fig. 13.5). When we entered the keyword "Accounting," we were presented with a list of three job postings (see fig. 13.6).

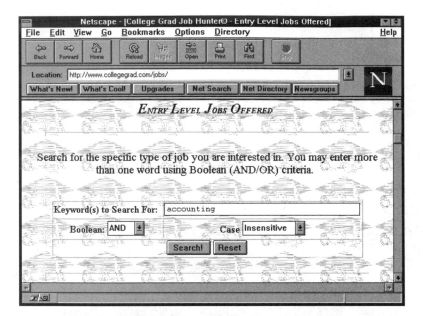

Fig. 13.6. *Search results showing three job postings.*

Check out the College Grad Job Hunter at

        http://www.collegegrad.com/

Online Recruitment Services

Many online recruiting services are available to you on the World Wide Web and the Internet. Many of these are free to job seekers. Others have a minimal fee for wide distribution of your resume or for special assistance in preparing it. Two services are profiled here.

JobCenter

JobCenter, located in upstate New York, is a vast database of jobs and resumes that is free to job seekers. JobCenter markets its services to colleges and university around the country. It posts information of interest to graduating seniors and reminds them of the need to start the job search process *early*.

JobCenter's Web site is simple to use. Let's find a job on JobCenter. Figure 13.7 shows JobCenter's home page.

Fig. 13.7. JobCenter's home page.

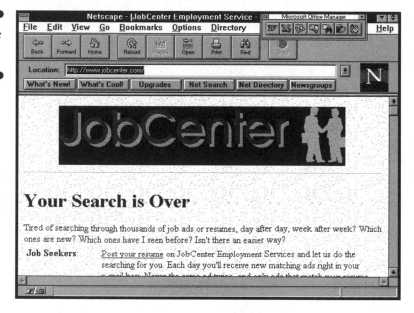

You can scroll down the page to an area containing the Search button (fig. 13.8) and select it. When you retrieve the Search screen, you may enter select keywords to begin your search, as shown in figure 13.9.

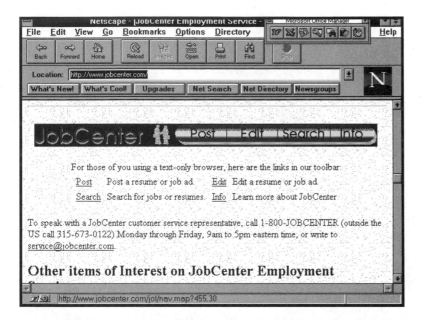

Fig. 13.8. *JobCenter menu of options.*

Fig. 13.9. *Search screen with keywords "BA Public Relations" entered.*

Figure 13.10 shows the initial screen of search results, which displays the first 10 of 284 ads containing the selected keywords.

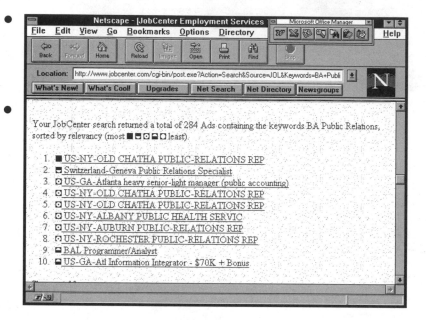

Fig. 13.10. Search results from "BA Public Relations" query.

You can access this extensive, easy-to-use database at

`http://www.jobcenter.com`

Online Opportunities

Online Opportunities is a commercial online recruitment BBS based in Exton, PA. Ward Christman, Executive Director of the company, says job seekers can access close to 20,000 jobs through Online Opportunities at any given time. There is no charge to job seekers for browsing jobs. However, there is a small fee for nationwide distribution of your resume. You contact Online Opportunities via their BBS phone number (610) 873-7170. However, Online Opportunities does have a Web page that lists some job openings, plus links to company sites containing their own referral areas. Here is a look at Online Opportunities' Web site. The home page is shown in figure 13.11.

Fig. 13.11. Online Opportunities home page.

Scroll to the area that reads Hot Links to Hot Companies, as shown in figure 13.12. We selected Pep Boys' home page (see fig. 13.13). From its site, we selected Career Opportunities (see fig. 13.14).

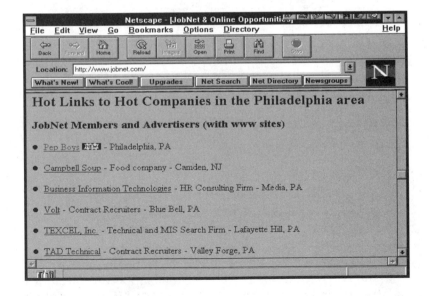

Fig. 13.12. Online Opportunities Hot Links page.

● ● ● ● ● ● ● ● ●

*Fig. 13.13. Pep Boys'
home page, accessed
by Online Opportuni-
ties.*

● ● ● ● ● ● ● ● ●

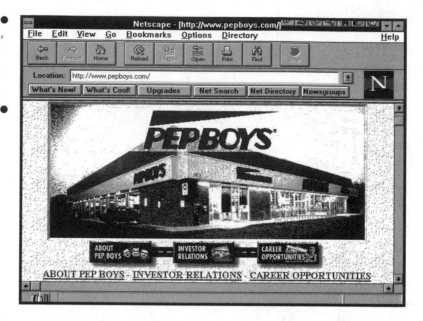

● ● ● ● ● ● ● ● ●

*Fig. 13.14. Career
Opportunities at Pep
Boys.*

● ● ● ● ● ● ● ● ●

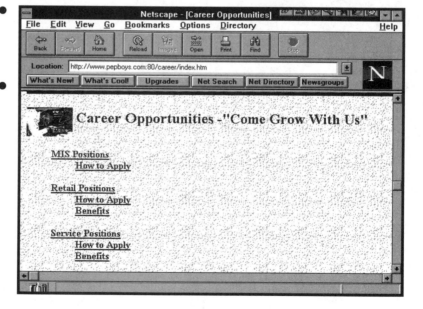

We then selected MIS Positions and got the screen shown in figure
13.15. From there, we chose the position System Support Applications
(see fig. 13.16). To find out how to apply, we selected How to Apply at
Pep Boys' Career Opportunities document (see fig. 13.17).

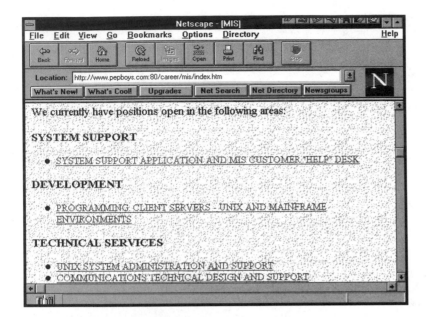

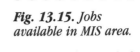

Fig. 13.15. *Jobs available in MIS area.*

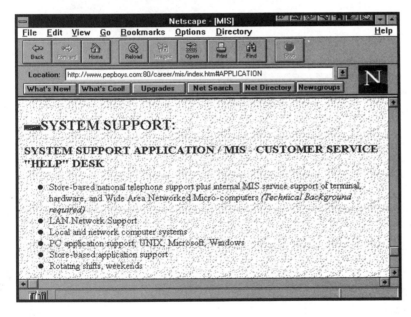

Fig. 13.16. *Detailed announcement for System Support position.*

Fig. 13.17. How to
Apply screen.

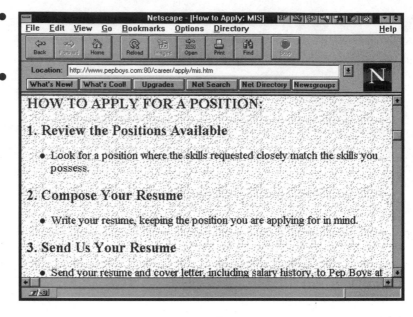

You may access Online Opportunities on the World Wide Web at

    http://www.jobnet.com

Insider Tips

Jim Shunk is the manager of Hewlett-Packard's Corporate College Recruiting Department. He has been with the company for 17 years, most of them in Human Resources. He joined HP right out of graduate school himself and has interviewed hundreds of college students and recent graduates, so he is a prime source of advice to student job seekers. Mary talked with Jim about college recruiting, and he offered several valuable insights into how students can prepare to succeed in the job interview.

MN: How should a college student or recent graduate compensate for a lack of career-related skills?

JS: Internships and/or co-op assignments are the best way to acquire career-related skills. While in school, honing one's skills in research, writing, public speaking, team projects, and project planning will come the closest to "mirroring" the work environment I see at HP.

MN: How do you regard internships?

JS: I think that a student's time spent in an internship or co-op assignment will be the most valuable time they have in school. We can't exaggerate their value or importance in competing for jobs. Here at HP, we hire a lot of summer interns, and it really gives the students a "leg up" on other students when it comes to getting a job with HP.

MN: What should a college student emphasize? GPA, honors, service, organizations—what?

JS: Schoolwork is #1. We and most other top companies I speak with still value the GPA highly as a predictor of success. We understand that a student with a 3.2 GPA and many other outstanding factors may be a better hire than a 4.0, but the GPA is used as a strong screening factor in determining who will get interviewed on campus and who will be "pulled up" on a computer search of candidates. After schoolwork, I would have to say that relevant work experience is next; either in internships or in a full-time position before or during school. Next would be leadership positions and contributions in school and/or student organizations. Finally, community service.

MN: What questions should an applicant ask *you*?

JS: A student interviewee should always be prepared with specific questions about the interviewer's organization, either at a corporate or divisional level. It is a real turnoff for a student to not have any questions. It is interpreted by recruiters as a lack of interest or knowledge. All recruiters and interviewers may not always leave time in the interview for the student to ask questions, but the student should always have five or six questions ready. The questions can vary greatly, but my favorites are these:

- Where is this organization headed? What is its vision for success?

- What are the main challenges this organization is facing?

- What do you see as the main opportunities to contribute in this or similar positions?

■ What are the opportunities for continued learning? What are the most common career paths? How does the organization support upward and horizontal career development?

MN: Is there anything a student can do while still in school to enhance employability after graduation?

JS: Work like a dog at schoolwork. Don't just learn areas of "knowledge," but improve skills, e.g., listening, speaking, writing, working in groups.

MN: What are some common mistakes students make in preparing resumes, grooming, and interviewing?

JS: Resumes can easily be too long and not include enough nouns–computer job searches are typically performed on nouns, e.g., ceramics, acoustics, computer architecture, SAP, etc. "Underdressing" for an interview is probably the most common mistake we see in grooming. Not coming with questions for the interviewer, and not showing that they have learned something about the company and thus are able to answer questions or ask questions with the company perspective in mind are the worst mistakes that can be made in interviewing.

MN: What do you see as a real "interview breaker?" (What will guarantee a student won't succeed?)

JS: For HP, behaving in an arrogant manner, not being able to demonstrate critical thinking or basic technical understanding, not listening well and thus not answering the question that was asked, and not demonstrating knowledge of and interest in what our company does are real "killers."

MN: How much interviewing do you do via e-mail? By phone?

JS: (E-mail interviews are) more for logistical information exchange (e.g., convenient times to have a plant trip). For HP, I don't think video interviewing or e-mail interviewing will ever replace our desire to have a face-to-face interview (both on-campus and at the plant site). Our hiring managers routinely conduct a 20- to 60-minute phone screen between the campus interview and an offer for a plant trip. We will be doing more video interviewing in the future. For us, it will most commonly be used for interviewing students for internships (we don't routinely fly internship candidates out for plant trips), for screening international candidates before offering a plant trip (a

European hiring manager conducting a video interview with a European student attending a U.S. school), or when several managers spread out all across the country want to interview a student simultaneously.

MN: What overall advice can you give students concerning career search?

JS: Be honest. Don't "oversell" yourself, or you may get in way above your head. Think about the kind of company you want to be associated with and be willing to make short-term sacrifices in terms of salary or geographic location in order to get a position with a company you want. The mid- and long-term opportunities will be there if it's a good company and you work hard. Find out who your manager will be; she or he will be the company to you, so it's important you know something about that person before you accept a job.

Tips for a Successful Student Job Search

When talking to recent college graduates, I am often reminded of the scene in "The Graduate" in which Benjamin's (Dustin Hoffman's character's) uncle has one word of advice for his newly graduated nephew: "Plastics." The meaning of that one-word admonition in the '60s was that Benjamin was assured a bright future if he landed a job in the plastics industry.

Unfortunately for today's graduate, no such assurance exists. With a tight job market and more companies downsizing, graduates today must be more competitive than ever to gain an edge in the labor market. This section provides insights on how to use your college degree and relative inexperience to your advantage.

Realigning Your Resume

Obviously, most recent grads don't have as much job experience as seasoned employees who have been in the labor market instead of school. You might think that this is problematic for writing a competitive resume. But you really only need to rethink the standard resume format and be more creative in job descriptions to write a proper and honest resume that attracts employers.

Education First

For starters, remember that as a recent graduate, you want to lead off with your education. Here, you will not use the standard two-line space that gives only the name and address of the university, degree, and graduation year. Education, after all, is your strongest offering to the employer. Elaborate. Indicate classes you think most closely match the company's needs. Include those special Saturday seminars and extra classes you took to really delve into advertising. Feature the paper you presented at a regional university conference. Discuss the special departmental honors you received. This is your big offering. Give it some attention. The employer will too.

Part-Time Jobs Are Still Jobs

You may not think that those part-time jobs you held during school have any relevance to your future career, but your employer is interested in them. You merely need to learn how to present them. For example, your experience as second assistant manager at the athletic shoe store, where you were in charge of two high school underachievers, can be mined for important generic job duties and attributes. You handled cash, budgeted, scheduled, controlled inventory, supervised, performed evaluations, opened and closed, served customers, and made sales. You had to be responsible, dependable, accurate, fair, organized, motivated, and adept at customer service, to name just a few. The same is true for your jobs in restaurants or the college bookstore. Look carefully at each of your part-time student jobs and think about the responsibilities you held. How do they relate to your future job prospects? Can you find something relevant to put on your resume? Employers appreciate this.

Internships and Special Projects

Now, what about the special projects you worked on as a student? Mary recently worked with an engineering student who had participated in two projects for private companies that had gone to his university for help with specific engineering problems. That was work experience, directly related to his job objective. Maybe you held an unpaid internship related to your major? It should go without saying that you include all internships and externships as job experience on your resume. They exist to give undergrads experience in the world of work for which they are preparing.

Your work experience is no less valid than any other job seeker. It is up to you to present it in a way that shows its relevance to your prospective employer.

Positive Qualities

Too many college students focus on all of the reasons why they won't be selected—which mostly revolve around experience. But employers hire candidates for a variety of reasons, not just experience. In fact, decisions are made every day to hire someone with less experience and better personal qualities, rather than more experienced candidates with other problems. Remember, employers want you to tell them why you would make a good candidate for the job. Applicants with experience need only point to work history examples that illustrate their fitness for a job. You can do the same thing using your experience as a student. Let's examine some positive qualities of student applicants.

Ability to Work with Deadlines

College students live in a world of schedules—papers due, projects pending, exams coming up. You are responsible for deadlines every day of your student life. Deadlines are also a reality in the work arena. You're good at meeting them. Offer this strength to employers.

Ability to Handle Multiple Tasks

During school, you worked on several projects for different classes simultaneously. "Why do they all want major papers and projects at the same time?" is a common student lament. This can be turned into an advantage in the job interview. Illustrate your ability to keep assignments straight and get everything in on time.

Ability to Achieve Goals

Your entire education revolved around the goal of graduating. You worked toward achieving that goal. You studied your head off to be top of the class. Employers like applicants with goals.

Ability to Work as Part of a Team

Remember those group projects in school that made you groan? It was difficult working with all those different personalities. You sometimes felt that not all members gave equally. In the world of work, you will frequently be part of a team effort. Many employers have adopted the Total Quality Management (TQM) philosophy of management. In TQM, teams work toward solutions of problems. You will already have similar experience from school.

Ability to Adapt

When that class you had to have closed, you somehow made the adjustment and still graduated on time. Your many professors exhibited huge personality differences, yet you managed to work successfully with all of them. You were able to fit your work schedule around your school schedule and survive on less sleep and money. Let's face it. The whole college experience involves adapting to many different conditions and changes.

No Bad Habits to Unlearn

All this time you've viewed your relative inexperience as a handicap, while employers often view it as a plus. Sometimes, seasoned employees want to do things their own way. This can cause real problems on the job. Inexperienced applicants are more easily molded into the company's way of doing things.

Enthusiastic Employees

Recent college grads burst on the work scene, eager to try out in the real world the theories they studied at school. Employers welcome enthusiasm and energy. It gets the blood of the organization going. Too often, long-term employees are set in their ways, out of ideas, and lack energy. Companies need the infusion of fresh ideas and dynamism of college hires to keep them going.

Knowledge of New Theories

College students get the whole picture when studying a discipline. They are often exposed to the latest theories and schools of thought in their field. Employers like to be in touch with cutting-edge information through their employees.

This is where your expertise with the Internet comes in especially handy. Colleges and universities had a real advantage with this new technology because they were among the first organizations to use it.

Two employers we spoke with said they had recently gotten online and were still feeling their way along. One department manager who had a job opening posted in a newsgroup told me he really wasn't the one I wanted to talk to. "This is the first time I've ever recruited for my department over the Internet," he said. "There are a couple other people here who have, but I'm not really knowledgeable or comfortable with it, yet." This is precisely the situation in which you would have an edge as a recent college grad with lots of Internet experience.

Writing Ability

Here's where all those hours spent slaving over a word processor or typewriter pay off. You can write that new policy statement. You can submit that press release. You can edit the in-house newspaper. Writing skills are important in the workplace. Many employees don't have the ability, and yours gives you an edge.

Remember that you will have already had a few chances to demonstrate your writing ability through e-mail correspondence with the employer. Do not throw those opportunities away. Construct your messages intelligently, with great care.

Fact Finding and Information Gathering

College students emerge from school adept at research. You had to be able to see all sides of an issue in order to present your own. Employers like employees who can research the information needed on some particular question and come back with an answer. Your education has prepared you for this.

The primary use of the Internet in colleges and universities is for research. Through the net, you can access libraries throughout the world. You can contact media producers and tap into information databases of all kinds. You can become the research source at work because of your experience on the net. This is a tremendous plus in your favor. Offer it at your interview.

Part of being a successful job seeker is knowing how to make the most of your assets. Examine your career as a student. Look for those things that made you a success at school; then translate them into employment terms.

Avoiding Mistakes

There are several mistakes to avoid as a job seeker. Consider those that follow.

What Can You Do for Me?

Mark, a human resource manager for a computer company, told me about an interview with a recent college grad. The applicant looked good on paper: He had a degree from a prestigious school with good grades. During the interview, though, he wanted to know all the "wrong" things.

> He asked me what time he had to be to work in the morning and how long he'd have for breaks and lunch. He also had questions about vacation and sick leave policy. I got the feeling he wanted to know just how much time he'd have to spend actually working. Time off seemed to be more important to him than time spent making contributions to our firm.

This is not your job as summer camp counselor or night clerk at the motel where you could do your homework. This could be your future, your second home, for years. The same questions you asked as a student no longer apply. You have to demonstrate real interest in the company and voice your plans for making a contribution to it.

Says Elaine, head of marketing for a manufacturing company,

> So often, inexperienced applicants ask me what we can offer them. The real deal is that we want to know what we're getting. I need to be sure that the person across from me will give me full value for the training time and expense I will be investing in him or her. Yes, I plan to offer profit sharing, a company car, and an expense account. But, neither my company nor I plan to do that for "free." Time in the interview would be best spent telling me what I'll be receiving in return for a good job with a bright future.

I'm Here to Fix This Place

That same wild-eyed enthusiasm that attracts employers to recent grads can also work against them. Sometimes in their zeal to make a contribution, new hires charge into the job with the attitude that they will make some changes and "rescue" the organization. Employers fear that they will upset the applecart, alienating existing staff, and perhaps valued customers. Don't be too quick to point out flaws of the organization, even if your intentions are good. If you have suggestions, pick your moment carefully. Go through the chain of command. Ask someone who knows the ropes to tell you the proper procedure for making a suggestion.

I Know Everything Already

Debby is an office manager who is responsible for training all new hires. She had the following to say about the know-it-all syndrome.

> Perhaps it's pride, but all too often, recent college grads are resentful of being corrected. At first, they are willing to take instruction and appreciative when their mistakes are corrected. After a while, even though they still have a lot to learn, they're not as likely to take constructive criticism willingly.

Good employees generally have the attitude that something can always be learned.

Grooming

Okay, when you were king of the "frat" at college, your earring with the omega symbol was a real fashion plus. But most human resource managers take a dim view of earrings on male applicants. True, you see some managers sporting gold or diamond studs in the entertainment or information systems industries. However, the fundamental rules for appropriate grooming in the employment interview are virtually the same for every industry across the board. Following are some tips for proper grooming choices.

For Men

Clothing

Degreed professionals are expected to wear a suit and tie to the interview. When you were an undergrad, you could get away with a neat shirt and slacks for the retail job at the mall. Not so, anymore. Your grooming choices are carefully inspected. The amount of care you have taken in dressing appropriately for your job interview equates in an employer's mind with how much respect you have for the proffered job.

Even with a suit, mistakes can be made. For example, the monochromatic look—the same color suit and shirt—will not work in most job interviews, especially black clothing. Choose a color that flatters you. Avoid large patterns. A conservative pattern such as a muted pinstripe is acceptable, but if you choose a patterned suit, even a subtle one, do not wear a shirt with a pattern or design. Shy away from ties that have words printed on them or that resemble a vivid test pattern. Men have a lot more latitude than before in choosing ties with colors and patterns, but somewhat conservative ties still work best at interviews. Don't wear "bolos," string ties, or bow-ties.

Choose a shirt in a pale color that complements both the suit and your complexion and hair color. Be certain that the suit is neatly pressed, collar and cuffs are not frayed, and all buttons are in place. Your shoes should be in good repair and polished. Athletic shoes are never appropriate, even if black or brown. Socks should be a solid dark color, without patterns and not sheer. Never wear white socks to an interview.

Most recent college grads aren't exactly "flush," what with student loans to repay and little savings from minimum wage jobs. It is not advisable to spend a fortune on clothes. Shop at discounted men's clothing stores, or do your initial shopping at thrift shops. You can purchase nice suits for little money. Mary often brings examples of interview clothes she has bought at secondhand stores to the classes she teaches, just to show it can be done. One suit she bought was a navy Brooks Brothers which she picked up for $7! A quick trip to the dry cleaners, and you'll look great.

Hair

Face it. It's time to lose the ponytail and let the "fade" grow in. Most employers are conservative about hair. Beyond extremes of style, however, your hair should be clean, neat, and out of your face. Facial hair doesn't pose as much of a problem. If you have a mustache or beard, it should be neatly groomed.

Hands and Nails

Years of talking to interviewers have revealed a common complaint from employers about male applicants: they do not like long nails on men. Include attention to your nails as part of your overall grooming habits. Also, be sure your nails are clean. Now, if you are an auto mechanic and an employer sees dirt under your nails, they think, "Yep. That's a mechanic." But if you are in, say, the health or food service industries, one speck of dirt under the nails can throw the interview.

Jewelry/Cologne

Limit the jewelry you wear—one ring, one chain, and so on. Instead of the earring, wear your Phi Beta Kappa pin. Use a tie tack or bar. Turn off your watch alarm! Cologne should be worn sparingly. This is an interview, not a date.

Hygiene

You should be freshly shaved. If your beard grows in very fast, shave just before leaving for your appointment. Use deodorant and mouthwash. Get a good night's sleep before the interview.

For Women

Clothing

The choices for business suits abound for women today. You are no longer limited to the navy suit with the white blouse and little scarf, once considered the "power suit" for interviews. By all means, use color. Choose shades that complement your coloring. However, you must wear a suit with a skirt. Slacks are not considered professional attire for interviews. Skirt length should be moderate, neither too short nor too long. Short skirts can be your undoing if you are constantly tugging at them during the interview. Your undergarments should fit properly, not slipping above or below your outfit.

The blouse you select can be any shade, as long as it goes with the suit. You can wear "shells" or button-front styles. Patterned blouses are not as professional as solids and you should never mix patterns of blouses and suits. Scarves are fine, as long as they don't overpower your appearance.

Polish your shoes. This is a grooming practice that is often overlooked by women. Be careful that your shoe heels are in good repair, with heel tips in place and no scuffing. Clean off the "black stuff" that gets on the backs of high heels when you drive. Heel height should be moderate. Hose should be the color of your skin tone. Do not wear colored, patterned, or seamed hosiery. Carry an extra pair of hose in the car. A run in the stocking is sloppy and distracting.

Hair

Avoid extreme hairstyles. Hair should be clean and controlled. It is distracting when an applicant fiddles with hair during the interview. If you are interviewing for a job in healthcare or food service, pull your hair back if it is long.

Hands and Nails

Manicure your nails carefully. Employers really look at hands. Keep nails at a moderate-to-short length. If you wear nail polish, choose a conservative color that complements your outfit. If you are in the food service or health occupations, you should wear clear nail polish or none at all, and your nails should be shorter. (A French manicure, with clean, white nail tips, works very well for these careers.)

Makeup

If the employer can see you from a block away, you have on too much makeup. Use a light touch when applying makeup for an interview. Less is more. Avoid bright eye shadow and blush. Your lipstick should complement your clothing and nail color. If you're not sure how to apply makeup properly, consult a fashion magazine for tips on daytime makeup application.

Accessories/Jewelry

Your bag should match your shoes. If you carry a briefcase, you shouldn't also carry a purse. Pare down the contents of your purse so you don't need to fumble for a planner or a pen.

Keep jewelry simple. Earrings should be close to the head, never dangling or extreme. Wear just a couple of pieces. Jewelry that is noisy or gaudy or moves is distracting to the interviewer. The idea is to keep attention focused on you, not your jewelry.

Be Professional

You have mastered some complex theories and principles during college. The world of work is waiting for you to make a contribution with your knowledge and training. But, unless you can convince the employer that you know how to be professional on the job, you won't get your shot. You look professional by making a strong showing in the interview with proper grooming, preparation, and communication with the employer. To do a good job of interacting with the employer, use the presentation skills you acquired in school.

Keeping the Job by Keeping Up

Now that the dust has settled and you're safely ensconced in your new position, take a good look around you. Take the measure of the company once again, this time from the inside. What does it take to get ahead and succeed in this new job? The task of *finding* a job required hard work and dedication. You will now need to apply that same determination and diligence to *keeping* it. Job retention is the final step in the job search process. Following are some tips to make you indispensable to your new employer.

Hone Your Skills

Whatever skills you brought to the interview were sufficient to get you the job. The problem is that many employees stop there. Doing just enough to get in the door and no more will keep you at a fairly plodding pace in the company. Employers look for employees who go out of their way to improve their skills and job performance. These are the ones who get the promotions and keep their jobs during crisis periods. Volunteer for new in-house training if it becomes available. Take extension courses. Practice your craft, whatever it is, and become an expert at it. Try to "best your best."

Stay Informed

You got this job by means of the latest technology. Don't let your cutting edge become dulled. Read up on the latest techniques and trends. Do periodic research on the Internet. Stay up-to-date on the most recent events and changes in technology.

Contribute

Get involved in the discussion at staff meetings. Make suggestions for improvements—at least for your own job performance. Give your input when asked for it. Take an active part in your company's future. Bumps on a log don't grow.

Be a Team Player

Of course, you want to be the one who stands *out* from the crowd. What you want to avoid is standing *apart* from the crowd. Share your ideas and always credit others for theirs. Be generous in praise for your coworkers. The prevailing management concept in business today is Total Quality Management, or TQM. In TQM, everyone has a stake in the success of the company. You need to know how to play nice and share with the other kids to make this work.

Keep Your Private Life Private

Don't bring your personal "stuff" to work with you. Employers don't like to hire problems.

Don't Become Involved in Office Politics

Stay professional and courteous to your coworkers and superiors. Try to distance yourself from petty grievances and conflicts between other people. Be the one who builds consensus instead of creating divisiveness.

Keep a Positive Attitude

Don't be the one who always says it can't be done. Rise to new challenges. Be open to change. Stay flexible and willing to grow. Help lead the way into the future, instead of being dragged into it.

Stay in Touch with the Internet

The Internet was your best buddy when you were looking for work. You developed many contacts there and discovered a whole universe of data on a wide variety of subjects. This information is invaluable to you now. Make frequent contacts with the Internet. Through it you can stay current on world events, learn about advances within your company's field, watch the stock market (including your company's holdings!), and nurture future job contacts.

Using Your College Experience to Your Advantage

Your college experience will serve you well as you enter the labor market of the future. At school, you have been exposed to some of the very latest in technological advances, particularly the Internet. This exposure is a distinct advantage in a competitive labor market. You bring with you a fresh approach and a willing spirit, something that longtime employees sometimes lack. Stay engaged and interested. Don't leave your education at the university—make it a lifelong pursuit.

Advice for Employers

Perhaps you have been considering using the Internet for recruitment but are daunted by the sheer immensity of it. After all, you keep hearing these huge numbers: "*TWENTY-FIVE MILLION PEOPLE NOW USE THE INTERNET.*" And you wonder, "If I put a job announcement on the Internet, how in the world am I going to interview and screen 25 million job applicants!?" You certainly don't have time to waste looking at all kinds of unsuitable applicants.

Electronic Recruiting

To many people the question is, what do you do now to prevent a crush of unqualified applicants? In the face-to-face world of recruitment and selection, employers are careful where and how they list position announcements. For example:

- They select agencies or "headhunters" who specialize in the kind of applicant pool they need.

- They pass the word through the "grapevine" to other employers that they are looking for good people.

- They write ads carefully, spelling out the minimum qualifications or setting the experience requirements very high.

- They place "blind" ads, where their name is not given.

- They begin with a "resume only" period, during which they do some preliminary screening to see how the applicant looks on paper.

- They contact college career centers where they think there might be a pool of graduates in their particular field.

These are the same steps you can take on the Internet. When you post your job opening in certain employment databases, you are asked to enter certain keywords. For instance, if your applicant must have a master's in marketing, ten years of experience, and live in the St. Louis area, your order would appear with the keywords: "MA Marketing, 10 years exp., St. Louis." You can narrow the field of applicants considerably just by adding specific keywords. This is akin to writing your ad with precisely defined requirements. Then, of course, within the body of the order, you may get even more detailed, thus further limiting your field of applicants.

Using an Online Employment Service

Recruitment is costly, both in money and time. The Internet and World Wide Web have whittled away at this major burden for many companies by providing access to a larger qualified applicant pool and by placing better control of the process in the hands of the hiring authorities. Resume management programs and online services have simplified the task of sorting through mountains of resumes. Employers can now search through hundreds of applicants and select the most qualified by typing just a few appropriate keywords. What once took a company months to accomplish can now be completed in a matter of days.

You can find applicants online in a variety of ways, with services providing differing options and levels of assistance. In the following section, we review a few of those services.

Overview of Services

A number of sources are available for posting your job openings on the Internet. Basically, these are Newsgroups, Bulletin Board Systems (BBSs), and commercial employment services. Which one you choose depends on a number of factors. Following is an overview of the various online recruiting services available on the Internet.

Newsgroups. Typically, newsgroups are places where people with common interests go to share information and resources. For recruiting purposes, newsgroups are arranged according to profession, degree of experience, or geographic location.

For example, there is a newsgroup for job seekers in the San Francisco bay area called `ba.jobs`. Job seekers looking in the `ba.jobs` newsgroup know that the jobs are limited to a certain geographical area. Similarly, there is an `atl.jobs` group just for jobs in the Atlanta area, a `balt.jobs` listing for Baltimore positions, a `dc.jobs` group for jobs in Washington, D.C., and so on.

Job seekers with one to three years of experience can seek work through the `misc.jobs.offered.entry` newsgroup. People in the field of Biology look for openings on the `bionet.jobs` newsgroup.

Before joining any newsgroup, it is necessary to read first the frequently asked questions (FAQ) posting for information governing use of the group. That way, you won't violate any rules of netiquette while you are dealing with the group. For instance, the `misc.jobs.offered` group is for the posting of job openings only. Thus, if, as sometimes happens, a person or group makes an inappropriate posting—say, a message or a resume—the group moderator or a reader will fire off a warning message, known as a "flame." The user will then be told which group to use for their purpose.

A major advantage to using newsgroups is that they are free, both to employers and job seekers. The main disadvantage is that they are not organized. Misc.jobs.offered, for example, contains a wide assortment of jobs that are not arranged in any discernible categories. Thus, job seekers must search through the entire list to find those openings that are most appropriate for them. Sales jobs coexist right alongside computer positions and clerical opportunities. Additionally, with newsgroups, the most recent posting appears first, with previous postings following in order of age. Lastly, newsgroups are not maintained, which means that your posting may remain on a newsgroup long after the position has been filled.

Bulletin Board Systems. A bulletin board (BBS) is also a place where people with common interests congregate to find and share information. They work much like traditional bulletin boards. People post a note to the board and other people read it and respond in some way, "tacking" up their own message on the board. BBSs are accessed through modem dial-up. If the BBS you call is local, it costs nothing for the call. However, you may incur telephone charges for time spent on a BBS if you use one outside your local dialing area. In addition to telephone charges, you may also pay an access fee to the person or people who run the board, although some BBSs are free.

One large BBS on the east coast is Online Opportunities, based in Exton, PA. On the west coast, you will find ECCO BBS, out of San Francisco, CA. D.I.C.E. National Network is located in Des Moines, IA. These three BBSs all contain a large listing of jobs all over the country. They are updated continually and accessed by thousands of job seekers daily.

Commercial Online Employment Services. Perhaps you have used an employment agency before to help you with a recruitment. These companies find "qualified" applicants for employers and charge a fee for the service. Sometimes these agencies deal only with management-level people and are known as "headhunters." Other times, they may supply only temporary personnel. Such services also exists on the Internet and World Wide Web. They are far easier to use, put more control in the hands of the employer, and bring in a much larger and better qualified pool of applicants from which to choose than traditional agencies. In general, they are also less expensive. Here's how they work.

When your company posts a job opening with a service such as the Online Career Center—one of the largest and most extensive of the online services—there is a section in which you can enter certain keywords, words that best summarize the qualifications needed for the position. You may then enter a full text job description, making it as detailed and concise as possible. You also give your instructions for applying, usually by fax, mail or e-mail. You may specify, "no phone calls" or "e-mail only" or "Please Fax a resume." You can even place your order as a "blind" ad, one that doesn't give your company name or address. This job order is then posted to the online service's list of openings.

When job seekers utilize the employment service, they, too, enter keywords that summarize their skills, knowledge, and abilities. The employment service's software searches the database of job openings and matches the applicant with the job. Thus, only qualified candidates, based on their own strengths in the form of keywords, are referred to your job.

Besides job postings, these online services also have resume databases. These work in much the same way when searched. When you are looking for a candidate, you can do a search of the resumes by use of keywords that best describe your job. Your query turns up only those candidates who have resumes containing those same keywords. Some online services charge nothing to employers for a resume search. Applicants are almost never charged for job searches.

Now that you know the basics of online recruiting, let's take a closer look at some actual services.

Newsgroups: One of the largest of the newsgroups is `misc.jobs.offered`. It contains a wide assortment of jobs. Again, the listings in this newsgroup are not arranged in any particular order, but the latest entries of jobs appear first. You are encouraged to put as much detail as you can about the job offered in the subject heading, including the location code for the job. That is what the job seekers use to scan the job postings. Bear in mind that applicants self-screen from newsgroups, so you really can't control the people who contact you through this medium.

Here are some sample jobs from the newsgroup:

• •

misc.jobs.offered:
FROM misc.jobs.offered

5/21 Reading . . . Sat, 05 Nov 1994 08:53:28 ab.jobs
Thread 1 of 8
Waterloo, Ontario, Canada

Position of International Marketing Director available:

Plastic household products manufacturing company, with
facilities in Canada and U.S., is looking for an individual
able to fill the position of International Marketing Director,
who will be directing marketing of the company products in
the worldwide market.

Salary between 60K-100K depending on experience, plus
other remunerations. Language aptitude and European
experience welcomed.

Please do not respond to this post,but fax your resume
directly to 000-000-0000. You can also e-mail your resume
to us <   >, while we cannot answer any questions,
we can forward your resume to the company. Please put the
words: "RESUME of <your name>" in the subject line.
Thank you.

• •

From misc.jobs.offered

Lines 24 Advertising Designer-Alkon Corporation-OH
No responses
occ@nero.aa.msen.com Online Career Ctr at Msen, Inc. –
Ann Arbor, MI (account)

Advertising Designer

Excellent opportunity for an individual to start up an
internal advertising department for a Columbus, Ohio-based
manufacturer of PC-based control systems. Ongoing projects
include company newsletter, print ads, brochures, direct mail
pieces, and related materials. Creative skills are a must, and
copy strength is a real plus. Candidates must have solid
experience with desktop publishing systems, purchasing skills
with outside suppliers, and the ability for self-direction.

Send resume and current work samples to:

(NAME OF COMPANY) Corporation
Attn: LB
ADDRESS
Advertising Designer
Columbus, OH 43204

No Phone Calls, Please.

OH 43204

• •

From misc.jobs.offered

misc.jobs.offered Thread 173 of 2924
Lines 37 Information Technology Consultants-CGA-MN
No responses
occ@nero.aa.msen.com Online Career Ctr at Msen, Inc. –
Ann Arbor, MI (account)

(COMPANY NAME), headquartered in New York City, is
part of a major transnational information technology
consulting firm. With annual revenues of approximately $2
billion annually and operations in 16 countries, (co. name)
maintains a worldwide, world-class professional staff of over
20,000 consultants.

The company's information technology service offerings
include custom software development, applications management, systems integration, outsourcing, reengineering,
training and professional services across a broad spectrum
of industries, including integrating manufacturing, financial
services, retail, pharmaceutical, and the telecommunications
industries.

We have needs for consultant to work in the MINNEAPO-
LIS, MN, area. We select only the most ambitious technical
professionals who are willing to do whatever it takes to help
solve our clients' business problems. You could qualify for
one of our Consultant positions if you've trained AND have
experience in one or more of the following: LOTUS
NOTES, C++, Oracle, Ingress, CICS, DB2, COBOL, Visual
Basic or Powerbuilder; IBM Mainframe, FoxPro, or Sybase.
Successful candidates will have demonstrated business
maturity, co-op or internship experience, leadership abilities,
as well as excellent interpersonal and communications
skills.

If you want to join a company committed to excellence and
client satisfaction, if you enjoy a challenge and teamwork,
and if you want to work with other exceptional people, we
want to hear from you. Please send your resume to:

(COMPANY SNAIL MAIL ADDRESS) Minneapolis, MN
55401; or 000-000-0000 (FAX).

We are an equal opportunity employer. M/F/H/V

misc.jobs.offered Thread 174 of 2924
Lines 25 Programmer/Analysts
occ@mail.msen.com Online Career Ctr at Msen, Inc. —
Ann Arbor, MI (account in)

(COMPANY NAME) currently needs:

- Sys38 RPG Analyst
(Will function as a Programmer/Analyst/Operator)

- Programmer Analyst
(Must have worked as a Programmer with ORACLE.)

Contact: Staffing Specialist
(COMPANY NAME)
Akron, OH 44308-1719
000-000-0000 - voice
000-000-0000 - fax

misc.jobs.offered Thread 277 of 2924
Lines 37 Laboratory Safety Spclst-Univ of Medicine
occ@nero.aa.msen.com Online Career Ctr at Msen, Inc. —
Ann Arbor, MI (account)

LABORATORY SAFETY SPECIALIST

Two (2) Positions:
One at Newark campus and one at Piscataway/New
Brunswick campus

UMDNJ, the University of Medicine & Dentistry of New
Jersey, the nation's largest comprehensive health sciences
university, is seeking a laboratory safety specialist. Reporting to the local Campus Safety Officer, this individual will
identify, evaluate, eliminate and/or minimize occupational
and environmental hazards in laboratories and related
premises.

In addition to a Master's degree in industrial hygiene,
environmental or occupational health sciences, chemistry or
a related technical discipline, a minimum of three (3) years
of professional work experience in the field of industrial
hygiene, laboratory safety, or occupational/environmental
health prevention programs is required. A Bachelor's degree
and five years of experience in laboratory safety, industrial
hygiene, or occupational/environmental safety and health
are also acceptable. Thorough knowledge of laboratory
safety principles is imperative. Considerable knowledge of
industrial hygiene equipment uses and methodology as well
as the ability to calibrate and maintain monitoring equipment is necessary. Knowledge of PEOSH/OSHA, NIOSH,
ACGIH, and NJ DEPE/EPA regulations is also necessary.

Ability to prepare clear, accurate, and informative reports including investigative findings, conclusions, and recommendations along with superior interpersonal and oral presentation skills needed.

UMDNJ offers a competitive salary and a comprehensive benefits package. Please send your resume to:

● ●

FROM misc.jobs.offered

Insect Management Discovery Research - Biology

Associate Biologist. We are searching for a scientist capable of working as a team member and collaborating on a variety of projects in a multidisciplinary environment. The successful candidate will be required to perform "in vitro" biochemical assays for insecticide discovery and mode of action studies. This person would maintain the equipment and supplies needed to run the assays, including maintaining insect and cell cultures and preparing media and buffers. Laboratory experience is required, and experience in performing receptor binding assays is preferred. In addition to these operational duties, computer literacy is essential.

Requirements: Candidates should have B.S. or M.S. in biology, i.e., pharmacology, biochemistry, neuroscience, or related disciplines.

Applicants should send their resume, including names of at least three references.

● ●

Remember, newsgroups are among the few places you can list your jobs online for free. Some college placement offices will also allow you to post your openings in their private database at no charge, but many of them will refer you to a fee-based service that they use, such as JobTrak. Still others charge a fee to employers to allow search of their resume database, just as they do when companies do on-campus recruitments.

Commercial Online Employment Services

There are many companies on the Internet and World Wide Web where you can post your job openings and search resume databases for a fee. Compared to conventional recruitment avenues, such as print ads, headhunters, and outplacement firms, the costs of these online services are relatively small. Remember that cost and assistance provided will vary among the different services. Let's explore a few of them.

Monster Board

First established in October of 1994, the Monster Board has become a major player in online recruiting. Thom Guertin, Associate Creative Director, says they are the "premier career site" on the World Wide Web. They use RESTRAC software that allows you to load your jobs from your desktop computer directly into their database. The same desktop program enables you to search their resume database. Monster Board boasts a database of more than 50,000 jobs.

Besides offering employers a job posting and resume-search, Monster Board renders some other special services. For example, they have held "Virtual Interviews" and Career Fairs. They provide what they call "corporate brochures," or company profiles on employers in their database. They also conduct "On-Line Open Houses" where your company may be "toured" by prospective employees.

The company logo and "mascot" is, not surprisingly, a monster, symbolizing the big idea that turned into a "monster" idea. According to Thom Guertin of Monster Board, the monsters function as "guides" to candidates and companies.

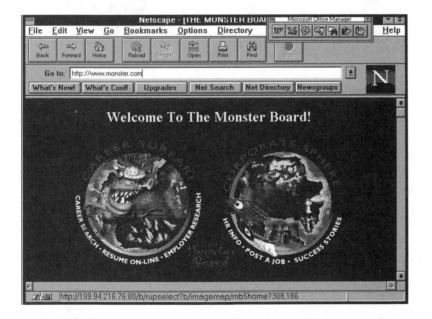

Fig. 14.1. Monster Board home page.

The cost to employers for Monster Board varies with the amount and kind of service you receive. "The Monster Board offers a number of corporate value packages to increase a company's online presence," says Guertin. "Individual job listings are priced at $125 each for the first 4 jobs, $100 thereafter. Each job runs for 8 weeks at a time."

You can access Monster Board at

> `http://www.monster.com`

Figure 14.1 shows the Monster Board home page.

Scroll to the bottom of the page and select Post a Job (see fig. 14.2).

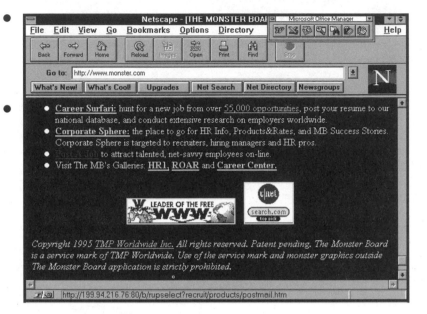

Fig. 14.2. Monster Board menu of options, including Post a Job.

This page contains a fill-in-the-blanks screen where you enter information and a sales rep from Monster Board will contact you about listing your job openings. This page also links you to the company's price list.

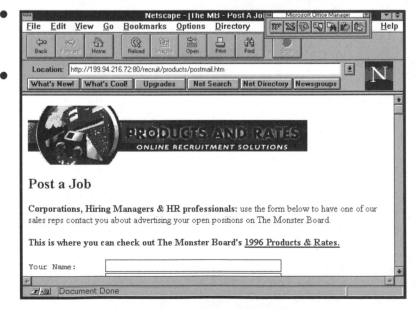

Fig. 14.3. Post a Job screen.

IntelliMatch

IntelliMatch On-Line Career Services serves both employers and job
seekers through a managed database of jobs and resumes. The company gathers applicant-supplied data into a resume database, which it
makes available to employers. It takes job openings from companies
and makes these available to job seekers. The database is mutually
accessible to both by means of a software system known as HOLMES
and WATSON. Job seekers use WATSON to structure their resumes.
Employers use HOLMES to access the resume data.

HOLMES (Hiring through On-Line Matching of Employment Specifications) provides direct access to IntelliMatch's applicant database via
the Internet. The software searches the applicant pool, based on
criteria that you set through your job description, and presents the
candidates to you in ranked order. Matches can be more exact because
of weighted and detailed data collection. A search of a qualified
applicant pool can be accomplished in a matter of minutes.

Doug Kryzan, Marketing Director of IntelliMatch says that the
IntelliMatch system goes well beyond traditional keyword searching. It
enables employers to create a structured query and match the
candidate's experience with the exact requirements of the position.
With HOLMES, you can find candidates with specific skills by setting
up your search using detailed criteria. It searches the data in the
WATSON-structured resumes and presents you with a ranked list of
top-tier candidates.

Here is an example of a query:

> Product Manager, M.S. in Computer Science. Preferred
> universities, CMU, Stanford, MIT. Five plus years
> experience with multimedia systems. Preferred compa-
> nies IBM, Disney or Apple. Good analytical, communi-
> cation and interpersonal skills. Salary under $100,000.

The WATSON candidate database is updated daily. IntelliMatch "deacti-
vates" resumes of applicants who have gone to work for member
employers. In addition, the company contacts its applicants quarterly
to update their status.

IntelliMatch uses an online fill-in-the-blank system to sign up employers. They also provide training in using the HOLMES software. There is
a User access fee in the amount of $3,500 for the primary user plus
$1,500 for each additional user. The cost for resume access varies
depending on how many contacts you make yearly. There are a variety
of pricing options available for posting your ads. For 3 to 9 ads, you
pay $100 per ad; for 10 to 49 ads, $50 per; for 50 and over, it's $45—all
based on a 30-day term. All include a free profile of the company and
product. Updated pricing information is available at the Web site.

IntelliMatch is located at

> http://www.intellimatch.com

The company is located in San Jose, CA. The phone number is (800) 964-6282; fax is (408) 441-7048. Or you may send e-mail to info@intellimatch.com

JobCenter

JobCenter is a large online placement center based in New York in a small town called Skaneateles, near Syracuse. JobCenter has an easy-to-use Web site where job seekers can look for work and businesses can list job openings and search resumes. The JobCenter has clients in the UK, Japan, Australia, Canada, and other locations worldwide. At the time we spoke with representatives, they were in the process of establishing a Web site in Russia. Their database includes all kinds of jobs. JobCenter has been rated by the Internet Business Network as the number-one site in the world that does any kind of matching. Gene Wolf is the energetic former president of JobCenter. He explains why:

> It's because of two reasons. First is our unique matching system. When an employer retrieves a resume or a job seeker receives a job opening from a JobCenter search, each of them already knows that the person on the other end already knows about them. They are, in effect, preselected. They're both JobCenter clients who know about each other. It's a two-way e-mail notification system. The job seeker is made aware of the employer, and the employer is made aware of the job seeker, both at the same time.

> The other reason is our unique approach at not trying to get someone at our site and keep them there forever. We get them in and out. We're trying to be a functional tool, not a publishing organization.

JobCenter's home page gets over 1,000 visitors every day.

JobCenter is careful of the postings it lists. The company wants to be sure that the job openings are not just taken from newspaper ads. The company markets its services widely, including over 700 college campuses nationwide. According to Wolf, it also utilizes the resource of newsgroups.

> We post to USENET newsgroups. One of the features of JobCenter is every ad and resume can have a unique distribution to various newsgroups. At the end of every ad placed in a newsgroup, we describe the services we can offer.

> When you post an ad in JobCenter, on the posting page, there's a list of 50 different newsgroups that you

can post to. You go through and select the ones you want to post to that are appropriate to your ad. It's a check-off thing. We then check to make sure that it's appropriate to your ad, and if it's not, we take it out.

The database of resumes is searchable by keywords. Additionally, JobCenter controls the flow of resumes to your business so that you don't keep getting repeats of resumes you have already seen. Wolf explains it this way:

> We allow you to define the type of searching you want to do, and then we do it for you. You enter your job ad, and then on a daily basis, we do a resume search for you. As an employer, when you come to our site and post a job ad, that first day, you get a bunch of resumes that might match and find a candidate right then and there. But, if you don't, every day after that, if you get a resume, that resume is guaranteed to be less than 24 hours old. You never get the old resumes (you've already read) again for that particular job ad. If new resumes get posted that match, you get first crack at them.

> We limit the number of resumes we send to companies to 25 per day until the cue wears a down a bit. We don't want to flood their mailbox. We tell them to write the ad carefully with lots of keywords and detail. Explain the ad. You've already got them reading the thing, now make them want to respond to you. Talk about benefits, where they're located, etc.

Wolf says that JobCenter will also provide a corporate page for your company at their site:

> Any advertiser on JobCenter is entitled to a corporate profile page. It can contain graphics, phone numbers, contacts, links back to their home page. Every job ad or resume on JobCenter is html-friendly. So if you post a job ad that has a link, and the job seeker clicks on the link, you can be taken to the corporate profile page on JobCenter, or you can be taken to the company's actual home page. So, it's like a mini-ad for the company. Wherever you happen to go, whether to news feeds or whatever, it becomes a link back to your site.

The company provides assistance with your posting and will even help you to make your page:

> If people are coming to our site and having trouble posting their ad, they can call the toll-free number for assistance, and we'll walk them through it. And we

make their corporate page for them. All they have to do is e-mail the text and the graphics. The whole philosophy behind JobCenter is to make things simple.

Wolf says that his service differs from others in its pricing structure:

The pricing is much lower. People can come to our site and search both jobs and resumes completely free of charge. Our ads cost $5.00 per ad per day, with a two-week minimum.

That's it. There is no password required, no annual fee. If an employer wants to come to our site and search through our resumes without paying a cent, that's fine. What we want is, we want to be a tool to everybody. We don't want to be in competition with recruiters, we want to be their tools.

Your ads on JobCenter can be as extensive as necessary to aid in screening applicants. According to Wolf, there is room for approximately 300 to 400 keywords—essentially no limit:

You can put in as many keywords as you want. We recommend that they put in different variations of the same thing, restated a number of different ways to get the best number of matches. You'll still get tremendous exposure on USENET newsgroups and our open Web site.

Wolf emphasizes the JobCenter philosophy of personal service and accessibility:

We want to make them aware that JobCenter is a little different from any other service they've ever used. We're really there as a tool to help them be successful—especially the small businesses that are just getting started. We don't want to be this monolithic entity that's so large that people can't call up and say, "Hey, what's going on with my job posting?" We want to be like the corner market that used to be around in the 1920s, where people can come in and talk to the president or talk to the owner and get a real person and get personal service and real feedback. That's what JobCenter is all about.

JobCenter can be reached by calling 1-800-JOBCENTER. Or simply call up its Web page at

```
http://www.jobcenter.com
```

The current president of JobCenter is Bradley LeRhonde. He echoes
Wolf's sentiments about accessibility and personal services. Brad reads
and answers all his e-mail. You can e-mail him directly at

> brad@jobcenter.com

Let's look at the JobCenter site:

At JobCenter's home page (see fig. 14.4), scroll to "Post a resume or
job ad" and select. This will send you to the Posting Information
screen (fig. 14.5), where you will fill in the blanks to complete your ad.
You will be asked to detail certain keywords to aid in finding the right
applicants. Figure 14.6 shows JobCenter's help screen for keywording.

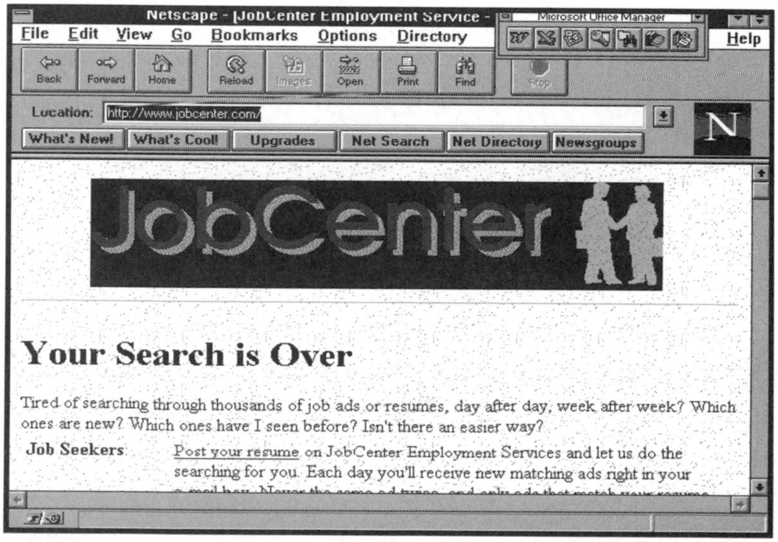

Fig. 14.4. JobCenter's home page.

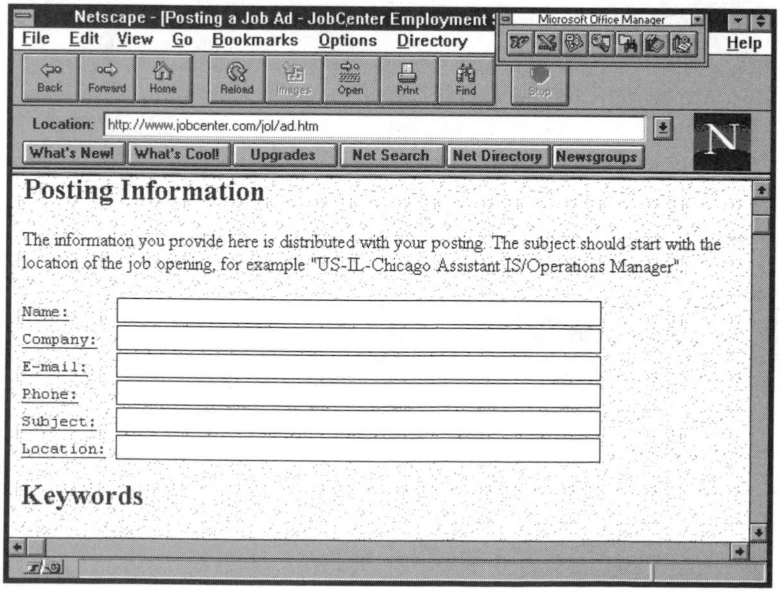

Fig. 14.5. Posting Information screen.

Fig. 14.6. *Keyword Information screen.*

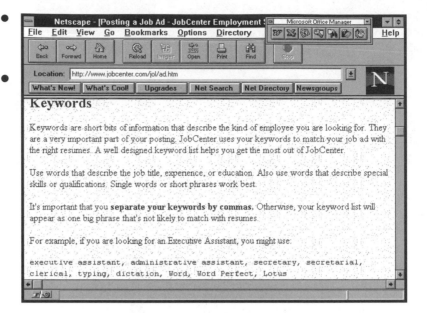

When you have finished entering your job criteria and indicating which newsgroups you want your ad posted to, you simply click OK, and it's in.

Fig. 14.7. *Submit Job Ad screen.*

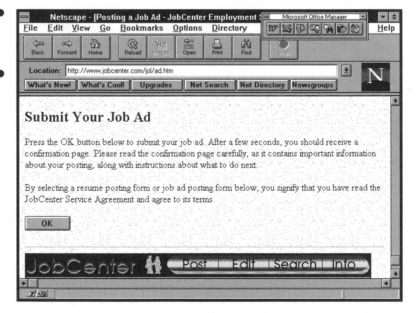

BBS

In our last book, we profiled Online Opportunities, a commercial online recruitment BBS based in Exton, PA. As well as posting its own job openings, Online Opportunities acts as sort of a clearinghouse for jobs from several different online recruiting services. At the time *Using the Internet in Your Job Search* was published, online placement services were just beginning to get established. In the year since then, there has been an explosion of growth. Online Opportunities has grown 800 percent in the last year!

Ward Christman is the Executive Director of Online Opportunities. He says there are several major reasons why a company should use online recruiting:

> The primary reason they should is to make sure they've left no stone unturned in looking for the best possible candidate in the most cost-efficient manner. Online Opportunities pulls together all the major players in online recruiting into one convenient place. We act as a distribution service for major online recruitment services. So, companies only have to go one place to cover all the bases.

Additionally, Ward says that company-run Web pages are not always the best alternative for businesses to use in recruitment:

> Many companies have opted to try to run their own recruitment area right in their company's own Web site. That's a good thing, but still limited. The vast majority of job seekers don't take the time to go from site to site, looking at specific companies. What they do is go to a service where they can access a bunch of them at one time and place. We provide access to a variety of different databases, besides our own job listings. We service Help Wanted USA and the Online Career Center, for example. And we also pull jobs from different USENET newsgroups.

The cost to access Online Opportunities' resume database is $2,400 per year. To post an ad, it costs $300 to run it for four weeks. Thus, says Ward, an employer can do a national search for approximately the same amount it would cost to run a local ad.

You can dial up Online Opportunities BBS at (610) 873-7170. They may also be contacted by phone at (610) 873-6811, or by fax at (610) 873-4022. In addition, they have a Web site where they list some job openings plus links to company sites containing their own referral areas. The URL for Online Opportunities is

    http://www.jobnet.com

Recruiting on Your Own Web Site

The other option for online recruitment is to use your own Web site to list openings within your organization. Environmental Systems Research Institute, known simply as ESRI, is a software company in Redlands, CA. Their business is geographic information systems (GIS). They design software that companies use to manage their own geographic data. Cities, for example, use their software to manage infrastructure, do street planning, locate utilities, and so on. ESRI is the world leader in geographic information systems and is ranked 34th in the world of all software companies.

Peter Moran is a Product Marketing Manager for ARC/INFO with ESRI. He is known as a "webmaster"–that is, the person who designs, builds, and maintains the WWW site for the company. They have developed a Web site to disseminate information about their company. Among the information links available is an area for applicant recruitment.

We asked him about recruiting on the World Wide Web.

> I taught personnel how to do online recruitment They find that it is basically another stream of input coming into the company. Because it is electronic, recruitment and hiring can occur much more quickly than it usually does using mail or paper. For example, we look for good C-programmers. These people are in great demand in the software industry as a whole. One way (online recruitment) has helped is that we receive resumes more readily from the Internet. Technological people are much more likely to e-mail resumes than send them by mail. Likewise, within our own organization, our technical people are much more likely to read their e-mail than to go through a stack of papers on their desks. What used to take two weeks now takes two hours, according to our personnel department. For example, the Leader of our software development group would get applicants for review from personnel. They would then make their recommendations and funnel them (back) to personnel. It's a pre-qualification process that goes much more quickly. Technical people are just more comfortable using electronic means than paper means. It just makes us as competitive as other people who are recruiting.

Peter tells us that the trend for online recruitment is growing, but that the company is not overwhelmed with responses.

> Part of it is the learning curve of our own people, but it is growing. We're receiving a growing number of resumes and inquiries in general electronically. It's not hundreds of messages a day as of yet. More like in the tens and twenties.

He says he spends one to two hours each day reviewing e-mail messages and applications. He includes reading, forwarding, and just dealing with "electronic transactions," as they call them.

In general, Peter credits the World Wide Web with helping them get better applicants.

> We're reaching people who otherwise would not have heard of us. The fishnet, if you will, has been greatly increased. In general, more people are being exposed to our company, our product and, yes, our job opportunities. As a software company, we are naturally looking for people who are computer literate. And since we are getting their resume over the 'net, it tells us they already are (computer literate,) which is fundamental to our business.

We asked Peter what advice he would give employers interested in running recruitment over their own Web site. He answered this way:

> If people want to do it, go for it. It's been a good experience that has benefited our business. But a company has to evaluate it before jumping in with both feet. There are good alternatives to creating your own site. AOL, for instance, will host your site. There are ongoing commitment and maintenance required to keep a Web site going, so consider what is entailed in looking after a Web page. First, it's on a computer, and computers don't look after themselves all the time. Sometimes they take a little kick in the side to get things going again. There could be a power outage, and the whole thing goes down, for example; and someone needs to boot the whole thing up again. There's all sorts of interactivity; even something as simple as submitting e-mail is a little programming on the server side. Simple thing, but takes just a little maintenance now and then. Having someone else host your site is also more cost-effective.

> Overall, I would say don't do it because of the hype. Do it for what you'll get out of it. Cautious optimism is what I'm trying to convey here.

ESRI's Web page is accessible at

```
http://www.esri.com
```

Peter Moran can be reached via e-mail at

```
webmaster@esri.com
```

Let's take a look at ESRI's home page and explore their recruitment area.

At the ESRI home page, we selected Jobs (fig. 14.8) and were sent to a screen called Jobs at ESRI (fig. 14.9). This screen provided a list of current openings at ESRI. We scrolled through the list and selected a job announcement (fig. 14.10). At the bottom of the ad, we clicked apply and retrieved the To Apply screen, which contained instructions for application (fig. 14.11).

Fig. 14.8. ESRI home page.

Fig. 14.9. Jobs at ESRI.

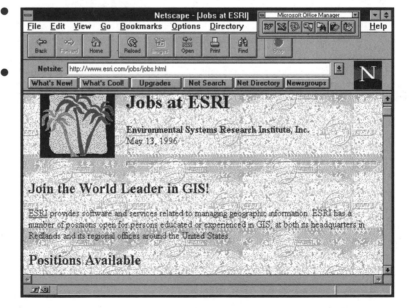

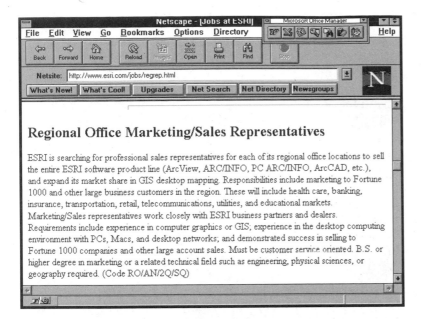

Fig. 14.10. *Job*
announcement at
ESRI.

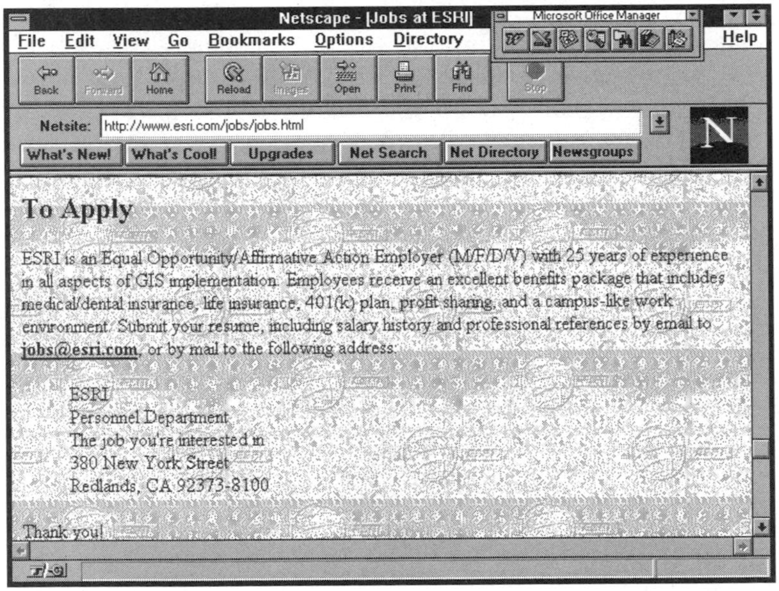

●●●●●●●●●

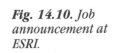

●●●●●●●●●●

Fig. 14.11. *To Apply*
screen.

●●●●●●●●●

Advantages of Online Recruiting

■ **E-mail.** The ability to use e-mail to conduct prescreening
interviews is a tremendous benefit to electronic recruiting. As
you respond to the resume postings, you do so through e-mail,
a much more expedient process than callbacks and "snail mail."
Through the ensuing messages between you and the candidate,
you get much more detail than you normally would in a single
phone call or by reading a work application.

The other advantage to e-mail is that the results are immediate. Generally, you can expect replies within eight hours, and usually even sooner because the job seeker is eagerly awaiting your "new mail" message. (Overseas responses usually take longer.) With e-mail there are no busy signals or answering machines or waiting on hold. You simply post your reply or request and go on with your business.

Note: Remember that a human being is waiting on the other end for your answer. It is disheartening and frustrating to be left dangling while waiting for an employer's decision. It doesn't take a minute to send an e-mail if you have decided not to consider the applicant. A good way to handle this unpleasant task is to compose a courteous rejection note in your word processor which can be easily uploaded to all your applicants. Be friendly and wish them success. It gives the job seeker closure.

■ **The Right People.** With conventional recruiting, you spend a lot of time interviewing the "wrong" people. Usually, when filling a position, you have first received a resume and maybe made a brief phone call to schedule the applicant. Often when you finally meet the applicant, you find he or she doesn't have the qualifications or qualities you really need. However, you are committed to that 15 or 20 minutes of an interview, after having brought the applicant in. It is a waste of your time and the applicant's. (Understand, applicants are no more willing to waste their time than you are. Indeed, with the expense of job hunting and no income to offset it, they are even less willing to sit through a futile interview.)

Thanks to e-mail prescreening interviews, you already have a "handle" on applicants before you ever meet them. You are able to delve into certain areas a bit more deeply, asking for examples or samples. These prescreening e-mails are a service to the applicant as well. They may be able to expand on some point in the resume that may have been overlooked at first glance. They get that "second chance" to impress you by giving you a little more than a mere piece of paper can provide.

Every employer we spoke with extolled the virtues of the e-mail prescreen. They found it a major convenience in terms of getting to the right people.

■ **The Lobby.** Electronic recruiting has it all over the face-to-face variety when it comes to the lobby of your company. During conventional recruitment, applicants—qualified and otherwise—crowd your office, making it difficult to conduct normal business. Entire weeks get blocked out on calendars, meetings get postponed, and alternative space arrangements have to be made when a company is in "hire mode."

Not so with electronic recruiting. Your "lobby" is the screen on your computer. You access it at your convenience. The business of your organization does not grind to a halt while your recep-tionist deals with a lobby full of applicants.

■ **Phone Time.** Thanks to e-mail, you won't be inundated with phone calls, as you are during conventional recruiting. Unless you have listed your phone number or have given it to certain candidates, job seekers will contact you by e-mail. It's a good idea to specify "no phone calls" in the job order and not include your phone number if you don't wish to get calls. (However, we received some complaints from applicants who wondered why employers recruiting in an e-mail medium would specify "no e-mails" in their postings, as sometimes happens. If you have a rational reason for not accepting e-mail submissions, by all means state it in your order. It will make more sense to applicants and spare some hard feelings.)

■ **Cutting Edge People.** All the employers and recruiters we spoke to were agreed on this point. If you find your applicant on the net, you are probably getting someone comfortable with technology, familiar with current developments, and not afraid to try new things. These are people who will know how to work with that new computer you just installed to help with invoicing and may even be able to help you troubleshoot problems with your system.

■ **You Control It.** With electronic recruiting, you call the shots. You decide when to pull your ad. You revise your announce-ment as needed. You can start recruiting immediately when you need to fill a position. You are not at the mercy of a newspaper ad or a busy calendar. Your computer can receive applicants 24 hours a day, 7 days a week, and hold them until you can deal with them. This puts considerably more control of the recruit-ment process in your hands and simplifies the task of finding your candidate.

Legal and Ethical Aspects of Electronic Recruiting

The Internet has grown so quickly that Congress and the judiciary have had difficulties in regulating what can happen. And with the even faster growth of the career portion of the Internet, it's no surprise that legal and ethical guidelines for recruiting on the Internet are ill de-fined.

What we can do is share the questions, experiences, and opinions of the job search professionals we have interviewed:

Question: How should I deal with those applications with photos attached?

Answer: Actors, models, and a few others are typically expected to submit photos, but today on the Internet an increasing number of applicants are attaching their photos on their electronic resumes simply because it can be so easily done. Most employers, of course, strongly recommend against it. We've seen resumes with what amounts to a family photo album attached!

It would be difficult to prove that an employer actually viewed a photograph, because most Web sites do not track the IP addresses of hits.

Additionally, the Web browser can easily be set to not load any images. You'll see only an image icon where the photo was located. Therefore, it would be difficult to prove that, even if an employer did download a resume, it was downloaded with photos. Our recommendation, however, is to set your browser to not load images. This way you won't even have the photos to deal with.

Question: Are electronic resumes any less or any more inflated than paper resumes?

Answer: No one can know, of course, but the consensus seems to be that resume fraud may well be more likely on the Internet. A fradulent resume can be circulated much faster and much wider than a paper resume. And it's much easier to make changes on an electronic resume. To be safe, remember this: There is no reason to believe every claim on an electronic any more so than on a print resume.

Question: Does the same need exist for keeping a paper trail of contacts with candidates?

Answer: It's so easy to move around the Internet and not keep record of what was done that documentation becomes even more important. The recruiter must be careful to keep a good document trail and thorough notes. This means saving e-mail correspondence and documenting within the e-mail message itself the date and time of contact.

Question: Is my company under any obligation to notify candidates we've found on the Internet that they're being considered for employment with us?

Answer: This concern opens up a broader area. Assume that a job seeker submits a resume in confidence to one company, and that this company subscribes to a service that provides automatic sharing of resumes. If one of the companies that now receives the resume is the job seeker's current employer and the job seeker is fired, does sharing a resume create any liability?

Question: The demographics of the Internet show clearly that some people typically do not have access. If our company recruits only on the Internet, regardless of the status of Affirmative Action laws, are we open to charges of discrimination?

Answer: First, give credit to the country's libraries that are moving as quickly as possible to provide Internet access to people who might not be able to afford it. Second, recognize that some community organizations are beginning to collect and post resumes in databases. Third, some job databases like Online Opportunities collect resumes at such places as Urban League job fairs.

Unless your business is closely tied to the on-line industry, you would be missing qualified candidates if you recruited only on the Internet. Until access is more widespread, we recommend that online recruiting should be one important part of your overall recruiting process.

Question: We're a privately-held business. We don't want our competitors even to know what positions we're recruiting for. Can we remain anonymous on the Internet?

Answer: There are several options here. Headhunters routinely post job listings without showing the employer's name. If the company didn't want to work with a headhunter, it could use its advertising agency and its e-mail address. If the company wanted to remain totally anonymous, there's always the option of having applicants reply through one of the anonymous mail servers.

Question: We're recruiting on the Internet and are getting applications from all over the world. Do we have any special problems to be aware of with the international applications?

Answer: It's the same with any type of recruiting. The same laws and policies apply.

Limitless Recruiting Opportunities

Recruiting over the Internet and World Wide Web can be the most expedient and rewarding means you have ever utilized for finding and hiring applicants. It is a cost-effective way of uncovering the best pool of qualified applicants available. This wonderful new technology has changed the face of the recruiting and employment process. Used properly, it can prove to be your company's most important tool.

Summary

The Internet is no longer an elite instrument of a few computer specialists or university personnel. In the last few years, it has become an indispensable tool for business and private citizens alike. The Internet—and the World Wide Web—provides an electronic marketplace for countless services and resources. As a job search and recruitment tool, it is unparalleled.

As members of the Internet community, you now have access to the most expansive assortment of jobs and applicants available anywhere. If you apply what you have learned about the process of job hunting on the Internet, coupled with a positive attitude, you cannot help but succeed in this or any other labor market.

In the parlance of the Internet:

`logon>` every day

`get>` motivated

`help>` your Internet neighbors

`DON'T>` quit

See you on the net!

`bye`

GLOSSARY

We offer this glossary as a limited glimpse of the information available about the Internet and World Wide Web. We have included those terms you will need to understand the information offered in this book. The rate of progression and change on the Internet is so rapid that we hope you will keep in mind that this glossary is by no means complete. A couple of glossaries are available on the Web. Take a look at

```
http://.matisse.net/files/glossary.html
```

from the Internet Literacy Consultants or

```
http://www.marketing-coach.com/mh-guide/
glossary.htm
```

from McGraw-Hill Internet Training Manual ©. As with most things on the Web, glossaries online are updated more frequently than those in print.

access A means of being able to connect (or "get on") the Internet

address One's computer address for receiving e-mail—for example, mnemnich@acme.csusb.edu, which is read as "M Nemnich at acme dot c-s-u-s-b dot e-d-u"

agents Tools that search out information on the World Wide Web; also known as "search agents" or "knowbots"

alt (1) newsgroups (sometimes called bulletin boards or discussion groups) that tend to be on controversial or lighter subjects—for example, alt.fishing; (2) the Alt key on your keyboard, used with another key to execute a command

America Online   One of the more popular commercial (for a fee) networks providing access to the Internet

anchor   Another word for hyperlink, the highlighted word or phrase that allows connection to another area or page

annotations   Your own notes, which you may attach to saved Web documents

anonymous   A way to logon to public storage sites on the computer

AOL   The abbreviation for American Online, read as "a-o-l"

application   Software used to perform tasks specific to the user's needs

Archie   A database of all the names of files stored at known public archive sites

Archive   A place where files are stored

Article   A message posted to a USENET newsgroup

ASCII   *American Standard Code for Information Interchange;* one of the two main types of files (binary is the other) also known as a text-only file containing no special formatting codes, such as bolding or underlining

AUP   An acronym for "acceptable use policy"; governs what activities may be permitted on certain networks

AU   Sounds a format for transmitting audio clips across the Web

authoring software   The software that allows creation of World Wide Web documents

bandwidth   The size of the frequency that determines how much data may be transmitted over a network; the greater the bandwidth, the greater the amount of data that may be sent

baud rate   The switching speed of a line, the speed data is transmitted over telephone lines: e.g., 2400, 14,400, 28.8

BBSs   (bulletin board systems) Services available through modem dial up that can include read-only information, conferences, e-mail, live chat, and Internet access

binary   One of the two main types of files (ASCII is the other); a program file rather than a text file, it is indecipherable without a computer program

bit   Short for "binary digit," smallest unit of information stored on a computer

bounced message   Undelivered e-mail returned to its sender

bps   Bits per second; a way of designating the speed of a modem

browser   Programs which search and present information on the World Wide Web in an easy and timesaving manner

bulletin board systems   Services available through modem dial up that can include read-only information, conferences, e-mail, live chat, and Internet access

bullets   (1) a dot for marking lines or otherwise calling attention to a part of a text; (2) a condensed statement of information on a resume

byte   (1) a character of data representing a single letter, number, or symbol; (2) a unit for measuring computer and disk storage capacity

caps   Uppercase letters

capture   To "grab" information off a file and store it in your computer

case sensitive   A warning that upper- and lowercase letters cannot be interchanged; for example, some computers can read only lower-case

CD-ROM   A disk with "read only memory"–that is, a disk for information storage and retrieval only

chat   Real-time interactive communication; that is, as you "type" your words, another person is able to read them

client   A computer having access to services over a network; services are received from a "server" computer

com   The part of an Internet address that indicates it is commercial; for example, jobnet@aol.com

command   Directions or orders entered into a computer

compressed   Files that are "squeezed" to conserve disk space and to make transfer time faster

CompuServe   One of the more popular commercial (for a fee) networks providing access to the Internet

configuration   The way in which you have your computer set up

cursor   A blinking indication of your position on the screen

CyberMall   A site at which several commercial concerns gather

cyberspace   A term created by sci-fi writer William Gibson for the electronic zone where information is exchanged and contacts take place through computers

database   A large amount of data stored in a well-organized format

Delphi   One of the commercial (for a fee) networks providing access to the Internet

dial-up   Connection means by which you connect from your home computer to the Internet via standard telephone lines

direct connection   A permanent connection to the Internet via leased telephone lines

directory   An index to a location of files

disk drive   A part of the computer that stores information on disks

DNS   *Domain Naming System;* system of names and addresses based on categories, such as Education (edu), Commercial (com), and Government (gov). System also translates names into official Internet Protocol numbers document on the World Wide Web; a document is a file containing text, hyperlinks, or media such as pictures and sound

document window   The "window" on the Web browser through which documents on the World Wide Web may be viewed and scrolled

dot   The word spoken for the periods in addresses

download   Transfer of information from one computer to another

electronic interview   An employment interview that takes place over e-mail rather than in-person

electronic job application   A computerized employment application form; information is entered by the applicant on-screen

electronic resume   A special type of resume for use in computer-assisted job search

elm   A mailreader on UNIX system

e-mail   (*Electronic mail*) a written message sent to one person or a group of people by computer networks

e-mail address   One's computer address (see "address")

emoticons   Facial expressions made up of punctuation marks used to convey emotion such as anger

error correction   A way of filtering out telephone line noise in modems

error message   A message from the computer that the user has done something incorrectly

escape   How one "gets out of" an application

Eudora   A system for handling e-mail

execute   To accomplish a command

exit   To logout or leave a session

external viewer   A program for viewing audio-visual and graphics files, such as GIF and JPEG

face-to-face   (or *ftf*) Communication that is face-to-face rather than by computer

FAQ   Frequently Asked Questions; answers to the most common questions compiled into one document

FidoNet   A large BBS network

file   A document or other collection of data

file server   A computer that stores data and programs that are shared by many users in a network

finger   A program for finding and displaying information about the users of a computer

firewall   Security system software that prevents unauthorized access to a computer or network

flame   An angry or hostile message or reprimand directed to an individual in newsgroups and IRC

floppy disk   A small disk used in a disk drive to record and store information

font   A particular style and size of letters or characters

freenet   Community-based bulletin board systems funded and operated by individuals and volunteers; many offer Internet access free or at low cost

ftp   File transfer protocol; program allowing you to connect to another computer and view and copy files back and forth between the two computers

GIF   *(Graphic Interchange Format)* format used to transfer graphics in a compressed form across phone lines

global village   The way in which our "real world" has been made smaller by computer and other communication technology

gopher   A fast and easy application using menus that organize and present Internet resources

gopherspace   The whole gopher network

groupware   Software that makes sharing work on documents easier

GUI   *(Graphical User Interface);* software that allows easy interaction between a particular computer application and the user hard drive– the memory storage device built into a computer

hardware   The computer itself and computer equipment; that is, modem, monitor, printer, etc.

header/headings   The identifying data at the top of an e-mail message; that is, date and sender

headhunter   A recruiter who charges a fee to an employer to find applicants

home page   The first document or page displayed when a browser accesses a site on the World Wide Web; usually contains the "welcome" message and a table of contents

host   (1) a computer with a permanent connection to the Internet; (2) a service provider

hotlist   A list of interesting or new Web sites and their addresses (URLs)

HTML   *Hypertext Markup Language;* the authoring language that allows creation of WWW documents; tells the browser how to read and display the various graphics, text, and links

HTTP   *Hypertext Transfer Protocol;* the basis of the World Wide Web, HTTP allows the transfer of linked hypertext documents; a hypermedia system allowing transmission of linked multiple media, such as sound, pictures, and graphics across the World Wide Web

hypertext   System of writing and displaying text in such a way that it can be transmitted and accessed by links that allow readers to jump from one piece of data to another

icon   A symbol for a computer program

inline images   Graphic images contained within a World Wide Web document

interactive   A means of "give and take" between the user and the computer program

interface   The connection between one compatible system and another

Internet   The interconnection among computer networks

InternetMCI   A new commercial network from MCI Communications

IP   *Internet Protocol;* the set of rules or standards that govern communication on the Internet

IP address   *Internet protocol address;* usually four groups of numbers separated by periods, such as 140.147.254.3–the IP address for the Library of Information System

IRC   *Internet Relay Chat;* a many-to-many live interactive discussion

job bank   A centralized listing of job openings

job search process   Includes on-line search, resume, application, interview, and hire

JPEG   *Joint Photographic Experts Group;* format used to compress and store images and photographs so they may be transferred over the Web

keyword   A word denoting an important job or applicant characteristic (such as "marketing") used to narrow search criteria

kill file   Tells your newsreader which articles to skip on USENET newsgroups

leased line   A phone line that is leased for an exclusive direct Internet connection

line length   The number of characters (letters and numbers) available on a line

links The hypertext connections used to jump between web documents

list Electronic mailing list or discussion group

list administrator The person who runs a list

LISTSERV *list server;* an automatic discussion list service capable of responding to requests for subscription

live An active link to another area of information on the World Wide Web

load To put information and data into the computer or memory

login (1) the process of signing on to a computer network (2) the prompt for your userid

lurker One who observes or reads a newsgroup or IRC without joining in the conversation

Lynx A text-only hypertext browser

megabytes One million bytes of information

megahertz An indicator of the speed at which a computer processes information

memory The capacity of a computer to store information

menu A list of sites, documents, or commands available

message An e-mail letter

Microsoft Network The commercial network from Microsoft

MIME *Multipurpose Internet Mail Extensions;* allows transmission of e-mail messages containing graphics, voice, and video

MIPS The number of millions of instructions a mainframe computer can process per second

modem (from *modulate-demodulate* device) the device for sending and receiving data over telephone lines

moderator Person who monitors and controls postings to USENET newsgroups

monitor The screen on which information is displayed in a readable form; monitors can be monochrome or color

Mosaic A hypertext browser with picture and sound capability

mouse A device used to point, select, and draw

MPEG *Moving Pictures Expert Group;* a digital compression format for motion media; requires a special application to view MPEG files on your computer

multimedia A combination of picture, sound, and text

NCSA *National Center for Supercomputing Applications* at the University of Illinois in Urbana-Champaign; developed Mosaic browser

net   A shortened form of Internet and USENET

netiquette   Internet etiquette; proper behavior on the Internet or USENET

Netscape   World Wide Web hypertext browser

network news   Discussion groups on USENET devoted to a single topic

networking groups   Traditionally individuals who work together to provide mutual support and job search assistance to other members

newsgroups   USENET discussion groups devoted to a single topic

newsreader   Program that allows you to read and respond to messages in USENET newsgroups

online   Being connected to the Internet or other computer networks

node   Access area for computer hook-up to a network; network access is limited by how many nodes it contains

Online Career Center   One of the largest job banks available online

online employment services   Fee-based employment agencies available online

page   A hypermedia document on the World Wide Web

password   A secret word used to verify userid

path   Menu choices selected to arrive at a particular information site

pc   Personal computer

point-and-click   Use the mouse to choose an option or select an action

POP   *Point of Presence;* the point, or location, where users may dial into their service provider's host computer for connection to the Internet

port   A dedicated line for linking up to a mainframe computer; a terminal for linking a peripheral to a personal computer

posting   A message or article on a newsgroup

POTS   *Plain Old Telephone Service*

PPP   *Point-to-Point Protocol* method, or protocol, that allows users to connect to the Internet by high-speed modem and telephone lines

Prodigy   One of the more popular commercial (for a fee) networks providing access to the Internet

prompt   The point where a command is entered

QuickTime   A digital viewer, developed for Macintosh computers that allows you to see video; requires special viewing applications

real-time   At the moment, as it is happening

router A device that finds the most expedient route for transmission of data between two networks

Scroll key The key to "freeze" and "unfreeze" the display scrolling or rolling on the screen

search engine A program that helps search out requested data

server A program to find requested documents

service provider An organization that provides access to the Internet

SGML *Standard Generalized Markup Language;* Internationally recognized standard for electronic publishing

shareware Software available through public networks, online services, BBSs, etc. Users may pay a small amount to the developer on the honor system

site Location on the Internet where information is available

SLIP *Serial Line Internet Protocol* allows connection to the Internet by phone lines and modem, rather than through a host

smileys Facial expressions made by using punctuation marks used to convey emotion in e-mail

snail mail mail delivered by the post office

spamming Repeating the same message posting to many different newsgroups; akin to junk mail

subject line A headline highlighting the most important part of a message

subscribe Adding your name to a list

synchronous connection A connection that can perform more than one process at the same time

sysop The person in charge of a BBS or other computer system

T-1 A dedicated line connection allowing high-speed data transfer

tags Formatting codes that tell how parts of an HTML document will look when it's on the Web; that is, whether parts will be bolded, larger or smaller, etc.

talk Real-time interactive conversation; that is, as you "type" your words another person is able to read them

TCP/IP *transmission control protocol/Internet protocol;* the basic set of procedures, or protocols, that allow linkage of different computers across varying networks; it governs all Internet applications

telnet What allows you to access another computer through remote login

Terminal emulation Enables a computer to recognize your terminal as a compatible terminal

thread   Various postings on a single topic on Usenet newsgroups

TIFF   *Tagged Image File Format;* a format for storing graphic images

TIN   *Threaded Internet Newsreader;* newsreader for reading postings on USENET newsgroups

UNIX   An operating system originally developed for networking individual workstations

upload   The transfer of information from one computer to another

URL   *Uniform Resource Locator;* the World Wide Web addressing system; the address of a World Wide Web site

USENET   User's Network; a very large distributed BBS that carries network news

userid   The name you use for login

user name   The name you use for login

Veronica   A way of searching gopher menus

viewer   A program used to display files containing graphics or video, or to play sound files

VRML   *Virtual Reality Modeling Language;* language that allows for the creation of virtual "worlds" for exploring the World Wide Web

VT-100   A standard terminal emulation

WAIS   *Wide Area Information Service*; an application using key-words to search databases

Web browser   The software used to access and view or "browse" HTML documents on the World Wide Web

Web document   An HTML document accessible on the World Wide Web

webmaster   the person in an organization who designs, administers, and maintains a Web site

Web page   HTML document that can be accessed or "browsed" on the World Wide Web

WELL   *Whole Earth 'Lectronic Link*; a BBS started by *Whole Earth Review*

World Wide Web   An organizing system with the Internet that makes it easy to establish links between computers; based on the concept of hypertext, the links between servers that allow fast and easy retrieval of data; also known as W W W and W3

Zipped file   A file in compressed form

INDEX